Scenes from Transatlantic Life / by Henry Bleby

Henry Bleby

ELIZA PARTED FROM HER LAST CHILD.

SCENES

FROM

TRANSATLANTIC LIFE.

BY HENRY BLEBY,

AUTHOR OF "ROMANCE WITHOUT FICTION;" "DEATH STRUGGLES OF SLAVERY;"
"SCENES IN THE CARIBBEAN;" "THE REIGN OF TERROR IN JAMAICA;"
"THE STOLEN CHILDREN;" "JOSIAH, THE MAIMED FUGITIVE;" "APOSTLES
AND FALSE APOSTLES;" "JEHOVAH'S DECREE OF PREDESTINATION;"
"THE WICKEDNESS AND DOOM OF POPERY;" "A MISSIONARY FATHER'S
TALES," FIRST SERIES, SECOND SERIES, ETC.

PREFACE.

---◆---

THE shorter tale in this volume embodies facts with which the writer became acquainted while pursuing his vocation as a Christian Missionary in the islands to which it refers. The incidents contained in the other and larger story were brought to his notice by an eminent Minister of one of the New England Congregational Churches, who was well acquainted with several of the parties mentioned therein. When the writer visited the United States, about 1858, this case of kidnapping was exciting considerable public interest, as showing that no person whose complexion was not of the favourite hue, was, in any part of the Union, safe from the grasp of the man-stealer. Though strictly a narrative of real occurrences, which might with truth have exhibited far more dark and revolting shadowings, the story partakes as largely of what is strange, thrilling and romantic as many a popular tale of fiction.   In this age of craving for stories and narratives, the writer does not doubt that he will in these pages awaken a lively interest in many youthful minds; while he contributes to their instruction, by placing in their hands these short and simple annals of the suffering and the poor.

CONTENTS.

———◆———

viii.

WRECKERS.

---•—•---

𝕬 𝕿ale of the 𝕭ahamas, and the 𝕱lorida Cays.

---•—•---

Homeward bound ! with deep emotion
    We remember, Lord, that life
Is a voyage upon an ocean,
    Heaved by many a tempest's strife.
Be thy statutes so engraven
    On our hearts and minds, that we,
Anchoring in death's quiet haven,
    All may make our home with thee.
                                PIERPOINT.

RECKERS, AND WRECKING, are terms that are associated in many minds only with scenes of horror, and deeds of cruel wrong—the decoying of vessels on to a dangerous shore, and the consequent sacrifice of human life, for purposes of rapine and plunder. That such villainous methods have been resorted to along the wild shores of the British isles, is too probable ; and many a luckless ship, lured by false lights and deceitful practices, has been drawn into the toils of wicked men, and their crews given over to a fate which is too dreadful to contemplate.

B

But this is by no means the idea of *wrecking* as
the term is used in the West Indies, especially in
the Bahama Islands, and along the Florida shore;
where it denotes a vocation that is both legitimate and
praiseworthy in itself, and duly regulated and protected by law.

There is one place in the West India Islands,
with which the writer is familiar, to which tradition
assigns the discredit of similar criminal practices to
those which are related concerning wreckers on the
coast of Cornwall, and elsewhere. A large castellated
building, with its extensive out-offices, stands upon
the seashore, which is there very low, and is in
close proximity to the sea. Stretching far out into
the ocean, in the direction from which the trade
winds generally sweep that part of the coast, there
lies a dangerous bed of rocks, upon which hundreds
of gallant vessels have found their last resting place,
and been dashed to fragments by the remorseless
waves, which roll and break with tremendous force
upon the treacherous shoal; for it lies just in
the way of vessels approaching the island, both
from America and Europe, if they should hug
the shore too closely.

Strange and thrilling tales are whispered concerning a former wealthy occupant of the great,
lonely mansion; the large number of wrecks
that occurred in his day upon that fatal shoal;
and the great and rapid increase of his wealth. By
the skilful exhibition of lights in the building itself,
or carried about on the shore, many a luckless

mariner was induced to believe that ships were sailing between him and the land, and was thus lured to destruction by running upon the fatal reefs. What measure of truth there was in these wrecking tales it is now impossible to say, as the actors have long since passed to their final accounts; but it is certain that the position of the mansion and its surroundings, was well adapted in all respects to the prosecution of such a nefarious scheme; nor is it easy, on any other hypothesis, to account for the placing of such a building as that dwelling is, in such a low and solitary situation.

The Bahamas form a very numerous group of islands, cays or islets, rocks and reefs, which lie on the east coast of North America, to the north of Cuba and San Domingo, and which, towards the east, encircle and almost enclose the Gulf of Mexico, leaving only three navigable outlets from the Gulf in this direction—viz., the Florida channel to the north, running along the coast of the United States; the Providence channels, passing through the group to the north; and the old Bahama channel, passing to the south of the Great Bahama bank, between it and Cuba.

The Bahama group is situated on two great coral banks of unequal size, called the Little Bahama Bank, and the Great Bahama Bank, and lies, for the most part, on the windward edge of those banks, or of the ocean sounds or tongues which pierce them. The whole of the trade from North America and Europe to the Gulf of Mexico passes by the north of

those islands. Steamers bound to the South stem
the rapid current of the Florida channel. Sailing
vessels pass between Abaco and Eleuthera through
the Providence channels, within forty miles of
Nassau, into the Gulf of Florida. All the return-
bound trade to the north, whether using steam
or sails, passes with the stream through the Florida
channel.

All the trade from North America to Cuba,
San Domingo, Jamaica, the Gulf of Honduras,
and the northern coast of South America passes
south, to windward of the Bahama group, and close
to the shores of Inagua. The return-trade, and
all the European trade from the same countries,
passes north, either through the Crooked Island
passage, or the Mayaguana or Caicos channels.
These islands, therefore, lie in the track of two
great streams of trade, and at times scores of vessels
pass daily by the " Hole-in-the-Wall," which forms
the south-eastern point of Abaco, and by the south-
western point of Inagua.

The vastness of the trade to and fro in the
direction of the Bahama group, and beyond it,
and the intricacy and difficulty of the navigation
through or near these most dangerous coasts, fringed
as they are with shoals, and bristling with cays and
rocks, and where strong and shifting currents, and
sudden and violent gales expose the most conscientious and wary navigator to unexpected perils and
trials, have led to the destruction and loss of
thousands of unfortunate vessels—ships of all sizes,

and of every description and character — which finished their voyages upon the treacherous sandbanks and deadly reefs of this widely-scattered group. But, in addition to dangers, natural and unavoidable, attendant upon the passage through these ocean labyrinths, there are innumerable localities and opportunities offering temptations to the dishonest ship-master wilfully to cast away his vessel for the purpose of defrauding the underwriters, or of obtaining, by secret arrangement with the wreckers, a share of the salvage. There is reason for believing that many ships and cargoes have been thus cast away, through captains of vessels betraying the trust reposed in them.

The large number of wrecks occurring in these dangerous seas, and along the Florida shores, where reefs and cays abound, rendering the navigation most perilous; and the rich prizes sometimes obtained by the wreckers, have led to a large number of the inhabitants in some of the islands, and along the coast of Florida, devoting themselves principally, though few, if any, exclusively to the occupation of wrecking; cruising about those places where accidents most frequently occur to shipping, or being ready to rush off as soon as they hear of a vessel stranded, or apparently in danger of stranding.

The writer has sometimes been amazed when looking from his piazza, which commanded an extensive view of a harbour from whence many wrecking schooners were fitted out, to see a strange commotion suddenly arise amongst all the vessels that happened to be in port—boats crowded with men hastily putting off from the shore, and every schooner and sailing boat with all possible haste hoisting sail and speeding away towards the entrance to the harbour, each evidently anxious to be ahead of all the others. The cause of the unwonted stir was soon understood; tidings had arrived that some unfortunate ship had got ashore, and all these were hastening away to the wreck—not to murder and plunder, but to give their aid in saving what they might be able, of the lives of the crew, and the cargo of the doomed vessel.

The wreckers of the Bahamas and of the Florida Cays are not, therefore, such monsters of depravity and crime as the term would seem to indicate to some minds not well-informed upon the subject, but men engaged in a pursuit which, abstractedly, is most commendable, and when not abused fraught with true benevolence and benefit to others. It is, however, not to be denied that it is an occupation which has had the necessary and usual effect of demoralizing the persons engaged in it, by diverting their attention from agriculture and other industrial pursuits; exposing them to the trials and temptations of alternate abundance and want; and accustoming them to rejoice instead of grieving over misfortunes which bring calamity and ruin to others. A remarkable illustration of the last-mentioned evil occurs to the recollection of the writer.

About the year 1870, I was on a visit to a cluster of small islands called the Biminies, lying right opposite to the extreme southern point of Florida; just where that point on the one hand, and the Bimini shore on the other, enclose the narrowest and most rapid portion of the Gulf Stream, as it emerges and rushes with greatly accelerated force from the Mexican Gulf to the Atlantic Ocean. From the Bimini shore, at a distance from one to two miles, the edge of the dark blue water of the Gulf Stream, clearly defined, was distinctly visible; between which and the land lay the smooth channel through which the multitudinous vessels of every class, closely hugging the land, threaded their course until they had weathered the last point of the island, and the wide-stretching waters of the Gulf itself lay before them. It was on a Saturday forenoon that, from the door of the cottage which formed my temporary home, I had watched with much interest a large number of vessels of different sizes and rigging, rapidly succeed each other in passing down the channel, with all their sails expanded to the strong favouring breeze which impelled them on their way. At length my attention was particularly arrested by the appearance of a very large full-rigged ship, probably a cotton ship bound to the Mississippi. I could see her at a considerable distance looming larger and larger as she drew nearer to the spot where I sat; and I could not help thinking that the course she was taking was in dangerous proximity to the island. Others, as it afterwards appeared, who were far better acquainted with the perils of that navigation than I was, thought so too. Many eyes were upon the large vessel, as, with every sail spread, she moved rapidly and majestically along the coast ; and the people all along the shore left their cottages in haste, expecting every moment to see her run aground. But onward she moved, until she seemed to the spectators behind her, to have safely passed the extremest point of land ; when in a moment her course was checked, and she stood perfectly still. She had grounded upon a sand-bank, stretching out some little distance beyond the shore.

Loud, long, and exultant was the shout that immediately went up from the crowd of spectators, who clapped their hands and danced about, and rejoiced exceedingly in the misfortune which seemed to have overtaken the noble ship. Most painful, and most unnatural and unchristian, were these demonstrations of delight over an event that must of necessity be fraught with loss and suffering, and possibly with utter ruin, to those who were interested in the safety of the vessel. In a few minutes all the inhabitants of the little town, men, women, and children, greatly excited, ran hastily to the shore, many of them laughing and congratulating each other, and crying out in joyous tones, " A wreck ! a wreck ! " anticipating large profits from the salvage of so rich a prize. But their exultation turned out to be premature ! The Captain, although he had been somewhat too heedless in running down so close to the land, proved himself equal to the emergency. The sails were backed and placed in the most favourable position to catch the steady breeze. All eyes were directed to the stranded ship; and half an hour had not elapsed when, to my great satisfaction, and the bitter disappointment of the excited islanders, she slowly drew off from the shoal, and spreading all her canvas to the winds, triumphantly pursued her voyage.

But, notwithstanding these well-founded objections to the wrecking system, and the demoralizing influence which it has exerted to some extent upon all who are associated with it, it is not to be denied that numerous lives and much property have been saved through the instrumentality of the Bahama and Florida wreckers; that large numbers of intrepid and hardy seamen are reared up; and that a large income is legitimately derived by the colonists from this source, which, however undesirable, is incidental to their geographical position, and almost inseparable from it.

Both in the Bahamas and the State of Florida, the Legislative authorities have endeavoured to bring the wrecking system under salutary control by enacting laws which require licenses to be taken out both for men and vessels engaging in the trade, provide for the appointment of wreck-masters, apportion the share of salvage which each vessel and its crew may justly claim, and impose heavy penalties for certain acts of misconduct. These laws are stringently enforced, especially of late years, very much to the advantage of underwriters, and probably to the lessening of the number of wrecks: the rapid and close investigation to which every case is now subjected, rendering it far more difficult than it formerly was for unprincipled ship-masters, in collusion with equally unprincipled wreckers, wilfully and designedly to run their vessels ashore.

For many years nearly half of the imports to the Bahamas consisted of goods saved from vessels wrecked within the limits of the Colony. During the seven years from 1858 to 1864, there were no less than 313 wrecks in the Bahama waters, of which 110 were British, 157 American, 13 French, 6 Spanish, and the remainder belonging to other nations. But of late years the number and description of wrecks have been considerably affected by the erection of light-houses to guide mariners through these devious and dangerous channels; so that one light has not been left far behind, before another of these friendly beacons is seen ahead, shedding its welcome radiance over the wild wastes of waters, and guiding the tempest-tossed mariner safely on his way. The men and vessels licensed for, and engaged in, the wrecking trade now, are probably not half the number that followed this occupation prior to the American civil war.

In the year 18— during the autumn, the good ship *American* sailed from New York, bound first for Mobile in the Gulf of Mexico, thence to a European port, and afterwards to the place whence she had originally taken her departure. She had been chartered for the voyage, to take the place of one of the regular packet-ships which, before the rise of steam had so largely driven packet sailing-ships from the ocean, were accustomed to perform these voyages, and convey passengers, mails, and cargo, to the different ports within the Gulf. At the earnest solicitation of the company who chartered her, Captain A. who had commanded the same vessel for many years, but after a long service at sea had retired for life, as he supposed, to his own quiet home in Massachusetts, was prevailed upon for this voyage, to quit his snug retreat and take charge of the ship. This he did with great reluctance, and once more prepared himself to face the hardships and perils of the stormy ocean.

The voyage promised to be very pleasant and prosperous; for it was a time of year when the weather is usually fine and balmy, unless a hurricane, originating eastward of the West India Islands bounding that side of the Caribbean sea, should happen in its mysterious affinity to the Gulf Stream to be sweeping obliquely across the Atlantic in that direction, carrying desolation and ruin in its train. But, happily no such unwelcome visitor appeared. The passengers, numbering about thirty ladies and gentlemen, formed a choice and agreeable company, and there was variety among them. The greater part were connected with trade, merchants and members of their families, and merchants' clerks occupying good and responsible positions, who were returning to their respective places of business from a pleasant visit to the various fashionable summer resorts and watering places in the North.

There was one of the passengers on board who

called himself a lawyer, but failed to commend himself to the good opinion of the Captain, who thought very lightly of the legal attainments of the somewhat forward and obtrusive gentleman, and considered him at best what he termed a "marine-court lawyer." The precise meaning he attached to the designation he did not explain, but it was manifestly used contemptuously as a term of depreciation. The Captain himself was one who commanded the esteem and confidence of all on board, and of whom one of the most intelligent of the passengers said, "I do injustice to none in assigning to our Captain a high place as a gentleman among others who worthily bore that honourable name. For my own part, I found in him my most agreeable companion on board, of whose leisure I was glad to avail myself in drawing from him the results of a varied and extensive observation and experience of men and things. He was a man of extensive reading and culture, and his modesty was equal to his literary attainments."

The region of Cape Hatteras, usually so rough and stormy, and the Gulf Stream, were safely passed; and what with reading and conversation, the oft-recurring meals, observing the "wind and weather," watching the ship's progress in dull or lively sailing, and the ever-interesting details of skilful navigation, with such spice of variety as head-winds and squalls could afford, and the excitement of "Let go and haul!" reefing, taking in, and making sail, that old method of sea-voyages before the innovation of ocean-steamers, though often tedious, was not without its interest and enjoyment. It was considered sufficiently good and comfortable when it was the best method of travelling then known. In due time the cays of Abaco, and the long straggling island of the same name, were sighted; one of the principal islands that form the Bahama group. No lighthouse then stood upon Elbow Cay as there is now, to inform the tempest-tossed mariner at what part of the low, monotonous coast he has made the land; but the weather was bright and fine, and running down the coast at a safe distance, the *American*, with all her passengers merry and cheerful, rounded the rock well-known as the " Hole-in-the-Wall," where a lofty lighthouse marks the extreme southern point of Abaco, and opens the passage into what is known as "the Providence Channel." Through this channel, and over the almost cream-coloured waters of the Bahama bank, the noble ship in a dark night beat in safely against a head wind, the most vigilant out-look being maintained on board to avoid the dangerous shoals surrounding them in all directions. The Berry islands were next passed; the several light-houses on Stirrup's Cay, Gun Cay, Cay Sal, or Double-headed-shot Cay, and the Great Isaacs, all contributing, as the mariners moved onward, to light them on the way.

Then came the Sabbath day, calling upon them to remember and render praise and worship to Him "who rides upon the stormy sky, and calms the roaring seas," a call which was readily and devoutly obeyed, and the day, under the salutary influence

which Captain A. exerted over all on board his
ship, was spent in a manner that was calculated to
awaken serious and solemn thoughts, and lift all
their minds above the perishing things of earth.

Passing close along the Bimini shore, and little
more than a mile from the edge of the Gulf Stream,
where its darker-coloured waters rush with almost
the rapidity of a torrent, through the narrow channel
between those islands and the Florida point, the ship
passed with a fine brisk wind, and all her sails gaily
spread, into the gulf, and without accident or harm
stood on her course, running along the line of the
Florida Cays, unconscious and unsuspicious of danger,
inasmuch as the worst perils of the voyage had
already been encountered, and now the ship had
plenty of sea room. Still there was need for the
exercise of all watchful care. The danger was less
than it had been; but danger still existed, as the
sequel painfully made manifest.

The last of the Florida Cays that lay in their course
after they had passed Key West was what is called
the *Dry Tortugas*, upon which the American government has erected a light-house, beyond which, to the
westward, taking care to give the light-house a wide
berth, ships bound to Mobile or the Mississippi turn
their bows more towards the north. The *American*
was now off the Dry Tortugas, the weather fine,
balmy, soothing—in a word, tropical, for the tropic
line was less than two degrees to the southward of
the course they were steering. All felt joyful in the
approaching termination of the passage to Mobile;

for the last turning point was at hand, when the ship would haul up for the north-west course that would bring her to the southern city to which she was in the first place bound. When the Tortugas light was nearly abeam it was ten o'clock, and with mutual pleasant congratulations and hopeful anticipations all retire below, saying to each other, "We shall see no more land until we make the Mobile light."

An hour passed after the passengers went below, and all was as quiet as sleep could make the occupants of the several cabins. It was a calm, starlight night, and the gallant bark, borne smoothly on her course by a favourable wind, was making easy progress, when suddenly she brought up all standing and hard-a-ground. Those who have not been taught by painful experience, can scarcely form an adequate idea of the mingled surprise, terror, and apprehension, caused by the vessel in which they have embarked running unexpectedly in the dead of the night upon a hard bed of rocks.

The harsh grating sound of the keel scraping upon the stones seems to thrill every nerve of the body; while visions of imminent peril rush before the mind, crowding it with startling images of shipwreck, disaster, drowning, and death. Those who have once passed through the trial never desire to feel it again.

In a moment all on board—passengers, and that part of the crew whose watch was below—started, terror-stricken, from their slumbers, and in such garments as they could snatch up and throw around

them at the moment, hastened upon deck to ascertain
the cause of the strange, startling noise which had
broken in upon their rest, and why the ship had
suddenly become so still. All was now bustle upon
deck. Soundings were made forward and aft, and in
all directions about the vessel; and it was soon
understood that the ship had kept in too close and
run upon a sunken reef.

The sails were backed, boats lowered and manned,
to try and carry out a kedge astern; and the windlass manned by some of the seamen and many of the
passengers. All possible efforts were made to clear
the reef, but in vain. The luckless bark had run
full sail upon the rocks, and there she stuck, hard
and fast, defying for the present all attempts to get
her afloat.

Soon the falling tide made more clearly manifest
the danger in which all on board were involved.
The ship careened more and more upon her side, and
showed that she had grounded during high water.
And now speculations became rife amongst those
who crowded the deck; for none thought of repairing
again to the berths from which they had so rudely
been summoned; and all, not excepting the female
passengers, remained on deck, cloaked and shawled,
to protect them from the dews of the night. Some
wondered how it was possible the ship could have
been drawn so much out of her right course, sug-
gesting that probably it was the effect of a strong
current which had set her upon the reef; others
spoke of a hazy atmosphere, though the sky was

clear and cloudless, and the stars shone out brightly—supposing that the haze might have dimmed the usually bright light on the Dry Tortugas, and made the distance from it to appear greater than it was; while two or three old hands suggested—a conjecture to which the circumstances gave strong probability—that the keeper of the light-house, in complicity with some unprincipled wrecker, had wilfully obscured the light, in hope of luring the ship, or some other unfortunate vessel, to her destruction upon the reef. This last hypothesis Captain A. considered the most probable; and after long and serious deliberation on the subject, exclaimed, " We are victims of the piratical Wreckers." Anxiously the crew and passengers waited for the morning, hoping that a rising tide would lift the ship from her rocky bed; but daylight brought very little encouragement, and dawned upon a seemingly hopeless wreck. The sea was still smooth, as it had been all through the night, but the vessel was hard-a-ground; no steamer was near which could be called to the help of the distressed mariners, and the prospect of getting the vessel afloat was exceedingly gloomy.

The morning was not far advanced when a small fishing-smack came alongside; and from her a rough specimen of humanity, who claimed to be her master, found his way to the deck of the stranded ship. He held a wrecker's license. His reception was not a cordial one, either with the Captain and crew, or with the passengers, when he announced his profession; for they all regarded it as a suspicious cir-

cumstance that the smack came from the direction of
the Tortugas light; and by this time the belief was
generally entertained that there had been some
tampering with the light, in order that those on
board any passing ships might be induced to believe
that the light-house was more distant than was really
the case, and so become entangled with the reef.
The wrecker was a stout, burly, red-faced, sun-burnt
sailor, whose only clothing consisted of a Guernsey
shirt, rough pantaloons rolled up to the knees, and a
slouched, weather-beaten hat. He described himself
as hailing from Connecticut; and as he stood by the
bulwarks, eyeing with evident satisfaction the unfortunate condition of the ship, presented by no means
an attractive appearance to those by whom he found
himself surrounded. The rough visitor was not
backward in making offers of assistance, but these
were refused by the Captain, not only because he considered the charge made by the man to be very high,
but chiefly because he disliked altogether the appearance and manners of the wrecker, and feared that he
might be drawn into still greater difficulties and
dangers; and the smack took her departure.

Moreover, the captain was not without hope that
high water might bring relief; and inspired by this
expectation, all that skill and ingenuity could devise
was done to save the ship. A kedge anchor was
again carried out astern, with the strongest hawser
the vessel could furnish; and as the time of high
water drew on, all hands were summoned to the
windlass. A powerful strain was applied to the

hawser, when, lo! to their grateful surprise, but almost contrary to all their hopes, the ship moved and floated! All was now joy and activity on board; sails were trimmed, and every man was sent to his post; but, unfortunately, it was found impossible "to fetch by" the reef, and again the ship grounded, driven further on to the rocks than she had been before by the force of the waves.

Another day came, and with it other plans for saving the ship; but with another day came a stronger wind and heavier sea, and the vessel began to thump somewhat heavily upon the rocks. As a last experiment the Captain determined to lighten the labouring ship; which, of course, could only be done by the sacrifice of valuable cargo—and at high water try to drive her with all sail right over the reef. Meanwhile, the wrecker again made his appearance on board, and in answer to the Captain's inquiries, gave advice as to a place of anchorage if required. Under a heavy press of sail, when the tide was at its height, the vessel was forced over the reef, but in the act of passing the rudder was unshipped and rendered useless. Now all was bustle and hurrying to and fro; but by skilful trimming of the sails, the ship was steered to the anchorage which had been pointed out by the wrecker, near a cay to the south-east of the light-house. Unhappily, during the night following, the wind rose to half a gale, and the ship, dragging her anchor, again took the ground; and when morning dawned was fast burying her stern in the sands of a lee-shore.

c 2

All hope of getting her fairly and safely afloat was now abandoned. The wind increased, and the wreck, driven stern-wise and striking more heavily, was thrown broadside upon the cay. The wrecker had left, and noon came; everything was ominous of danger; and it made the Captain's stout heart ache within him, as he felt the noble vessel lift and strike, grounding heavily upon the coral reef beneath. Almost in despair, he exclaimed, " I would rather that my body instead were grinding upon those rocks."

Preparations were now ordered to be made for leaving the ship, as it might be unsafe to remain on board through another night, and a raft was begun, upon which to float the passengers to the shore where the light-house stood.

These preparations were stayed by the timely return of the wrecker and his smack. His opportunity, for which he had been patiently waiting, had now arrived.

With some difficulty, he succeeded in taking off the passengers and their luggage, and landing them on the Dry Tortugas Cay; but it was after dark when they stepped ashore. The only dwelling on the Cay was that of the light-house keeper; it had only two rooms, and these were given up to them. One of the rooms was assigned to the ladies; the other, and the piazzas, were occupied by the gentlemen, who distributed themselves as best they could. Stores were brought from the wreck the next day, for the use of the whole company.

Now, according to the usages of the wrecking system, the voyage was ended; the wreck belonged to the underwriters, and the wrecker who had first come must have the first opportunity of saving the property, for the benefit, first of the underwriters, and secondly for his own profit, together with those who formed the crew of the smack.

The wrecker, with his crew of two or three fishermen, amongst whom the deputy light-keeper was prominent, had gained their object, and obtained full possession of the prize.

Captain A., anxious to secure the interests of the underwriters,* requested the principal wrecker to assist him in sending intelligence of the wreck to Key West, the chief rendezvous of the wreckers, in order that he might obtain more help in saving, with little delay, all that was possible of the cargo. The vessel having bilged, admitted the sea water, and the value of the goods she contained was hourly diminishing; but the Captain's proposal did not suit the views and purposes of the wreckers. The only means of conveyance was the lighthouse boat—a small, sloop-rigged craft, undecked, of about five tons burthen; this boat, they assured the Captain, should be immediately dispatched, according to his wishes; but there the matter ended.

Three days elapsed, and no movement was made to send away the boat; meanwhile, the wrecker and his associates were busy about the wreck. The Cap-

---

* The parties by whom the vessel and cargo were insured.

tain then became impatient, and insisted that the promise of the wrecker should be fulfilled : and, seeing how determined he was, it was resolved that the next day the boat should be sent away in charge of the deputy light-keeper.

Some of the passengers volunteered to accompany the expedition, among them the talkative lawyer, who thought it a good opportunity to display his zeal and courage, but who was really anxious to get away from the unpleasant predicament in which they were all involved, and secure his own safety. Not without some foreboding of failure Captain A. saw the party off, wishing them a safe and speedy passage. It was rather a risk to undertake the passage—a distance of sixty or seventy miles—in so small a vessel. All were hopeful, but none so confident and boastful as the lawyer. "The thing," he said, "can and shall be done." Owing to a prevailing calm, the boat, after her departure, remained long in view, but at length a breeze sprang up; and the adventurers were wafted out of sight.

Relieved of this anxiety, which had worried him greatly for several days, the exposure and excitement to which he had been subjected began to tell upon the Captain, and he was prostrated by a severe paroxysm of fever. He had taken up his quarters, for the sake of quiet, on the ground floor of the light-house ; and, at his request, one of the passengers bore him company, and attended upon him.

He was sick both in mind and body. "How foolish I was," he exclaimed, " to leave my home for this voyage ! Yet, now I would like to make another, only to give the Dry Tortugas a wide berth."

As evening came on the unwelcome news spread among those at the light-house that the boat was returning, and soon the whole party, boasting lawyer and all, landed at the Cay. It soon became evident to Captain A., from the story they told, that this had been planned beforehand, and that the deputy light-keeper had been tampering with the fears of those who were in the boat. The same night this was singularly confirmed. While the Captain and his companion lay quietly on the floor of the light-house, the deputy keeper and the principal wrecker passed in and ascended to the top of the building. There they talked in their ordinary tones about the incidents of the preceding day. Evidently they were not aware that the winding staircase formed a sort of whispering gallery, so that what was uttered in the lowest tones at the top could be distinctly heard below. They listened while the light-keeper stated how he had represented to the travellers in the boat the obstacles and perils they would encounter before reaching Key West—calms and head winds, a long and tedious passage at the best—and their liability to meet with heavy squalls and northers. The effect he designed to produce was accomplished, and they became terrified, and resolved to return.

Over this result the two rejoiced and laughed heartily ; they spoke of the prospect of a rich harvest of gain being brighter than ever, and in view of it the wrecker said with marked satisfaction, " If the boat can be kept back another day, I shall be able to get all I wish, and then she may go." On hearing this, the Captain whispered to his companion, "Now, the boat shall go, and that to-morrow morning, even if I am obliged, sick as I am, to go in her myself."

In further planning for the proposed trip, the Captain urged his companion, who, like himself, had heard the conversation between the two conspirators, to accompany him, to which he assented.

The next morning the light-keeper, who offered no resistance, with a boy to assist in sailing the boat, together with the Captain and his companion, embarked a second time, for what proved a successful experiment. The early morning was calm as the previous one; soon, however, a breeze arose, but it was dead ahead.

Their first stretch was on a starboard tack, by which they stood out into the Gulf; late in the afternoon they tacked again, and stood across the line of Cays, passing to the northward of them. At midnight the weather became squally; the first two or three squalls were comparatively light, then followed one which came down upon them with terrible fierceness. The first blast from it sent the boat down upon her beam-ends, and to increase the danger, the halyards were found to be foul, and they were for a few moments in imminent peril; indeed, the boat would have been capsized, had it not been that, by dint of the greatest exertion, the peak was lowered sufficiently to shake the wind out of the sail, and so they were saved. After this the Captain and his friend took

A Wreck and Wrecking Schooners.

matters entirely into their own hands, and kept a sharp look out for themselves. This squall over, they had light and baffling winds during the rest of the night; but as morning approached, a regular norther set in, which, under shortened sail, carried them on very rapidly; and for the last few miles, being north-ward of their port, they ran down to it under bare poles, unable to carry any sail at all.

While still at some distance, the boat was descried by the people at Key West, and the light-house boat being recognised, a crowd soon gathered on the dock awaiting her arrival.

The visit of the boat being unexpected, the people at once conjectured the truth. This was shown by the inquiries which greeted their arrival. "A wreck?" was shouted by many voices; and this being answered in the affirmative, was succeeded by the cry, "Where? where?" The answer to these questions pretty well fulfilled the purpose of the boat's voyage, and soon speedy help was sent to the wreck. Although a gale was blowing, in a few minutes all was bustle and preparation, and several wrecking schooners were hastening their departure to the spot which had been named. Some got under weigh, but the severity of the norther compelled them to put back. Amongst them was a fishing smack just arrived from Havanna with a deck-load of oranges; the fruit, without any hesitation, was thrown overboard, to clear the vessel for her wrecking voyage, and the Captain and his companion, secure of obtaining the help they came to seek, and having tasted no food for twenty-four hours, were glad to repair to a comfortable hotel, and order breakfast. With sharpened appetites, they sat down to a plentiful repast of Key West beef-steaks (*alias* green turtle), with suitable accompaniments ; not failing to render their thanksgivings to Him who had delivered them out of great perils, and brought them to a secure haven.

The next business which claimed their attention was to engage a suitable vessel to proceed to the Tortugas light-house to take the shipwrecked passengers to their destination at Mobile. The next day the chartered vessel was ready, and the Captain and his companion proceeded in her to the scene of the wreck, where their fellow-passengers were soon embarked with their luggage, and on their way to their homes. At the earnest request of Captain A., the one who had been with him when he overheard the conversation at the light-house, before mentioned, remained behind, in order that he might give evidence on that subject, when the salvage suit should come before the Admiralty Court, at Key West.

It was a fortnight, or more, before all the goods were got out of the wreck and dried, and the ship stripped of her sails and cordage, and whatsoever was movable. Then the whole was shipped on board the several wrecking vessels, and conveyed to Key West.

The first wrecker having precedence of the rest, as is usual in such cases, had succeeded before the arrival of other vessels in discharging all, or nearly all of the dry and undamaged goods, and thus made his profit sure ; then came the more difficult work of breaking up the cargo from the lower hold and out of the water, which at the flow and ebb of the tide rose and fell in the bilged vessel. The last and most difficult of all the business was that of the divers, who had been trained in the waters around New Providence, and who now persevered in their work, deep in the vessel's hold, making fast ropes and hooks to submerged boxes and bales of merchandize, and to the casks which usually form the lowest stowage of a large cargo ; and this, notwithstanding the water was discoloured, and rendered insupportably nauseous by dye stuffs, drugs, medicines, and poisons washed out of the various packages by the ebb and flow of the sea.

After everything was done that was practicable at the wreck for the benefit of the underwriters, and all the goods were conveyed to Key West, Captain A. and his companion returned to that port to await the issue of the salvage suits in the Admiralty Court. There they found the place all astir with the additional excitement growing out of the stranding of another large merchantman, with a full cargo of assorted merchandize, on one of the Florida Cays.

Following in the established order of things, a public sale of all the goods, sails, and rigging of the wrecked *American* took place under the orders of the Admiralty Court : the saving of each wrecker, or association of wreckers, being kept distinct from those of other parties, which is the ordinary usage both in Florida and the Bahamas; the laws governing the wrecking system being closely assimilated under both Governments. Then came on the proceedings in the above-named Court, which were regarded with special interest by all concerned, involving, as they did, the amount of salvage or compensation to be awarded to the several parties of wreckers.

The Admiralty Court at Key West was presided over by a judge of eminent ability and probity, whom the wreckers regarded with the profoundest reverence, holding him in the highest respect for his judicial sagacity, and standing, as they had reason to do, in salutary fear of his strict and impartial justice. Captain A.'s friend having inquired privately of this gentleman how such a rough class of men as the wreckers could be effectually controlled and held in check? "Oh," said he, "that is easily done. If they commit any offence against honour or justice, instantly I take from them their licenses, which are always subject to the control and revocation of the Court. It is well-known among them that the penalties of any abuse of privilege, or dishonesty in the prosecution of their business as wreckers, involve not only the revocation of their licenses, temporarily, or for ever, at the discretion of the Court, but also a forfeiture, or reduction of the salvage fees, as may seem fitting to the Court."

In the case of a wreck on Corrysfort Reef, it

was charged that a certain wrecker had received from the wreck certain goods which he had failed to deliver at Key West; and further, it was proved that this wrecker had stopped at his home on J—— Cay by the way. The main facts having been established, he was deprived of his wrecking license, and denied all salvage for his four vessels which he had employed about the wreck.

The percentage of salvage varies according to the circumstances of each case. In most instances it may appear to be extravagantly high; but a large compensation is necessary as an inducement to the wrecker to undergo the hazard, expense, and toil, which are inseparable from the business: and when it is considered how much of the wrecker's time is unemployed, what risks and hardships they undergo, and how small the amount and value of the goods saved often are, it is not at all surprising that from thirty to sixty or seventy per cent. is often awarded to the wreckers. There have been cases—probably few and far between—in which the whole of the proceeds of the goods saved have not been thought by the Court too much to reward the services of the wreckers.

The attention of the wreckers, as a rule, is first directed to the preservation of the passengers and their luggage, and the lives of the crew; and for this no reward is *claimed*, although frequently bestowed voluntarily. A brig laden with sugar, bound from Havanna to a port in Europe, was wrecked upon a reef to the eastward of Key West. On board her, beside the crew, were four or five passengers; only one boat belonging to the wreck was left fit for use, and that too small to hold all the company in escaping from their perils. A raft was, therefore, constructed and the party divided, some entering the boat and others embarking on the raft which was attached by a rope to the boat, to be towed by her to the nearest place of safety. The attempt failed. No progress could be made through a rough sea against a head-wind and current, and the raft with the people on it, had to be cast adrift.

The boat alone reached the island, and falling in with a wrecking schooner by the way, reported the wreck and the abandoned raft.

The wrecker went immediately in search of the raft and its freight of human life ; and for two days anxiously cruised about for it in all directions, until it was found and the people rescued.

Then, and not till then, the schooner proceeded to the wreck. Of the perishable lading nothing could be saved, for the sugars were all washed out of the brig : and after stripping her of all available rigging, sails, chains, &c., the wreckers proceeded with them to Key West. "In this case," the Admiralty Judge said, "I awarded to the salvors all the avails of the articles saved—not over three or four hundred dollars—as a just, though inadequate, compensation for their praiseworthy efforts."

It was a great relief to Captain A. and the passenger he had detained as a witness in the case of the *American* when the last act of the business was completed by the decrees of the Court fixing the amount of the salvage, and the disbursement to the several wreckers, and associations of wreckers, of the several awards made in their favour.

The residuum, of course, went to the underwriters. But in the case of the unfaithful, scheming wrecker —the first who had presented himself on board— Captain A.'s friend had been detained in order that he might give his testimony in the Court as to the sinister part he had played, in conspiring with the deputy light-keeper to hinder the boat from reaching Key West to summon other greatly needed help. To the great amazement of those worthies, the whole conversation that had been held at the top of the Tortugas light-house was related and sworn to before the judge, furnishing undeniable, but wholly un- expected proof of their criminality : and for his guilty interference the wrecker was justly punished ; his share of the salvage, which otherwise would have been very considerable, because of the favourable opportunities he had had of selecting the best and most valuable portion of the cargo, being cut down by Judge W. from sixty, to thirty-five per cent. upon the amount of the goods saved by his vessel. Thus, he was taught by severe experience, that " honesty is the best policy." Captain A.'s companion took an early opportunity of going on to his destination ; while the Captain returned as soon as possible to New York and home, regretting that he had been so unwise as to undertake the voyage which had ter- minated so disastrously ; but often expressing the wish to try another trip to the Gulf, only for the opportunity it would afford him to give " a wide berth to the Dry Tortugas."

The foregoing narrative will serve to show those who may be uninformed on the subject, that the wrecking system, as it exists among the islands of the Bahamas and the cays of Florida, is not the wild, criminal, cruel system of deceit and plunder and murder which many suppose "*wrecking*" to mean. On the contrary, it involves much that is wise, humane, benevolent, economical, and effective, saving human life from the perils of the sea, and rescuing much valuable property from total and inevitable destruction.

But liable, as it is, to be perverted and abused by unscrupulous men, there is an obvious necessity that all its operations should be narrowly watched, and faithfully controlled and guarded. This is done both under the British and the American Governments, and such a rigid investigation instituted into every wrecking case that comes before the Admiralty Courts, as to secure ample protection to the rights of the owners and underwriters of merchant vessels. It is now a very difficult matter for an untrustworthy captain and dishonest wreckers to conspire successfully, as they used to do very frequently, to cast away a ship and cargo for their own profit and the injury of the owners.

VICISSITUDES
OF A LOWLY LIFE.

Heaven but tries our virtue by affliction,
And oft the cloud which wraps the present hour
Serves but to brighten all our future days.

DR. BROWN.

CHAPTER I.

Free-Born.

T is a wise and beneficent arrangement that shuts the future from our view, and keeps us ignorant of events which are about to transpire. If the dark shadows of coming events were permitted to fall across our path, and impending calamities to exhibit their threatening outlines in the dim mists of the future, how fatal would this be to the happiness of human life! All the brightness of man's existence would be obscured; and the enjoyments and comforts of the present would be absorbed and forgotten in the corroding anxieties and cares of approaching sorrow and trouble!

Thus would it have been with the subject of the present sketch. Could he have looked into the future and foreseen that he, a free American citizen, born to an inheritance of liberty, would, through the wickedness and cupidity of some of his fellow-citizens, be stolen from his native land, deprived of his birth-right, and consigned for many years of his

D

life to the multiplied horrors of slavery, how effectually would all the happiness of his pleasant home
have been blighted! and how completely would the
dreary anticipation have embittered every earthly
comfort, and rendered his future only a gloomy scene
of wretchedness and woe. ·

For some years before the providential extinction
of slavery in the United States of America, no man
who had the slightest mixture of African blood in his
veins was secure from the cupidity and villainy of the
slave-holding fraternity in the South. Although he
might be born free, in a free State, and of parents
who for several generations had known no bondage
and were well-known free citizens of the Republic ;
yet was the individual who had the misfortune to be
of coloured parentage liable to be entrapped by some
nefarious scheme even in the free land, lured away to
the slave territory, and there, hopelessly cut off from
all communication with his family and friends, consigned to all the miseries and oppressions of slave
life. When Abraham Lincoln's proclamation, for
ever abolishing human slavery in the United States,
was promulgated as a measure calculated to bring to
an end the sanguinary civil war then raging, how
many kidnapped human beings were scattered over
the slave-holding South—men and women who had
been born free, and even, according to the oppressive
laws of the Slave States themselves, were justly entitled to their liberty—is only known to Him from
whom no secrets can be hid. Many ruffianly men,
whose nature had become utterly corrupted under the

blighting and hardening influence of the slave system, made kidnapping their trade, and devoted themselves to the evil work of man-stealing and slave-hunting. Many a coloured man, lured and stolen away from his home and friends by such agents of wickedness, was sold to the South, and sent to wear out a wretched and hopeless existence in the rice-swamps of Georgia, the cotton-fields of Alabama, or the sugar-plantations of Louisiana, under the merciless lash of the slave-driver.

In the year 1841, there was residing at Saratoga Springs, in the State of New York, celebrated as a place of great fashionable resort, a coloured family of the name of Northup. Solomon, the head of the family, was in complexion a Sambo, that is the offspring of a black and a mulatto, his father being a pure negro, his mother, half white and half black. Anne, the wife of Solomon, was a coloured woman possessing considerable personal attractions, having the blood of three races flowing in her veins, the Indian blood being mixed with that of the African and European. Of graceful form and handsome features, possessing a clear yellow skin similar to that of the quadroon, and the flowing hair inherited from Indian progenitors, Anne Hampton was one of the belles of the neighbourhood, and sought after by many suitors. Solomon's susceptible heart was subdued by the charms of the coloured maiden, and he entered as a competitor for her favour. For some reason or other, he obtained the preference, and on Christmas day, 1829, they were married, Solomon

D 2

being then only twenty-one years of age, and his bride several years his junior.

The ancestors of Solomon, on the paternal side, were slaves in Rhode Island. They belonged to a family by the name of Northup, one of whom removing to the State of New York, settled at Hoosie, in Rensselaer County. He took with him Mintus Northup, Solomon's father. On the death of this gentleman which occurred early, Solomon's father became free, his emancipation being provided for in the master's will. He had previously been married to a free coloured woman.

After his liberation from slavery, Mintus Northup devoted himself to agricultural pursuits, being employed on various farms in different parts of the State until his death, which took place in November, 1829. He left a widow and two children, Joseph, and Solomon, the subject of this narrative.

Though born a slave, and labouring under all the disadvantages incident to such a condition, Solomon's father was a man respected for his industry and integrity. While he continued to be a slave, he enjoyed the respect and confidence of his owners, and after he became a free man, entitled to enjoy all the fruits of his own labour and industry, he commended himself to the respect and esteem of all who knew him by his diligence in business, and the unswerving truth and honesty with which he conducted all his affairs. He governed his family wisely, and gave to his children an amount of education surpassing that of most children around them who were in a similar condition of life; and by his diligence and economy, he acquired sufficient property to entitle him to the right of suffrage—the property qualification required for voters by the law.

"He was accustomed to speak to us," says Solomon, "of his early life; and although at all times cherishing feelings of kindness and even of affection towards the family in which he had been a bondsman, he nevertheless abhorred the system of slavery, and dwelt with sorrow on the degradation of the race to which he belonged. He endeavoured to imbue our minds with right and Scriptural sentiments, and to teach us to reverence and to place our confidence in Him who regards the humblest as well as the highest of His creatures. How often since that time has the recollection of his paternal, loving counsels occurred to me while lying in a stone hut in the sickly regions of Louisiana, smarting with the undeserved wounds which an inhuman master had inflicted, and longing only for the grave which covered the loving adviser, to shield me also from the lash of the oppressor. In the churchyard at Sandy Hill a humble stone marks the spot where he reposes, after having worthily performed the duties appertaining to the lowly sphere wherein God had appointed him to walk."

Solomon was employed with his father in the labours of the farm, until the father's death broke up the household and scattered it. His leisure hours during the intervals of farm labour were, under his judicious father's direction, devoted to his books and such branches of study as were within his reach, occasionally diversified by practising on the violin, an amusement which soon became the passion of his youth. He was soon somewhat proficient as a player on this instrument; and this, as the sequel will show, became to him a snare and a source of much danger and suffering, as well as the means of relieving the bitterness of many a weary hour of oppression and despair. It was probably the possession of this accomplishment that gave him the advantage over many rivals in securing the heart and hand of Anne Hampton. Little more than a month elapsed after his father was laid in the grave, when the blooming Anne was saluted by Solomon as his bride.

Three children were the fruit of this union, two girls and one boy. The young couple were warmly attached to each other, and both contributed their share to provide for the expenses of the household. Anne had resided for several years at a place well-known as the Eagle tavern, and had acquired considerable skill as a cook, being a clever and handy girl. After her marriage this accomplishment was turned to profitable account, and during Court weeks, and on other public occasions, she found employment at high wages in the principal boarding-house of the neighbourhood.

Solomon laboured industriously in the farming line, and his musical talent was in frequent requisition. He and his industrious little wife earned considerable sums of money; "so that," as he himself remarked, " with fiddling, cooking and farming, we soon found ourselves in possession of abundance, and leading a happy and prosperous life."

Solomon was, however, like many other Americans, of a somewhat restless disposition, and given to change and speculation. Soon after his marriage, and during the winter months when farm labour was not much in demand, he accepted an engagement to labour on the Champlain Canal. This was lucrative employment; and by the time his engagement terminated and the canal was opened in the spring, he was enabled, from the saving of his wages, to purchase a pair of horses and other things required in the business of canal navigation; and thus his energies were turned into a new channel.

Having hired several efficient hands to assist him, he entered into contracts for the transport of large rafts of timber from Lake Champlain to Troy. Many trips were successfully accomplished ; and during the season he became perfectly familiar with the art and mysteries of rafting. Little did he dream that he was then acquiring knowledge which should enable him many years after, when a slave, to render in this way profitable service to a worthy and kind master, and astonish by his readiness and skill the simple-witted slave lumbermen on the banks of Bayon Bœuf, in the far-distant swamp regions of Louisiana.

In one of his voyages down Lake Champlain, he was induced to make a visit to Canada. He extended his travels to Montreal, visiting the Cathedral and all the other lions of that large and beautiful city, and continued his excursion to Kingston and the Thousand Isles which beautify the St. Lawrence River, where, near to Kingston, the Lake Ontario contracts and forms the head of that majestic stream which flows on with its numerous rapids, receiving the copious streams of many other rivers, until it is lost in the Gulf which bears its own name.

Solomon completed his contracts on the canal, with profit to himself and satisfaction to his employers ; and then engaged with one, Alfred Gunn, to cut a large quantity of timber, which afforded him remunerative employment during the whole of the winter of 1831-32, and enabled him to support his wife and family in great comfort.

But again a change came over the spirit of his dream. He had been all his life accustomed to the labours of a farm, and it was an occupation more than any other congenial to his tastes. He resolved, therefore, with the concurrence of his wife, to employ his energies in that direction. Accordingly, in the spring of 1832, he entered into arrangements for a part of the old Alden farm, on which his father had formerly resided. The results of his winter's toil enabled him to purchase a cow and some other animals ; and, what was more important than all, a fine yoke of oxen. With these and other useful items of property which his wife's industry, combined with his own, enabled them to obtain, they proceeded to their new home near Kingsbury. The first year Solomon planted twenty-five acres of corn, sowed several large fields of oats, and commenced his farming operations on as large a scale as his means would allow. Anne diligently looked after affairs at home, while Solomon laboured industriously in the field. The end of the year proved to them that they had entered upon what was likely to turn out a prosperous speculation.

Here they continued, doing well, until 1834; and if Solomon had been of a more settled disposition, and less given to wandering and change, he would, no doubt, have become a prosperous and wealthy agriculturist, and acquired the means of purchasing a farm instead of paying rent for one. But being well-known as a skilful player on the violin, he had frequent calls to render his services at parties, and on festive occasions; and this tended to foster in him that indisposition to settle quietly down in his own peaceful home, which is characteristic of Americans, whatever may be their complexion. " Well, indeed, would it have been for us," Solomon remarked, " had we remained on the farm at Kingsbury; but the time came when the next step was to be taken towards the cruel destiny that awaited me."

Saratoga Springs had become a place of great attraction. Immense hotels were erected there, and vast crowds of the votaries of fashion flocked thither from all parts of the Union during the summer months. Especially from the hot, swampy regions of the South, to escape from the deadly influence of the maleria exhaled by the sun's fierce rays from June to November, the wealthy and haughty planters with their families hastened to the watering-places of the North, crowding the hotels, and lavishing in revelry and dissipation the wealth obtained for them by the hard toil of their slaves. Of all these scenes of pleasure and recreation Saratoga was, at the time we are writing about, the favourite place of resort to the fashionables of the South.

No doubt the anticipation of a rich harvest from the exercise of his musical talents amid scenes of so much gaiety, had its influence in tempting Solomon away from the peaceful and profitable culture of his farm. And his wife also conscious of her skill in the kitchen department, imagined that her services in that line of things would be much in demand at a place like Saratoga Springs, and that larger gains would thus be realized than by the slower and more laborious labours of the farm and the dairy. So they resolved to go to Saratoga.

This proved to be an ill-advised step, and ultimately led to consequences involving unutterable misery and distress. They went into house-keeping, and soon obtained sufficient employment. Anne was generally engaged during the visiting season at the United States Hotel, one of the largest and most fashionable in the place. Solomon was engaged by the keeper of a large boarding-house to drive a hack, and worked in that capacity for two years, receiving a high rate of wages. When the winter season came on, the company departed, and the hotels were shut up. Lacking more congenial employment, Solomon wrought upon the rail-road, then in course of construction between Saratoga and Troy. But his chief dependence during the intervals of more regular employment was his violin.

Their removal to Saratoga did not at all fulfil the sanguine expectations they had formed, and they often saw cause to regret the ·giving up of the peaceful and happy life they had experienced on the farm at Kingsbury. Though earning plenty of money, and always living in comfortable circumstances, they had not prospered. The riches they had fondly anticipated had not been gained, and seemed to be as far off as ever. The associations they had formed, and the society in which they had · mingled at the renowned watering place, were not calculated to foster and strengthen the simple habits of industry and economy to which they had been accustomed; but, on the contrary, had led them into a style of living, and the adoption of habits, tending to what the Americans call "shiftlessness" and extravagance.

While living at the United States Hotel, Solomon frequently met with slaves, who had accompanied their master's families from the South; and he held many a conversation with them on the subject of slavery. These were, generally, favourite, trusted slaves, who stood high in the favour of their masters. Although they were always well dressed, and well provided for, when thus in attendance on the family far from home, leading an easy kind of life, and with few cares to perplex and trouble them, he nevertheless found that, almost uniformly, they cherished a secret desire for liberty. Some of them expressed the most ardent anxiety to escape, and consulted Solomon on the best means of effecting it. But when it came to the point, the fear of the punishment which they knew was certain to attend their recapture and return home, in almost every case, was sufficient to deter them from making the attempt. Solomon had all his life breathed the free air of the North, and could hardly conceive how any man who had the smallest chance of making his escape could be content to live in the abject condition of a slave. He saw clearly the injustice and wrong done to the individual who was held in slavery by another man, and compelled to live and labour at that man's pleasure, and for his benefit, and, he, therefore, never failed to counsel those who consulted him, to watch their opportunity and strike for freedom. He had yet to learn from painful experience how slavery depresses the mind, and enervates the whole man, depriving him in many cases of the energy required to make a bold effort for freedom, especially in those early days when very few successful efforts to get off to a free land were heard of. The Underground Railway had then no existence, which in after years enabled so many thousands of fugitives to evade all attempts at recapture, and furnished them with facilities for reaching the happier land under the North Star, where they found protection, security, and employment under the shadow of the British flag waving over the Canadian shore.

CHAPTER II.

Betrayed and Stolen.

SOLOMON continued to reside at Saratoga until the spring of 1841. At this time his wife, to whom he was most fondly attached, was the mother of three children, who filled their home with joy and gladness, and whose lively prattle was like sweet music in their ears. Elizabeth, the first-born, was in her tenth year; the second, Margaret, in her eighth; while little Alonzo, the pride and pet of the household, had just completed his fifth year. The engagements of the mother took her away from home more frequently than the father, to whose care the little ones were a good deal consigned; both of the parents building many an airy castle concerning the destiny of these loved ones, for whom the future could in their estimation supply nothing that was too good or too great. It was always a gilded, happy future that they pictured out for their children.

Solomon was a devoted, loving father; his whole soul wrapped up in the children. During the intervals of his labour, when Anne was pursuing her vocation in the kitchen of some neighbouring or distant hotel—her services being much in demand—it was Solomon's delight to deck his children in the best that their wardrobe afforded, and wander with them through the streets and groves of Saratoga, or take them on some longer excursion into the country, where the most beautiful scenery abounded, training them to appreciate and delight in the beauties of nature. Nor was any expense spared upon their education; all such advantages as were then within the reach of persons of dark complexion being freely secured for them.

Thus far the history of Solomon presents little that is out of the ordinary current of events—nothing unusual—nothing but the common hopes, and cares, and labours of an obscure coloured man, having to contend, not only with the ordinary difficulties of life, but with the prejudices of caste, making his humble progress in the world more rough and painful than that of the man boasting of a fairer skin. But he had now reached a turning point in his life, and without the slightest suspicion of it stood upon the threshold of unutterable wrong, and sorrow, and despair. All appeared calm and bright around him. He had never been more happy in his family, who were all in the enjoyment of robust and vigorous health. He had never been more prosperous in his circumstances: though far from rich, he was surrounded with all worldly comforts, and enjoyed the blessing of a happy home. But he was now entering within the shadow of a thick cloud, in the dense darkness of which he was soon to disappear; thenceforward to be hidden from the eyes of all his kindred, and shut out from the sweet light of liberty for many a weary year.

One morning in March, 1841, towards the latter end of the month, as Solomon was walking about the village, looking for some employment by which his time might be profitably filled up, until the arrival of the busy season should bring back the usual engagements by which the summer and autumn months were fully occupied, he fell in with two strangers, who by some means engaged him in conversation. They appeared to belong to the rank of gentlemen, both of them being well-dressed, and the younger of the two habited in the extreme of the prevailing fashion. They seemed free and easy in their manners, not differing much from many others he was accustomed to meet at that place of gay resort. The first to address Solomon and engage him in desultory talk was a short, thick-set man, apparently about forty years of age, whose countenance indicated a considerable degree of shrewdness and intelligence, not to say sharpness. He wore a black frock coat, with a stylish hat, and other garments in accordance with them. He afterwards gave his name as Merrill Brown, and stated that he resided either at Syracuse or Rochester. His companion did not appear to be more than twenty-five years old, of fair complexion and light hair and eyes. He was somewhat effeminate in appearance, tall and slender, yet prepossessing, and making the impression that he might be some youthful sprig of fashion brought up in the luxurious habits of the South. He gave his name as Abram Hamilton, but did not mention where he came from.

That they had obtained some previous knowledge of Solomon was evident from the fact that, after they had succeeded in opening a conversation with him, they referred to his knowledge of music, and his expertness as a player upon the violin. If any feeling of suspicion for a moment arose in his mind when he found that he had by some inexplicable means become an object of interest and attention to these strange gentlemen, it was adroitly lulled to rest by the subtle flattery with which they assailed him on the subject of his musical powers. This was Solomon's weakness. His vanity inclined him to believe that in the use of his favourite instrument he was much more skilful and accomplished than he really was. They dexterously plied him with compliments concerning his performances, which completely won the heart of the simple-minded Solomon, and disposed him to do whatever such intelligent and well-informed gentlemen might require of him. Like the boa-constrictor of the South American swamps and creeks, which, after having enclosed its victim in its coils, covers it over with its slimy saliva before proceeding to the task of swallowing it; so these designing strangers, by fulsome flatteries, prepared their unsuspecting victim to yield himself up to their selfish and treacherous purposes.

After a somewhat lengthened conversation, the strangers gradually approached their object, and gave Solomon to understand that they were connected with a large circus company which was then in Washington City, and they were now on their return to that place to rejoin the circus, which they had left for a short time for the purpose of taking an excursion to the North, and seeing the country. If Solomon had been disposed to be suspicious of his new friends, he might have thought how unlikely it was that gentlemen, as they appeared to be, would be taking a pleasure excursion to the North, and indulging in sight-seeing at such an inclement season of the year, when everything as yet was in the iron grasp of winter. But Solomon was too much blinded by their flatteries to perceive any incongruity in the account they chose to give of themselves.

They gave Solomon to understand that they paid the expenses of their journey by giving an entertainment or exhibition in the places where they stopped; but they had found much difficulty in procuring music to accompany and enliven their performances, which had been a great drawback to their success. They then intimated that being well satisfied concerning his proficiency as a musician, they would like to engage his services for their future exhibitions; and proposed to Solomon to accompany them as far as New York City, and play on the violin wherever they found it practicable to give one of their entertainments. They offered as an inducement to give him a dollar a day as regular wages, with his board, and three dollars additional for every night he might play at their performances. They also offered to pay his expenses on his return from New York to Saratoga. It was, as the result showed, no part of their plan to part with Solomon at New York. But, not

E

to excite suspicion, no word was spoken about his going beyond that city.

If Anne had been at home, her advice might possibly have induced her husband to decline the tempting offer of these strangers. Women instinctively read human character much more readily than duller-witted man. And if she had had the opportunity of looking these men in the face and listening to their conversation, she would, no doubt, have discovered enough of discrepancy and false pretension to put her on her guard, and induce her to counsel her husband not to put too much confidence in these strangers, and to be cautious about putting himself in their power. But the faithful wife was away from home. It was Court week at Sandy Hill, some twenty miles distant; and Anne had been summoned, as for some years past, to take charge of the culinary department at Shenill's coffee-house, and minister to the comfort of judges, and jurors, and witnesses, who were in attendance upon the Court. Elizabeth, the eldest daughter, had gone with the mother to assist her in her labours, being now thirteen years of age or thereabouts. The other two children were on a visit to an aunt at Saratoga. Thus the family was scattered. If Solomon had had the opportunity of consulting his wife concerning this engagement, as he was in the habit of doing concerning all things affecting the family interests, he would have done so, but he did not expect his absence from home would extend beyond a few days, and supposed that he would be back from New York before the termination of her present engagement; he therefore did not even write to inform his wife of the expedition he was about to undertake. Thus it happened that none of his family knew whither he had gone; and when he was missed it seemed almost as if he had suddenly vanished into non-existence; leaving no trace of his departure behind.

Solomon accepted the tempting offer of the strangers the more readily, as he had a strong desire to see the metropolis of American commerce—the New York, of which he had heard such glowing accounts. His new employers were anxious to leave immediately after the engagement was completed, as if they were waiting only for that, as doubtless they were. So taking only a single change of clothes and the cherished violin, he was ready to depart within a very short time from his first meeting with the strangers in the street. The carriage was ordered round, a handsome vehicle drawn by a pair of noble bays, and forming altogether a handsome turn-out, not much in keeping with the pretensions of their owners. Their baggage, consisting of three large trunks, was attached to the vehicle; and then Solomon, mounting to the driver's seat, while the gentlemen took their places inside, drove away from Saratoga on the road to Albany, all unconscious that he was driving away to slavery and misery the entrapped victim of two unprincipled man-stealers. Solomon said, " Elated with my new position, and the bright prospects before me, I was as happy as I had ever been on any day in all my life."

They arrived at Albany the same day, and in the evening Solomon had an opportunity of gaining further knowledge of the real character of his travelling companions: for there they gave a performance, the only one during the whole period that he was with them. Hamilton was stationed at the door; Solomon formed the orchestra with his violin; while the man called Brown provided the entertainment. It consisted in throwing balls, dancing on a rope, and various tricks of ventriloquism and legerdemain. The whole performance was confined to this man. The audience was small, without being at all select, and the proceeds so trifling as to afford a very small remuneration to the parties who were interested.

The next morning they resumed their journey, Solomon on the driver's seat, and the other two occupying the interior of the comfortable carriage. The conversation of the two confederates now began to indicate great anxiety to rejoin the circus without delay. They pushed on their journey without stopping anywhere to give another entertainment, and in due time reached the City of New York. They took lodgings at a private boarding-house in a street running from Broadway to the North River. Solomon now supposed his journey to be at an end, and expected after he had seen something of the city to set his face again toward Saratoga, which he knew he could soon reach by journeying up the Hudson in one of the river boats to Albany; from whence he would have no difficulty in finding his way to

Saratoga. But now Brown and Hamilton commenced to importune him to go on with them to Washington and see the capital of the nation, together with the cities that they would pass through on their way. They stated that immediately on their arrival, now that the summer season was approaching, the circus would set out to take a circuit in the northern towns and cities. They promised that a situation in the circus and high wages should be given to Solomon while on their northern tour, and expatiated so largely on the advantages that would result to him that, overcome by their flattering representations, though not without some misgivings that the better course would be for him to return to his home, he was at length induced to comply with their wishes.

Whether it was that they saw cause for lulling to sleep fears and apprehensions in Solomon's mind, or that they feared there might be some interference with their designs on the part of any abolitionist friends he might possibly fall in with, they suggested that, inasmuch as they were about entering a slave state it would be well before leaving New York to obtain papers certifying his freedom. The idea struck him as a prudent one, although it had never occurred to him in the slightest manner that there would be any danger as to his personal safety where he was going. He accompanied his new friends to a building which he understood to be the Custom House. After certain preliminaries had been gone through, which he did not very clearly comprehend, a paper was filled up and handed to them with the

direction to take it to the clerk's office. This was
done; and the clerk having added something to the
paper and received a fee of six shillings, they all
returned to the Custom House. Here other for-
malities were gone through, and a further fee of two
dollars paid to the officials. Placing the papers in
his pocket, Solomon accompanied Brown and
Hamilton to their boarding-house, profoundly impressed with the conviction that the papers were not
worth the cost and trouble of obtaining them. He
never could understand this part of the conduct of
his associates. That it was part of a deep-laid
scheme of villainy he had no doubt, but the motives
for this procedure he could never penetrate.

Losing no time, the next day after their arrival in
New York, they crossed the ferry to Jersey City, and
then prosecuted their journey to Philadelphia. Here
they stopped one night, and then pushed on to
Baltimore, their anxiety to rejoin the circus seeming
to become intensified as they approached their
destination. All this time they travelled with the
carriage and the bays, Solomon being the driver.
In this occupation he was perfectly skilled, having
had the practise of several years at Saratoga; and
under his management the horses were well cared
for, and made to perform their duty cheerfully and
efficiently. At Baltimore they left the carriage and
horses, Solomon being kept in ignorance of the way
in which they were disposed of. Stopping one day
and night at Baltimore, they proceeded by the railway cars to Washington City, where they arrived

at nightfall, stopping at Gadsby's Hotel on Pensylvania Avenue.

After supper the two employers called Solomon to their apartments, and paid him forty-three dollars, a sum exceeding somewhat the wages he was entitled to. This act of generosity, they stated, was intended as a compensation for their not having given an exhibition so frequently as they had led him to anticipate during the journey from Saratoga. Their design was probably to render their intended victim perfectly unsuspicious; their plans being already laid for repossessing themselves of the money, together with the price of their victim's liberty.

Brown and Hamilton informed Solomon that the circus was to have left Washington for the north on the following day; but that was the day appointed for the funeral of General Harrison, on which account its departure would be deferred. On this occasion their treatment of him was exceedingly—not to say ostentatiously—kind. They had never shown him anything but kindness; but at this time they were profuse in their expressions of approbation and kindly interest in his welfare. " On the other hand," said Solomon, " I gave them my confidence without reserve, and would freely have trusted them to any extent. Their bearing and manner towards me— their foresight in procuring for me papers recognizing my rights as a free man, and many little acts of attention, too numerous to be repeated—all seemed to indicate to me that they were friends indeed.

Even when terrible experience had shed fresh light upon the subject, Solomon found it difficult to believe that there could be such inhuman monsters in the shape of men as could designedly, for the sake of gold, lure him away from home, and family, and liberty, and consign him to the indescribable miseries he was afterwards called to endure. But afterwards, on carefully revolving in his mind all the facts of the case, he was forced to the conclusion that these seeming friends were really such monsters of iniquity, that all their apparent kindness was but intended to lull him asleep in fatal security, and that he had through them, and for their profit, been wickedly betrayed, and plundered of all his rights as a citizen and as a man.

Solomon thought it strange that he saw nothing of the circus, nor any traces to show that it had a real existence. After receiving the money from his employers, they advised him not to venture out into the streets, as he was unacquainted with the customs of the city. This advice he thought it well to act upon, and was soon after shown by a coloured servant to a sleeping room on the ground floor in the back part of the hotel. He laid him down to rest, thinking of home, and wife, and children, and the long distance by which he was separated from all his loved ones. As he lay meditating upon the past and the strange situation in which he found himself, some uneasy, undefined apprehensions of impending evil floated through his mind until he fell asleep. But no angel of mercy in his dreams suggested to him to fly from the evils and trials which were close at hand.

The next day there was a grand pageant in the city, to which vast crowds flocked from the country as well as from all parts of the city, until the streets were blocked up and nearly impassable. Death had entered the White House, and laid low the Chief Magistrate of the Great Republic; and that day was to see the remains of General Harrison borne to the grave. The roar of cannon and the tolling of bells filled the air; many houses were shrouded with crape, and the streets were black with crowds clad in the garb of mourning. At the appointed hour the funeral procession made its appearance, moving slowly through the Avenue. A multitude of carriages followed the richly decorated hearse, while thousands upon thousands attended on foot; military bands at distant intervals playing the Dead March in Saul. There was genuine mourning as the remains of President Harrison were carried to their last resting-place, for all felt that in his premature and unexpected removal the nation had sustained a great loss, and that a truly great and good man had disappeared from among them.

During the whole day Brown and Hamilton were careful to keep Solomon near to them. He stood by them, watching the procession as it passed by, and amusing himself by noticing how, when the heavy guns were fired, windows were broken by the concussion, and showers of shattered glass came rattling to the ground. He walked with them to the Capitol, and for a long time strolled about in the public grounds and other parts of the city, where his companions pointed out to him various objects of interest which attracted their notice. In the afternoon they strolled as far as the President's House, and thus the day passed away. Still Solomon saw nothing of the circus, nor of any persons professing to be connected with it except his two companions. The excitement of the day served in a great measure to occupy his attention and divert his thoughts from other matters; but still, as the evening drew on, he could not help being impressed with the feeling that the non-appearance of the circus was somewhat strange; and stranger still, the great anxiety of his companions to rejoin the circus had entirely passed away! Since their arrival in Washington not a word had been spoken by them concerning it, except when, on the evening of their arrival, they referred to the funeral of General Harrison as the reason why its intended departure towards the North had been deferred.

Although they had given Solomon no reason, while he travelled with them, to believe that they were addicted to excessive drinking, he thought it somewhat remarkable that, several times during the afternoon, his two companions entered drinking saloons and called for liquor. On all these occasions, having helped themselves, they filled another glass and handed it to Solomon, and were careful to see that he drank the whole of what they gave him. He did not become intoxicated; but after the last of these potations towards the evening, he began to experience very unpleasant symptoms, and felt extremely ill. A dull, heavy, disagreeable pain in the head, accompanied by excessive drowsiness and other disagreeable sensations pervading his whole body, excited the suspicion that something unusual had been mingled with what he had drank. When he reached the hotel he could take nothing at the evening meal; the sight and smell of food were repulsive, and he turned away from it in disgust. His two friends appeared to commiserate his suffering and advised him to go at once to bed, expressing a hope that he would be better in the morning. And this was the last he was ever to see of them—they crossed his sight no more.

The same servant conducted him to the room he had occupied the previous night, where, divesting himself only of coat and boots, he threw himself upon the bed. But he found it impossible to sleep. The racking pain in his head increased until it became almost unbearable. In a short time he became thirsty : but there was nothing within his reach that would allay his thirst, and there he lay until he became delirious, and could think of nothing but water—of lakes and flowing rivers, of brooks where he had stooped to drink, and of the dripping bucket, rising with its cool and overflowing nectar from the bottom of the shaded well. After enduring this torment for some time until he was on the verge of madness, he resolved that he would endeavour to find his way to some part of the house where he could obtain relief from his agonizing thirst. Groping about in the dark, for he had no means of obtaining a light, he found his way to the head of a stair-case leading to the basement. Discerning a light, he made his way towards it, and at last entered a kitchen where he found two or three coloured servants still moving about, for it was not so late as he had supposed. One of these, a woman, gave him two glasses of cool water which afforded him momentary relief, and he found his way back to his apartment.

But he had scarcely reached his room when the burning thirst returned. It was even more torturing than before, as was also the excruciating pain in his head; and he rolled and tossed about, suffering such agony as he had never endured in his life before. "The memory of that night of horrible suffering," he observed, "will follow me to my grave."

How long he continued in that condition he did not know. He could not sleep; but wearied out with the intensity of his suffering, he sunk into that state of semi-unconsciousness in which the soul perceives very dimly the images of persons and things that are moving around. He had not lost all recollection of the place where he was; but after what appeared to him an interminable period of anguish and horror, he was conscious of persons entering his room. There seemed to be several of them, and a mingling of different voices; but how many, or who they were, he had no idea. Whether Brown and Hamilton were among the persons in his room he could not tell. He was partially aroused, though still in a delirious and dreamy state, when some one told him that it was necessary to go to a physician and procure medicine.

Too much enfeebled and confused to resist or object, Solomon allowed himself to be invested with his boots, and then, without coat or hat—which no doubt fell into the hands of his former travelling companions, enabling them to repossess themselves of the money they had paid him, and the free papers which they well knew were deposited in the pockets —he was conducted through a long passage way or alley into the street. They did not pass through any part of the hotel, the door of the room he had occupied opening immediately into the narrow passage way. This led into what appeared to the confused faculties of Solomon to be Pennsylvania Avenue, with which he had become familiar the day before. On the opposite side there was a light burning in a window, which Solomon imagined to be the window of the physician's office to which he was going. There appeared to be three persons with him, as far as he could observe. But from that moment all became a blank, and he sank into a state of utter insensibility. The drug which had been administered to him in his drink by his betrayers had produced its effect, and their helpless victim was now entirely in their power. How long he remained in that state of unconsciousness he could never tell or ascertain— whether it was only during that night, or for many days and nights he was never able to learn. But when consciousness returned, he found himself alone, in darkness and in chains.

The pain in his head had subsided to a considerable extent when he awoke to a sense of his condition;

but he felt excessively faint and weak. He found himself in a strange place, very different from the one in which he lay down. He was seated on a low bench made of rough boards, running along the wall of what appeared to be a cell, or dungeon, with scarcely a ray of light penetrating the gloom that filled the place. He was without hat or coat and upon his wrists were a pair of hand-cuffs. Around his ancles were fetters attached to a heavy chain, the other end of which was fastened to a large iron ring in the floor.

It was some time before he recovered the use of his faculties sufficiently to enable him to think over his circumstances with any degree of clearness or consistency; and when the power of consecutive thought returned to him it seemed as if he was in, or just waking from, a painful trance. "Where am I? what is the meaning of these chains and fetters? where are Brown and Hamilton, my employers? what can I have done to deserve imprisonment in this wretched dungeon?" such were the questions that suggested themselves to his mind. He could not comprehend it. All was darkness and mystery. But he began to fear that he had been made the victim of some fearful treachery.

A long time elapsed—hours it seemed to Solomon, and he still remained in the dreary solitude of the dungeon, which nothing occurred to interrupt. He listened attentively for some sign or sound betokening life; but nothing broke the oppressive silence, save the clinking of his chains whenever he chanced to move. He spoke and called out aloud; but the sound of his own voice startled him, and there was no response. After awhile he bethought him to feel in his pockets so far as his handcuffs would permit, but only to ascertain that nothing was there. He had been robbed and stripped of all he had in the world. His coat and hat, his money and free papers, all were gone, and he had been deprived of his liberty also. Then the appalling idea began to take possession of his mind that he had been kidnapped. The circus was nothing more than a pretence; Brown and Hamilton, with all their pretended kindness, were unprincipled betrayers; and he had been lured away from home, and wife, and children, to be made the victim of some atrocious scheme of villainy of which these deceivers would reap the profits.

Still he would not give way to despair. It might turn out better than he feared. It was incredible that these men, so attentive and kind, should be kidnappers! There must have been some mis-apprehension—some unfortunate mistake—which had brought him to that unhappy condition! It could not be that a free citizen of New York, who had wronged no man, nor violated any law, should be dealt with thus inhumanly! But the more he reflected upon the incidents of the past few days, and connected one circumstance with another; the more he thought of those visits to the drinking saloons, and the suspicious circumstances attending the sudden sickness he had experienced, the fainter became his hopes, and the more his worst suspicions were confirmed. It was a desolate thought indeed! He felt that there was no trust in man; and commending himself in prayer to the God of the oppressed, he bowed his head upon his fettered hands, and wept most bitterly.

CHAPTER III.

The Slave-Pen.

HOURS passed away—how many Solomon could not tell—and he remained seated on the low bench, absorbed in painful meditations, and feeling miserably ill. He was disposed to think that he had remained in a state of stupefaction and unconsciousness through one whole day and far on into the second night; for after being a long time occupied with painful thoughts and reflections, when he came to himself, he heard the crowing of a cock; and then he heard a distant rumbling sound as of vehicles passing along the streets. From these circumstances he knew that it was day; but no ray of light penetrated to the dungeon in which he was imprisoned. After awhile he could perceive the sound of footsteps immediately overhead, and distinguish the distant sounds of voices as of persons moving to and fro. From this it occurred to him that he was in some underground apartment, or dungeon; and the damp, mouldy odours of the place confirmed the supposition.

These sounds overhead, and the rumbling of vehicles in the streets, had continued for some time —at least an hour or two—when at last he heard

F

footsteps from without evidently approaching the place of his imprisonment. A key grated and rattled in the lock; a strong door swung back on its hinges, admitting a flood of light into the gloomy cell; and two men entered and stood before the manacled prisoner. Both were strangers whom he had never seen before. The one who was evidently the principal was a man whose whole appearance was sinister and repulsive in a high degree. A glance was sufficient to show that brutality had set its mark clearly upon him; his every movement indicated the accomplished ruffian, while every word that passed his lips was flavoured with blasphemy and profaneness. He was a large, powerful man, not less than forty years of age, with dark, chestnut-coloured hair and whiskers, slightly interspersed with grey. His face was round and full, his complexion flushed, as of one who was familiar with intoxicating beverages, and his features exceedingly coarse, expressive of nothing but cruelty and cunning. He was about five feet ten inches high, of full habit, and altogether a strongly-built muscular man. Solomon knew nothing of him when he thus first presented himself to his notice; but afterwards he had occasion to know him as James H. Burch, a notorious slave-dealer in Washington, well known for his habitual and unrelenting cruelty, and connected in the nefarious slave-dealing business, as a partner, with a man of kindred spirit, Theophilus Freeman, of New Orleans, both subsisting on the wrongs and miseries of their fellow-creatures.

The other person who entered Solomon's cell in company with Burch was an employee of that worthy person, acting in the capacity of attendant and turnkey. His name Solomon afterwards learned was Ebenezer Radburn, who, without the same remorseless energy as his employer, was equally unscrupulous and indifferent to human suffering and wrong.

The light admitted through the open door enabled Solomon to observe the room in which he was confined. It was a cell constructed of solid masonry, chiefly underground, with one small window near the ceiling crossed with strong iron bars, and with a strong wooden shutter securely fastened on the outside. The floor was of heavy plank, and the cell eleven or twelve feet square. On one side was a strong iron-bound door, which Solomon afterwards ascertained admitted to an inner cell, wholly destitute of windows, or any means of admitting light or air. Both places were well adapted, as doubtless they were frequently used, for kidnapping men and women. Shut up in these horrible cells, such victims of man's cruelty and cupidity would strive in vain to make themselves heard ; and if by any means they should chance to do so, all inquiry was easily stifled by representing the voice as proceeding from a refractory slave.

In Solomon's cell the light revealed only the wooden bench on which he sat, and an old-fashioned disused, dirty box-iron-stove. Besides these there was not in either cell bed or blanket, or any other thing whatsoever. The door through which Burch and his companion entered, led through a small narrow passage, up a flight of steps into a yard surrounded by a strong brick wall, not less than ten or twelve feet high, immediately in the rear of a building. The yard extended about thirty feet. In one part of the wall there was a strongly-ironed door, which opened into a narrow covered passage, leading along one side of the house into a street; but what street of the city Solomon could not tell. The doom of the coloured man upon whom the door leading out of that passage once closed was sealed. Over it might have been written—"*He that enters here leaves all hope behind.*" Drugged into insensibility, poor, unsuspecting, unresisting Solomon had been conveyed, under cover of night, to a slave-pen, kept by as hardened and unprincipled a ruffian as ever trafficked in the liberties and agonies of the down-trodden children of Africa—betrayed and sold by the men who had professed to be his friends.

The building to which the yard was attached was two stories high, and its front overlooked one of the streets of Washington. Its outside presented the appearance of a quiet private residence. No stranger looking at it from the street would have dreamed of the execrable purposes to which those premises were devoted, or the cruelties that were often practised there. Strange as it may seem, within a comparatively short distance of this place, and looking down from its commanding height upon the spot, was the Capitol, where eloquent declaimers often dwelt upon the glories of that land of liberty. Strange inconsistency! The voices of patriotic representatives and dignified senators boasting of freedom and equality, and the rattling of the kidnapped slave's chains almost commingling! A slave pen within the very shadow of the Capitol—the Temple of Liberty! Yes! it was a slave-pen. The top of the high wall surrounding the yard supported one end of a roof, which descending inwards formed a shed open to the yard, the front being only a few feet from the ground. Underneath the roof there was a crazy loft constructed all round, where the unhappy captives, if so disposed, might sleep at night, or in inclement weather seek shelter from the fury of the storm. In some respects it was like a farmer's barn-yard; only it was so constructed that the outside world could never see the human cattle that were often herded there. This horrible place Solomon ascertained was known in Washington as "Williams' Slave-Pen." And here it was that Solomon found himself immured in a loathsome dungeon, when he recovered from the effects of the drug with which he had been poisoned.

"Well, my boy, how do you feel yourself now?" said Burch, in a brutal, swaggering tone, as he entered the open door.

"I am very sick, and suffering much pain," was the reply of Solomon. "But I wish to know why I have been treated in this cruel way, and what I have done to deserve imprisonment, and to have these handcuffs and chains put upon me?"

"Oh, there is no mystery about that. The long

and the short of it is that you are my slave. I bought and paid for you, and I intend to have my profit out of you. I shall send you to a good market in New Orleans."

All this was plentifully interlarded with fierce, brutal oaths, which it would answer no good purpose to place on record here. But wherever an oath could be thrust in there it failed not to make its appearance.

"But I am a free man," Solomon affirmed, "and you have no right to buy and make a slave of a free man. I was born free. My father and my mother were both free. I was born in New York State, and have been living for some years at Saratoga in that State. My name is Northup, and I am well known there as a free man; and I have a wife and children living there who were all like myself born free. I have been shamefully and unlawfully treated, robbed of my money and the papers which would prove me to be a free man, and wrongfully imprisoned without any cause. When I obtain my liberty I will have satisfaction for the injury that has been done to me, and cause the wrong-doer to be justly punished."

"Shut your mouth; you are a liar. You are no free man, but a runaway slave from Georgia." This was spoken with fierce blasphemous oaths that almost seemed to curdle the blood in Solomon's veins. He had heard profane swearing before; but he never listened to such indecent and horrible blasphemies as flowed from the lips of this slave-dealer, Burch. But again and again he asserted that he was no man's slave ; that he had never been a slave, and had never been in Georgia in his life ; and demanded of Burch that he should release him from his chains at once, and restore him to the liberty of which he had been so unjustly deprived.

Solomon became excited and loudly demanded to be set free. The slave-dealer endeavoured to hush and quiet him, as if he feared Solomon's voice might be overheard. But Solomon would not be silenced, and loudly denounced the authors of his imprisonment, whoever they might be, as unmitigated villains. Finding his efforts to quiet his victim vain, Burch flew into the most ungovernable rage ; with fearful oaths he denounced him as a black liar, a runaway slave from Georgia, heaping upon him every profane and vulgar epithet which the most indecent and depraved fancy could invent.

During this time the lackey, Radburn, stood silently by. As Solomon afterwards learned, he was the hired overseer of this horrible den, whose business it was to receive the slaves brought there for security or punishment, and to feed and take care of them, or to whip them according to the orders of those who owned them. The usual fee was two shillings currency per day for feeding and taking care of the wretched denizens of the place. Turning to this agent of oppression, Burch said with a fierce oath :

" Bring in the paddle and the cat, and we'll soon teach this black liar who and what he is and what he has to look for."

"I'll fetch 'em," was the prompt reply.

He disappeared, and in a few moments returned with the instruments of torture that had been called for.

The cat was the ordinary instrument of punishment known by that name; a whip with a stout handle somewhat more than two feet in length, with numerous strands or lashes made of stout cord or leather, capable in experienced hands of inflicting fearful tortue upon the sufferer. The paddle, which Solomon had never seen or heard of before, was a piece of hard-wood board, eighteen or twenty inches long, shaped like a paddle, being about eight or nine inches at the widest part, and tapering off so as to form a convenient handle. The wide portion of the instrument, which might be about the size of a man's two open hands laid together, was bored in numerous places with a small augur, that whenever the paddle was used with a sufficient degree of violence blisters might be raised on the flesh of the victim, and the torture fearfully enhanced.

As soon as these formidable weapons were brought in, Solomon was at once roughly seized by his persecutors and divested of all his clothing. He could offer no effectual resistance, crippled as he was by the handcuffs and with both feet securely chained to the floor. He was then drawn over the bench with his face downwards, and Radburn placed his heavy foot upon the fetters between his wrists, holding them painfully down upon the floor utterly heedless of the severe pain he inflicted. Burch then took up the paddle, and with his whole strength, stimulated by

THE SLAVE PEN.

the fierce rage into which he had been wrought, laid a series of blows upon the naked trembling body of the victim. Blow after blow fell with all the power of which the burly ruffian was capable until his arm grew tired. Then he stopped, and stooping down, said :—

" Well, my fine fellow, what do you think of it now ? Have you found out, you——liar, that you are not a free man from Saratoga, but a cursed runaway black nigger from Georgia ? "

" I am nobody else but what what I told you. My name is Solomon Northup, and I am a free citizen of New York State ; where I was born, and where my family are living now."

Groaning and writhing with pain, Solomon contrived with difficulty to get out this reply; and then the blows were renewed as fast and energetically as before. Again, when his arm grew weary, Burch desisted, and stooping down, cursing the obstinacy of his victim, repeated the question. Receiving only the same answer, he went on cursing and flogging till he resembled an incarnate fiend, foaming at the mouth with fury and the sweat running in streams from his face. At length the paddle broke short off, leaving the useless handle in his possession; while the other part flew to the other side of the room. Still Solomon would not yield. All the brutal punishment to which he had been subjected could not force from his lips the foul lie that he was a slave.

Casting away from him with horrible imprecations, the fragment of the paddle that remained in his hand, Burch pounced upon the other instrument of torture, which he began to use with terrible effect. " This," said Solomon, " was far more painful than the other. I struggled with all my power, but it was in vain. Chained and manacled as I was, with my hands most painfully held to the ground by the heavy foot of the other tormentor, I was unable to move. I prayed for mercy, but my prayer was answered only by curses and stripes. I thought I must die beneath the lashes of the unfeeling brute into whose power I had fallen. Even now (fourteen years later), the flesh crawls upon my bones as I recall the scene. I seemed to be all on fire, and thought surely my sufferings can be compared to nothing else than those burning agonies of hell, of which I have heard ministers sometimes speak in the pulpit."

Exhausted by pain and suffering Solomon became silent, too feeble to return any answer to the repeated questions that were put to him. Still the merciless lash was plied without stint upon his poor body, until it felt to him as if the lacerated flesh was being stripped from his bones at every stroke. How long this scene of cruelty was continued Solomon could never tell: it seemed to him to be almost interminable. At length Radburn said, " It is useless to whip him any more—he has had what will make him sore enough for a long time to come." Thereupon Burch desisted from his labour and laid aside the cat, the victim being lifted by Radburn from his prostrate condition so that he could recline upon the bench.

Burch then clenched his massive fist and shook it in Solomon's face, hissing through his firmly-clenched teeth with bitter imprecations, "If ever, you black devil, you dare to say to anybody, or any where, that you are entitled to freedom, that you have been stolen or kidnapped, or anything whatever of the kind, the flogging you have just received will be nothing in comparison with the cutting up I will then give you." Then grinding his teeth, with an expression of hellish malignity on his countenance, and fiercely stamping his foot upon the ground, he said " ———— you ; I will conquer you, or I will kill you." After these—anything but consolatory—words had been uttered, Radburn removed the handcuffs from the sufferer's wrists, leaving his feet still fastened to the heavy chain, and the shutter of the little barred window, which had been opened to assist the operations of the kidnappers, again closed and made secure. The two worthies then departed, locking the heavy door behind them; and poor Solomon, with every fibre of his lacerated body twitching with agony, was left to the solitude and the darkness of his cell, and to that God who is the Hater and the Avenger of oppression and wrong.

An hour or two had elapsed in great suffering, when the key rattled in the lock of the door again, and Solomon's heart seemed to leap to his throat. He who had been so lonely and longed so ardently to see some one, he cared not who it might be, now shuddered at the thought of a human being approaching him. The very idea of a man's face, especially a white one, was fearful to him : and it was with a feeling of terror, that he listened to the sounds at the door which indicated the approach of some visitor. His apprehensions were somewhat relieved when he found that it was Radburn, and that he was alone. The door swung back and the man entered, bearing in his hand a tin plate, on which were a piece of shrivelled fried pork, a slice of bread, and a cup of water, which he set down within reach of the prisoner. The visitor asked Solomon in a not un- kindly tone, how he felt, remarking that he had received a pretty severe flogging. He then sat down and proceeded to remonstrate with Solomon against the folly of asserting his claim to freedom as he had done, observing, " You see that it has brought upon you a very heavy punishment : and you are not likely to gain much by it but many a severe licking, for you have got into the hands of one who will keep a strong grip upon you, and give you very little chance of asserting your claim to be a free man." In rather a patronizing and confidential manner he gave it as his opinion that the less he said on that subject the better it would be for him, and advised him to keep his own counsel. Whether the man was touched at the sight of Solomon's wrongs and sufferings with a feeling of pity, or was desirous to save himself future trouble by pre- vailing on Solomon to abstain from all future asser- tion of his rights, he could not understand ; but the man evidently wished to appear kind and friendly for some reason or other. When he retired he unlocked the fetters on the sufferer's ancles, leaving his feet at liberty as well as his hands, and opened the shutter of the little window, so as to admit both light and air. He then left him again alone.

After a few hours he became very stiff as well as sore. His body was covered with blisters from the use of the paddle, and with livid wheals and gashes caused by the cat, so that it was with great pain and difficulty he could move at all. From the window he could discern nothing but the roof resting on the adjacent wall—not even a strip of sky could be seen. He had nothing to sleep on but the hard, rough, damp floor, and no pillow or covering of any kind. There, in the dreary solitude of that miserable cell, with nothing to relieve the monotony of such a wretched existence, he was left for many days—how many he could never tell. But the misery he endured there might have been sufficient for a life-time. Punctually twice a day Radburn made his appearance, with the usual allowance of pork and bread, and water. Solomon had little appetite for the food served out for him, but he was tormented with continual thirst. His festering wounds would not permit him to remain long in any one position, so that every few minutes he was compelled to seek for ease by changing it. Thus, disabled for taking anything like refreshing rest day after day and night after night, now sitting for a brief spell, now stretching out in a recumbent posture for a minute or two, now moving slowly about the cell, now gazing dreamily through the window at the opposite shed roof, he lingered out a painful existence.

But the chief source of misery was within—his own gloomy thoughts. He was heart-sick and discouraged. He thought of his wife and the children, and the misery and uncertainty in which they would be involved by his strange and mysterious disappearance. He thought of his comfortable and pleasant home in Saratoga, from which he had been so cruelly and wickedly lured away. He pictured to himself the pleasant scenes and landscapes of that charming locality, and the groups of relations and friends who must now be wondering and inquiring, " What can have become of Solomon." When for a few moments his senses became locked in sleep, visions of home and its endearments were floating in his imagination ; he heard the familiar voices of Anne and the children ; and once more he felt himself the free-born American citizen, seated upon the driving-box of his familiar hack, with a pair of noble horses obedient to every inflection of his well-known voice. Then he would awake up to the stern reality of those dungeon walls, and the misery of feeling that he had been entrapped and betrayed and consigned to cruel hands, a fettered and degraded slave. And he would groan and weep, and literally water the floor with his tears.

Still, his spirit was not broken, nor had hope entirely deserted him. He still indulged the anticipation of escape from the doom that seemed to be impending over him, and that speedily. " It was impossible," so he reasoned, " that men could be so unjust as to detain him in slavery when the truth of

his case should be known." He thought that Burch
had been imposed upon by some plausible tale about
his having made his escape from Georgia, and when
he came to know the truth, that he really was a free
man from Saratoga, he would certainly let him go.
Hope whispered to him the flattering tale that Brown
and Hamilton might not be, after all, the false and
treacherous men he had believed them to be, and
that when they missed him, they would certainly
seek him out and deliver him from his thraldom.
Surely, after all the friendship they had shown him,
they could not have been parties to his imprisonment
and cruel treatment, and they would come to his
rescue. Alas! Solomon had not then learned,
painful as his experience had already been, as he was
afterwards to learn, the measure of "man's inhumanity to man," nor to what limitless extent of
wickedness he will go for the sake of gain.

After being closely immured in his cell for many
days and nights, the outer door was thrown open,
and the captive was allowed the liberty of going into
the yard. There he found companions in misery—
three slaves, two of them young men of about twenty
and twenty-five years of age, the other a lad of ten
years. He was not long in forming acquaintance
with them and learning their names, and the sad
particulars of their history.

The eldest was a coloured man several removes
from black, and he said his name was Clement Ray.
He had lived in Washington; had driven a hack
carriage, and worked in a livery-stable there for a

long time.   He was an intelligent young fellow, and
fully comprehended his situation and the gloomy
prospect that lay before him.   The thought of going
South overwhelmed him with grief, for there he
expected to endure the evils of slave life in an
aggravated form.   Burch was his master now.   He
had purchased him a few days before, and had placed
him there in that slave-pen until such time as he was
ready to send him with others to the New Orleans
market.   From him Solomon learned that he was in
Williams' slave-pen, a place he had never heard of
before.   This young man described to Solomon the
uses for which the place was designed, and the
cruelties and villainies that were enacted there
towards the oppressed children of Africa.   Solomon
in return detailed to his companion the particulars
of his unhappy story ; but he could only give him the
consolation of his sympathy.   He also strongly
advised Solomon to be silent henceforth on the
subject of his freedom : for, knowing the brutal
character of Burch, he assured him that to speak of
it, would only be followed with renewed cruelty.
But how could he take such advice ?   How could he
resolve to give up his hopes of freedom, and quietly
submit to be shipped off to New Orleans, there to be
subjected to a hopeless life of slavery ?

The next eldest of his fellow prisoners was named
John Williams. He stated that he had been " raised "
in Virginia, not far from Washington.   Burch, he
said, had taken him in payment of a debt, and he
entertained the hope that his former owner, who was

not by any means an unkind master, would redeem him and not allow him to be shipped away to New Orleans, far from his home, and far away from all his relations and friends. This hope was subsequently realised. Before Burch had made up his gang for the Southern market, his old master came and took him away; and John Williams was carried back to his former home, and saved from the misery it was well-known awaited unfortunate slaves in the swamps and on the plantations of the far South.

The boy was a sprightly little fellow, who answered to the name of Randall. Most of the time he was playing about the yard in all the forgetfulness of childhood; but occasionally he would burst into fits of crying, calling loudly for his mother, and wondering why she did not come to fetch him home. His mother's absence seemed to be the only sorrow that touched his heart; for he was too young to realize the sad realities of his condition, and the gloomy prospects that lay before him. When the thought of his mother was not in his mind, he amused his fellow captives by his clever childish pranks.

At night Solomon was carefully locked in his cell, while the others clambered up to the loft of the shed, where they slept. After several days a coarse horse-blanket was dealt out to each of the prisoners, which was all the accommodation Solomon was destined to know in the shape of bedding for many years to come, and which he found to be a miserable contrast with the well-furnished and comfortable bed he had been accustomed to at home, before he fell into false

G

and treacherous hands.   Ray and Williams asked
him abundance of questions about New York State
and the treatment which coloured people experienced
there.   It seemed to be above their comprehension,
and almost to be in the category of things impossible,
that persons of dark complexion like their own
should live in comfortable homes and possess houses
and land, with none to disturb or oppress them. The
effect of such conversations was only to intensify
their longings for freedom, and sometimes to overwhelm them with sorrow that no prospect of gaining
such a state of happiness was possible for them.
They were careful that their talks on such subjects
were not overheard by Burch or Radburn.   It would
have been regarded as a crime, and would certainly
have brought down the lash of the merciless whip
upon their backs.

" I had had such liberty as the limits of Williams'
slave-pen permitted between two and three weeks,"
said Solomon, " when a woman was brought into the
horrible place, leading by the hand a little child. She
was weeping bitterly, and seemed to be well nigh
broken-hearted. As soon as he saw them, little
Randall gave way to the most extravagant transports
of joy, for in these strangers he at once recognised
his mother and sister. He ran to the woman and
clung to her dress, and fondled and kissed the child,
crying, ' O my mother, how glad I am that you are
come. My dear sister, my dear Emily.'" The mother
clasped him in her arms and warmly embraced him,
gazing at him tenderly and fondly through her tears,

while she lavished upon her boy every endearing name that a warm-hearted mother's love could suggest. The little girl also clung fondly to her brother, and he returned her embraces with equal warmth, showing that, although under the blighting influence of slavery, there was in that case " Love at home."

Emily, as Randall called her, was a beautiful child about seven or eight years old. Her complexion was very light and fair, and her light-coloured hair fell in a profusion of curls upon her neck. She was richly dressed and in the newest fashion; her whole appearance indicating that she had been brought up in comfort and wealth. Whether it was the contrast with the sordid wretchedness of everything around that rendered the contrast more striking he could not tell; but as Solomon gazed upon this vision of youthful beauty, he thought he had never looked upon a sweeter child in all his life.

The woman also was arrayed in silk, the other articles of her dress corresponding with it. Costly rings adorned her fingers, and rich, golden ornaments hung from her ears. Her whole appearance was that of a lady belonging to a respectable class of society; only her complexion, which seemed to be that of a quadroon, showed that she was connected with the degraded race. But her air and manners, and the propriety and correctness of her language, clearly showed that she had stood above the common level of a slave.

After the first emotions caused by finding her little

G 2

son Randall had subsided, she began to feel amazed
at finding herself in such a place, and she looked
around with a feeling of wonder upon her surroundings, still holding her two children closely in
her arms. It was clearly some sudden and unexpected turn of fortune that had brought her to that
wretched place. But the time came when all must
retire to their sleeping places; and filling the air
with her complainings and shrieks, the woman—
whose name was Eliza—was hustled with her two
children into the cell, whither also Solomon was
conducted, that as usual he might be locked up
securely. Language cannot convey an adequate idea
of the moanings and outcries to which the wretched
woman gave utterance, when forced with her children
into that gloomy and filthy cell. Throwing herself
upon the ground, and clasping the two children in
her arms, she poured forth over them such touching
lamentations as only a mother's anxious love and
tenderness could suggest; and the children nestled
closely to her, indifferent to the discomforts of the
place, as if only there in that mother's arms was
there any safety or protection for them. At last
they fell asleep, their heads resting upon the mother's
lap.

While they slumbered she smoothed back the hair
from their foreheads and talked to them incessantly.
Too much engrossed with thoughts of her unhappy
fate to sleep, she fondled and talked to them, as they
slept, the whole night long. She called them " her
precious darlings "—" her sweet babes "—" poor

innocent things that had no idea of the miseries they were destined to endure. Soon they would have no mother to comfort them—they would be taken from her. What would become of them with no loving mother to care for them and watch over their comfort? Oh! she could not live away from her darling boy and her precious little Emmy. They had always been good, loving children, and had such sweet and loving ways. It would break her heart, God knew, if they should be taken from her. She knew they meant to sell her darlings, and they would be separated and taken away she knew not where, and they might never see one another again." "It was enough to melt a heart of stone," Solomon said, "to listen to these wailings of a mother's love, who felt herself desolate and distracted.

Eliza's history was that of many a female slave in the Southern States; a history of sin, and disappointment, and misery. She was the slave of a rich man in the neighbourhood of Washington, born on the plantation of which Elisha Berry was the owner. Berry was a married man and had a daughter; but his dissipated habits produced quarrels between himself and his wife, and eventually led to their separation. One of the main causes of the domestic strife was Berry's conduct with regard to his handsome slave, Eliza, and the birth of the boy, Randall. When the separation took place, he left his wife and daughter in the house they had always occupied, and built another on a distant part of the plantation, where he placed Eliza, promising that she and her children should be emancipated and placed beyond the danger of future suffering from slavery. Here he had resided for nine or ten years with abundance of servants, and heaping all the luxuries of life upon Eliza and her children. Emily had been born nearly two years later than Randall.

In the course of time the young mistress, Berry's daughter, who had always lived with her mother, was married to a Mr. Jacob Brookes; and some complication having taken place in Berry's affairs beyond his control, a division of his property was made; and in the final arrangement Eliza and her two children fell to the share of Brookes. Berry had always intended to execute papers that would give them their freedom; but he had procrastinated about the business, leaving it to a more convenient season, until the power of carrying his intention into effect had gone, and the future destiny of Eliza and her children had passed into other hands. Very merciless hands they proved to be. Berry, Eliza represented as a man of kind heart and benevolent disposition, and she had no doubt that it was his purpose to set her free; and even after the division of the property occurred, she still cherished the hope that he would find means of fulfilling the promises he had so often made.

But this was not to be. The position she had been compelled to occupy was always hateful to her, and she would far rather have been engaged in some menial domestic employment. But a slave, body and soul completely in the power of her owner, she was powerless to resist his will. And this exposed her, as might have been expected, to the fierce hatred of Mrs. Berry and her daughter. When, therefore, she was thrown unexpectedly into the power of Mrs. Brookes, she was made painfully to feel the effects of her displeasure. And beautiful as was the little Emily, so nearly related to her by blood, she took no pains to conceal the malignant feelings she cherished towards the child.

On the day that Eliza and her little daughter made their appearance at Williams' slave-pen, Brookes had brought them to the city under false pretences. He told Eliza that the time had come when her free papers were to be executed in fulfilment of her master's promise, and it was necessary that she and Emily should go to Washington for that purpose. The boy, Randall, had already been taken away from her very quietly, and she knew not what had become of him. Overjoyed at the prospect of immediate liberty, she dressed herself and little Emily in their best apparel, and entrusted herself to the direction of the deceiver with a grateful heart. The prospect of escaping from the hatred of the family, and enjoying with her children the blessings of freedom, was almost too much happiness to be borne. And, oh! how readily would she submit to the hardest toil, to earn for herself and her loved ones the bread of honesty and virtue! But who can tell the misery of her disappointment—the despair that seemed to lay its withering grasp on all her faculties—when, on their arrival in the city, instead of being made free from the yoke of slavery, she was handed over to the slave-dealer, Burch, one of the most hateful and degraded beings disgracing the form of man.   The paper that was executed was not a deed of emancipation but a bill of sale.   The hope she had been fondly cherishing for years was blasted in a moment.   From the height of the most exulting happiness she was cast down to the lowest depths of wretchedness and despair. Her life was terribly blighted.   No wonder that she wept, and filled the slave-pen with wailings and expressions of heart-rending woe.

At intervals during that long night, Eliza complained bitterly of Jacob Brookes and the cruel treachery he had practised towards her, in beguiling her by false representations and promises into the horrible place to which he had brought her.   She declared that had she suspected his purpose, he should never have got her to the place alive.   They had chosen the opportunity when her old master, Mr. Berry, was away from home.   He had always been kind to her, and she knew that if he had been aware of the cruelty designed against her and her children, he would have found means to prevent it.   But now it was too late, and even he could not rescue her, for he did not know where she had been taken.   Wringing her hands in anguish after uttering these complaints, she would again begin weeping over her children and kissing them, talking first to the one and then to the other, as they lay slumbering in her lap, unconscious alike of her griefs and their own. So wore the dreary night away, and when morning dawned, and when night had come again, still without tasting food, she kept moaning on and could not be consoled even by the endearments of her children.

Poor Eliza! Her worst anticipations were to be realized. Torn from her precious little ones, and knowing not what had become of them, she mourned night and day, and like Rachel weeping for her children refused to be comforted. As she had so often in her bitter despair predicted, her heart did indeed break with the burden of a bereaved mother's sorrow. Far up the Red River, where its sluggish waters flow through the pestilential low-lands of Louisiana onwards to the Mississippi, she laid down life's weary load and found a solitary grave, far away from all whom she had loved.

CHAPTER IV.

"Down South."

ABOUT midnight following the second day of Eliza's imprisonment, the cell-door was suddenly thrown open, and Burch and Radburn entered with lanterns in their hands. Burch, with a volley of brutal oaths addressed to the whole party, ordered them to roll up their blankets without delay and get ready to go on board the boat. He seemed to be in a great hurry, rushing about and swearing that they would be all too late unless they made great haste. With a rough shake and many curses he aroused the children from their slumbers, wondering what could make the brats so sleepy. Going out into the yard he called for Clem Ray, ordering him to come down from the loft and bring his blanket with him into the cell. When Clem made his appearance, Burch placed him alongside of Solomon, and fastened their wrists together with handcuffs—Solomon's left hand to Clem's right. The two manacled captives were ordered to march, Eliza and the children following. John Williams was not of the party; his master having redeemed him, to his very great delight, a day or two before.

They were conducted into the yard; from thence into a covered passage, and up a flight of steps

through a side door into the upper room, where
Solomon supposed he had heard the footsteps on that
memorable, miserable morning, when he awoke from
the stupor into which he had been drugged. It was
a whitewashed room, without any carpet on the floor,
and seemed to be a sort of office.   Its furniture was
a stove, a ·few old chairs, and a long table covered
with papers scattered carelessly about. In one corner,
by a window, there was a rusty sword hanging, which
attracted Solomon's attention. Burch's trunk was there
already packed for removal; and to take this appeared
to be the principal object in coming to the room.   In
obedience to peremptory orders from Burch, not
unaccompanied by an oath, Solomon took hold of one
of its handles with his unfettered hand, while Burch
took the other, and passing through the front door of
the house into the street they marched on in the same
order in which they had left the cell.

The night was dark, and all was very quiet.
Solomon could discern the lights, or the reflection of
them, over towards Pennsylvania Avenue ; but there
was no one, not even a straggler to be seen.
Solomon must have been somewhat cowed by the
painful discipline of the paddle and the cat to which
he had been subjected in the cell at Williams' pen, or
he would now have made an effort to effect his escape.
He was almost resolved to break away and attempt
to gain his liberty, but the handcuffs rendered it
difficult and placed him somewhat at the will of his
companion, and unless he also entered into the
attempt to get away, it could not be accomplished, the

fetters which bound him to Clem being too strong for him to break. Radburn was in the rear bearing a huge bludgeon, and doubtless both he and Burch were armed with revolvers. These considerations caused Solomon to hesitate, and while he hesitated the opportunity passed away. Radburn hurried up the children behind, while Burch pressed forward the men in front, and so they passed on in silence through the streets of Washington—the Capital of a country whose theory of government was based on the principle that life, liberty, and the pursuit of happiness are the inalienable rights of every human being—a company of captives, deprived by violence and fraud of their liberty, and borne away into interminable and hopeless bondage under the sanction of that country's laws.

A short time elapsed ere the party reached the steam-boat lying at the wharf ready to receive them. They were all quickly hustled into the hold, amongst barrels and boxes of freight. All was dark at first, and each took the place into which he or she had been pushed. Soon, however, a coloured servant brought a light, the bell rang, and the vessel started down the Potomac River, carrying the enslaved ones they knew not whither: they were driven and disposed of just as if they had been cattle. When the steamer reached that part of the river where, upon its banks, is to be found the tomb of Washington, the bell tolled as a mark of respect to the memory of the illustrious man who, while he freed his country from the yoke of British Government, helped to establish among her people that system of human slavery which has entailed upon millions such aggravated woe. This is the one blot that stains the memory of Washington.

None of the party slept that night, except the two children. Clem Ray was now for the first time completely broken down with grief. To him the idea of going South was terrible in the extreme : but hitherto it was an evil dimly seen in the distance. Now the sad reality was come. He was leaving all the friends and associations of his youth—everything that was dear and precious to him in life—in all probability never to look upon them again. He was actually on his way to the hated South, of which he had heard such terrible accounts concerning the oppressions and cruelties practised upon slaves amidst its swamps, and on its sugar and cotton plantations. His grief was uncontrollable, and he shed abundance of tears. Eliza moaned and wailed the whole night, the burden of her lamentation being the dreaded separation from her children. Solomon endeavoured to keep up his spirits, as he said, though he found it very difficult to do so. He revolved in his mind a hundred plans of escape, determined that he would make the attempt the first opportunity that offered. He had come to the conclusion by this time that his wisest policy would be to say nothing about his having been a free man by birth, as it was only likely to expose him to further maltreatment, and diminish his chances of liberation, if he adopted a different course. He was resolved to keep a sharp look out for any chance that might occur. But he forgot that every hour was now increasing the difficulty, not to say the impossibility, of getting away, being borne as he was into the very heart of the slavery region.

The morning dawned very beautifully; the fields along the banks of the river were clothed in living green, far in advance of what Solomon had been accustomed to see in the North at that season of the year. He looked upon them with a farmer's eye. The sun shone out brightly and warmly, and the birds were singing very sweetly as they hopped from branch to branch in the trees that lined the banks of the Potomac. The happy birds! How greatly did Solomon envy them! How he wished that he had wings like them, that he might cleave the air, and transport himself to the happy home where his own birdlings vainly looked for their father's coming, amongst the cool and pleasant hills of the home-land!

Immediately after sunrise, the party of slaves were summoned on deck to get their breakfast. Burch took their handcuffs off, and they sat down to a tolerably good breakfast spread out on a rough table. The slave-trader was sagacious enough to understand that if he would gain a good profit on the unfortunate creatures that fell into his hands, he must carry them to market in good condition. So their food was pretty good and plentiful. Burch invited Eliza to take a dram; but this she declined, politely, but with an expression which showed that she did not feel herself complimented by the offer. The meal passed in silence; for the hearts there were too heavy for conversation, and not a word was spoken by anyone to the other. A mulatto woman attended upon the table, who seemed to feel a kindly sympathy with the party of sufferers. No doubt she well understood the case— a party of slaves going to the South! Poor creatures! So she seemed to feel, for she attended to them, and more especially to the children, with tender assiduity, telling them to "cheer up and not to be so much cast down. Things may turn out better than you expect." When the breakfast was over the handcuffs were restored to their wrists, and Burch ordered them to sit down together in a certain place on the deck. They took their places as directed and remained silent, none of them speaking a word in his presence. Occasionally one of the passengers would walk out to where the miserable group were sitting, look upon them for awhile, and then silently return.

In the forenoon the steamer arrived at Acquia Creek. There the passengers left the vessel and were transferred to stages—a large, rough, lumbering kind of stage-coach. One of these was occupied by Burch and his prisoners entirely. During this journey some of his bearishness was laid aside, and he talked and laughed with the two children; and at one of the stopping places went so far as to purchase for each of them a piece of gingerbread. Speaking a little less roughly than usual, he addressed himself to Solomon, telling him to "hold up his head and look smart;" adding, "you may perhaps get a good master if you are a good boy and behave yourself well." Solomon gave him no reply: the bloated face of the tyrant had become hateful to him, and he could scarcely bear to look upon it. He sat quietly in his corner, but with feelings of hatred and revenge rankling in his bosom, and cherishing a hope that he might one day meet with the ruffian on the soil of his native state.

Arrived at Fredericksburg, which has since been the scene of several sanguinary conflicts between the two parties concerned in the civil war which was destined in the Lord's good Providence to overthrow and abolish the hateful institution of slavery, the whole party were placed in a railway car; and before it became dark they arrived at Richmond, the Capital City of the State of Virginia, beautifully situated upon several hills. There they were taken from the cars and driven through the streets to a slave-pen situated between the railroad depot and the river, and kept by a man named Goodin. This place was larger then Williams' slave-pen in Washington, and there were two small houses standing at opposite corners of the open yard. These houses Solomon found were used as rooms for the examination of human chattels by purchasers before making a bargain. Any unsoundness in a slave, as in a horse, detracted from the value of the article. Sometimes no warranty would be given, when a thorough examination became necessary on the part of the negro jockey; and to this purpose the houses were devoted, as well as to the locking up of slaves who were disposed to be noisy and refractory.

Arrived at Goodin's pen, they were met at the door by that respectable gentleman, whose appearance was the reverse of prepossessing. He was a short fat man, with a round plump face and black hair and whiskers; his complexion being almost as dark as that of some of his own negroes. He had a hard, stern, merciless look, as if he had been accustomed to gaze with pleasure on human suffering. He appeared to be about fifty years of age. Burch and he met each other with great apparent cordiality. They were evidently old friends and seemed to be kindred spirits. They shook each other warmly by the hand, and Burch remarked that he had brought some company, and inquired at what time the brig was to leave. He was informed that she would probably leave the next day at a certain hour which was named. Goodin then turned to Solomon, and taking hold of his arm turned him partly round, looking at him sharply from head to foot with the air of one who considered himself a good judge of such property, and was estimating in his mind about how much the specimen before him was worth. When the inspection was over he asked:—

" Well, boy, where did you come from ? "

" From New York," Solomon replied promptly, entirely forgetting himself for the moment.

" From New York !—What have you been doing there ? " The oaths accompanying this exclamation showed that he was quite as proficient in profanity and blasphemy as his friend Burch.

This outburst of surprise on the part of Goodin at once reminded Solomon that he had committed a mistake in his reply. Yet, what else could he say ? Looking at Burch he saw his countenance covered

H

with a fierce, dark, malignant scowl which it was not difficult to understand. After a little while it was explained that "he had only been up that way a piece, he had travelled as far as New York," and the impression removed which Solomon's words were calculated to convey, that he had lived in a free State.

Goodin turned to Clem and put a few questions to him. He then spoke to Eliza, whose lady-like appearance seemed to surprise him a little; although the neatness and elegance which marked her first appearance at the Washington slave-pen had been somewhat lessened by the events which had since transpired. He next turned to the children, and with as much of softness and tenderness as such an embruted nature could exhibit, put to them a variety of questions as to where they came from, who they belonged to, and the way in which they had been brought up. He seemed to be particularly pleased with little Emily, as was everyone who looked upon her fair, sweet countenance. She was by no means so neat and tidy as when she made her first appearance with her mother: her dress was somewhat disordered, and her hair a good deal dishevelled. But through the soft profusion of unkempt, neglected ringlets, there beamed a face of surpassing loveliness, every feature and every smile being expressive of an amiable and lovable nature within. "Altogether they are a fair lot," he said at length, when he had completed his survey; "a devilish fair lot." This expression he repeated more than once very energetically, and enforced it by many an adjective not to be found in the Christian vocabulary.

The slave party then passed into the yard, where they found quite a number of slaves, not less than thirty or forty, who were moving about or sitting on benches under the shed by which the yard was surrounded, like the slave-yard at Washington. They were all cleanly dressed—the men with hats, the women with handkerchiefs tied about their heads.

Burch and Goodin, after the party was turned into the yard amongst the other slaves, walked away, and ascending some steps at the back part of the main building, sat down upon the doorstep, and entered into conversation. What the subject of discourse was Solomon could not hear, but it was probably the brief conversation that had taken place between Goodin and himself; for after some time had elapsed Burch came down, and taking the fetters from Solomon's wrists, led him into one of the small houses before described. Shaking his huge fist in Solomon's face, and with a fiendish scowl upon his countenance, he said with a bitter oath :—

" You told that man you came from New York."

" I told him," Solomon replied, " that I had been to New York, but I did not tell him I belonged there, neither did I tell him that I am a free man. I spoke without thought. I don't think I should have said that if I had had time to think for a moment ; but I was quite taken by surprise."

He looked at Solomon for a moment with intense malignity, as if he was ready to murder him, turned round and went out. In a few minutes he returned, and stepping up to the trembling slave, and thrusting

H 2

his clenched fist again in his face, ejaculated fiercely with a volley of oaths, " If ever I hear you say a word about New York again, or about your freedom, as God is in Heaven, I will be the death of you—I will kill you, you may rely on that."

He understood better than his captive did the penalty and the danger of selling a free man into slavery. He felt the necessity of Solomon's mouth being shut concerning the crime he knew he was committing. Of course, the life of a man like poor Solomon would not have been regarded as a feather's weight where his own safety was concerned. He meant precisely what he said; and if any emergency had arisen likely to bring his villainy to light, he would not have scrupled a moment to murder his captive, and thus put him and his evidence out of the way.

After this colloquy Solomon returned to the yard. Under the shed on one side a rough table had been constructed, while overhead were lofts for the slaves to sleep in, the same as those he had seen at Washington. On the table just mentioned the coarse supper of the slaves was served out, consisting of pork and bread. After partaking of this meal, Solomon was handcuffed to a large yellow man, who was stout and fleshy, and who exhibited a countenance expressive of the utmost melancholy. Solomon found him to be a man of intelligence and enlarged information. Chained together, as they were, it was not long before they became acquainted with each other's history, and Solomon found in this

new acquaintance one whose experience enabled him
to sympathise with Solomon's wrongs and sufferings ;
for he, too, born free, had been robbed of all his
rights as a man—kidnapped and sold into slavery.

His name was Robert. He stated that he had
been born of free parents at Cincinatti, in Ohio,
where he had a wife and two children. Two men,
with whom he had met in his native city, had hired
him to travel with them to the South, offering him
large wages to go and return with them. Suspecting
no wrong he had accepted their offers ; but when
they arrived at Fredericksburgh, in Virginia, having
no free papers, he was seized and placed in confinement as a slave. He had been treated very much as
Solomon was, except that he had not been drugged.
He had claimed his liberty, affirming that he was a
free-born citizen of Ohio, but was beaten and cruelly
treated, until he had learned the policy of being
silent on that subject. From Fredericksburgh he
had been transferred by rail to Richmond, and had
been in Goodin's pen about three weeks when
Solomon first became acquainted with him. He and
Solomon could understand and sympathise with each
other, both having suffered the same wrong at the
hands of unprincipled kidnappers ; and never again
was Robert destined to look upon wife, or children,
or native land ; for a few days after he and Solomon
were brought together he found a watery grave in the
wide Atlantic.

Solomon found considerable variety of character
amongst the new associates with whom his unhappy

fate had made him acquainted in Goodin's slave pen. Robert and himself, with Clem, Eliza, and her children, were sent to sleep in one of the small houses in the yard. There were four others also sleeping in the same place. They were all from the same plantation, and had been sold, probably for debt, and were now on their way to the Southern market. David and Caroline were man and wife, both bright mulattoes. They were in deep affliction, and greatly dreaded what they feared was the fate impending over them, that of being put to labour in the cane and cotton fields of the South. But their greatest trouble was the thought of being separated and sold in different directions. Mary, another of the party, was a tall, lithe, well-made girl, jetty black, but apparently utterly listless and indifferent. Like some others of her class, she scarcely knew there was such a thing, or such a word, as "freedom." Brought up in utter ignorance, she possessed scarcely more than a brute's intelligence. She was one of those who feared only the master's lash, and whose only idea of duty was to obey his will. She did not appear to have heard of God, or to have any idea of religion at all. Solomon thought that he had never before met with a human being who appeared to be so utterly destitute of all the nobler attributes of humanity as this girl, Mary. The other was named Lethe, a girl of an entirely different character. She was good-looking, and had long, straight, coarse hair, bearing more the appearance of an Indian than of a negro woman. She had sharp, piercing,

spiteful eyes, and was continually giving utterance
to sentiments of hatred and revenge. From the
bitter feeling she manifested, and the ferocious
language she uttered, it might have been inferred
that she was possessed of an evil spirit. She had
been happily married to the man she loved—and she
loved with the greatest intensity—but her husband
had been sold away from her, and she knew not
where he was, or what had become of him. This had
turned all the great love that filled her heart towards
her husband into a feeling of hatred and revenge
towards all others. She had become utterly desperate, and did not care what might become of her.
They might carry her where they pleased; a change
of masters could not be for the worse. She had
evidently been cruelly treated in the vain attempt
to subdue her bitter, ungovernable spirit. Her person
bore abundant marks of the severe discipline to
which she had been subjected; but she cared not for
it. Pointing to the scars upon her face and elsewhere, the desperate creature would often wish she
might see the day when she could wipe them off in
some man's blood. It was not a matter to excite
surprise that one so vixenish should be sent to the
South.

While Solomon was making himself acquainted
with his companions in misfortune and their history, and giving them an account of his own sorrows,
Eliza sat apart in a corner with her children, praying
over them and weeping, and occasionally singing at
their request a verse or two of some little familiar

hymn, which she had taught them at home. Thus a great part of the night was consumed, until at length sleep stole over the whole party, and they lay and slumbered until morning; when at earliest dawn they were aroused by Goodin. Having washed and dressed themselves under his superintendence in a place arranged for the purpose, he made them sweep the yard, and then ordered them to roll up their blankets, and make ready for the continuance of their journey.

But here they were a little surprised to learn that a change had taken place as to the destination of Clem Ray. He was to proceed no further with them, Burch having for some reason or other resolved to take him back to Washington. Solomon was glad to hear that he was no longer condemned to the hateful presence of Burch, whose very appearance excited feelings of loathing; and he rejoiced that Clem was to be delivered from the fate he so much dreaded, that of going to the South. They parted in Goodin's slave-pen at Richmond, and Solomon, as he shook hands with him, wished him a speedy deliverance from bondage. This wish was fulfilled. Solomon saw Clem no more; but they had not been thrown together in vain. They had talked much of the North, and the comforts and privileges enjoyed by coloured people there, and they had discussed the means and chances of escape. After his return home, Solomon learnt that his former companion had so availed himself of the knowledge he acquired in this way as to succeed in making his escape to Canada. Solomon never learnt the particulars of his flight; but he had made his way to Saratoga, where he was sheltered for a night at the house of a brother-in-law of Solomon, who was living there. From Clem Ray Solomon's family first heard how he had been kidnapped, and of the place and condition in which he had left him. They had, however, before this, received a few hurried lines, which Solomon contrived to get written and posted at New Orleans on his arrival there.

In the afternoon all the slaves in Goodin's pen, except Clem Ray, were called up and ranged two abreast, Solomon and his companion, Robert, being placed in front, Eliza and her children bringing up the rear. In this order they were driven by Burch and Goodin through the streets of Richmond from the slave-pen, until they came to the place where the vessel lay that was to convey them further on their journey. She was a large brig, named the *Orleans*, full rigged, and freighted principally with tobacco. To each of the company, amounting to about forty, Burch gave a tin cup and an iron spoon.

With a small pocket knife, of which he had retained possession, it having been left in one of his pockets when they were rifled in the slave pen at Washington, Solomon began to cut or scratch the initials of his name upon his cup. This attracted the attention of the others, who all flocked around him, wondering at his skill, and requesting that he would do the same for them, and put their own mark upon their respective cups. He gratified them all, of which they did not appear to be forgetful, evidently considering that a great obligation had been conferred upon them.

They were all on board by five o'clock, and when night approached were ordered down into the hold, where they stowed themselves on boxes or barrels in any convenient place they could find, no kind of accommodation for their sleeping being provided. There each one looked out for himself, all seeming ready and anxious to forego their own convenience that Eliza and her children might be made comfortable. The hatch was then placed on and barred down.

Here Solomon saw the last of Burch, until he met him more than twelve years after in the police-office at Washington, when that worthy was brought up on a charge of kidnapping and selling him into slavery, which will be more particularly referred to hereafter. It was a relief when he took his departure, and Solomon seemed to breathe more freely when he knew that the brutal tyrant was gone, and was not expected to return again. This Burch was a slave-dealer—a disreputable calling even at the South. He was a speculator in human flesh, buying men, women, and children at low prices, and selling them at an advance. For this business Burch was well fitted by nature and training, being utterly destitute of all the kindlier attributes of humanity, callous to human suffering, and utterly unscrupulous as to the injury and suffering he might inflict upon others.

CHAPTER V.

A Plot Defeated.

SOON after all the slaves were put aboard, the brig proceeded down the James River. Passing into Chesapeake Bay, she arrived next day oppposite the City of Norfolk, and came to anchor. Whilst lying there a lighter came alongside bringing four more slaves. One of these was named Frederick, some eighteen years of age; another, Henry, who was several years older. Both of these had been born to an inheritance of slavery, and both had been house servants in the City, their owners having been compelled to part with them to a slave-dealer, for the Southern Market. Maria was a good-looking coloured girl, seemingly a quadroon: she had a very graceful form, but was excessively vain, indulging the most flattering visions as to the great advantages which her beauty was to secure for her in the South. The idea of going to New Orleans was very gratifying to her, as she entertained an extravagantly high opinion of her own attractions. She mounted to the deck of the brig from the lighter without the slightest degree of reluctance.

But it was very different with the fourth of the party. He was another victim of the kidnappers. As the lighter approached he struggled stoutly with those who had him in charge, fettered as he was with handcuffs. It was only by main force that he was got on board the brig. He protested with a loud voice against the treatment he was receiving, affirming that he was a free man, and demanding to be released. He was forced in the most brutal manner into the hold of the brig, and there firmly secured. His face was fearfully swollen, and covered with wounds and bruises; indeed one side of it was almost entirely raw. Solomon learnt his history afterwards. His name was Arthur, and he had been born free, residing for many years in the City of Norfolk. He was a mason by trade, and had a family who were still living there. One day, having been detained by his work to a later hour than usual, he was returning to his home in the suburbs of the City, when, as he was passing through a rather unfrequented street, he was suddenly attacked by a gang of men. He fought with them until his strength failed him; when being overpowered by numbers a gag was placed in his mouth, and being firmly bound with ropes he was beaten until he became insensible. In that condition he was borne to a slave-pen in Norfolk—a common institution in all Southern cities—and there he was secreted for several days. When the brig *Orleans* came to anchor, having first been subjected to severe discipline to quiet him, he was taken out of the cell in which he had been chained and put on board the lighter. Still protesting and struggling he was carried as a slave on board the brig.

After being forced below and secured there, he still continued loudly to protest against the wrong that was being done to him, and demanded as a free man to be set at liberty. At length, exhausted by the violence of his own struggles, he became silent. He sank into a thoughtful mood, and appeared to be taking counsel with himself. The expression of his face was such as to indicate that his thoughts and feelings were of a desperate character. Shortly after the lighter took her departure the anchor was lifted, and the brig pursued her course.

After leaving Norfolk the handcuffs were taken off, and during the day the slaves were allowed to have their liberty on deck. The next day after the new slaves came on board, the Captain arranged the order in which they were to serve on board the ship. He selected Robert as his own waiter to attend upon himself. Solomon was to superintend the cooking department, and act in the capacity of steward for the slave passengers, distributing to them food and water; Jim, Cuffee, and Jenny being appointed his assistants. Jenny's business was to prepare the coffee; which consisted, not of the fragrant berry known by that name, but of Indian corn-meal scorched in an iron pot, then boiled and sweetened with molasses. Jim and Cuffee baked the hoe-cake, and boiled the bacon. A rough table was formed of a wide board resting upon the ends of barrels. At the head stood Solomon, who cut for each a slice of the bacon, and what was called a " dodger " of the cake; and from Jenny's kettle he dipped out for each a cup of the coffee. Plates were dispensed with, and sable fingers served as knives and forks. Twice a day was a supply of food dealt out to the slaves, at ten and five o'clock, the fare being always the same both in kind and quantity; and the above was the routine always observed. As night came on they were all driven into the hold and securely battened down.

Shortly after they lost sight of land a violent storm came on, when all experienced the horrors of sea-sickness, aggravated by their being so closely shut up. The brig rolled and plunged until it was feared she would go down. Some were utterly prostrated by the sickness until they cared not what might become of them; some were praying and calling upon the Lord to have mercy upon them, and save them; while others were fast clinging to each other utterly paralyzed by fear. "It would have been a happy thing for most of us," Solomon afterwards said, "if the brig had foundered in the storm. It would have saved the agony of many a hundred lashes, and prevented a vast amount of suffering and some miserable deaths, had the compassionate sea snatched us that day from the clutches of remorseless men. The thought of Randall and little Emmy sinking down to a quiet resting place in the deep, is a more pleasant contemplation than to think of them passing through those scenes of pollution and cruelty which in all probability awaited them, or dragging out lives of misery and unrequited toil."

When they arrived off the Hole-in-the-Wall, or Old

Point Compass, the southern point of Abaco, in the Bahamas, they were becalmed three days, and there was scarcely a breath of air. They were surprised to find the water on the Bahama banks presenting a singularly white appearance like lime water, an effect caused only by the reflection of the white sand on the bottom, the water there being very shallow. The navigation amongst these banks is very dangerous, and formerly the wrecks in these seas were very numerous. But since the erection of additional light-houses clearly marking the passage for ships, wrecks have been much less frequent, and the occupation of multitudes who gained their living by giving assistance to wrecked ships has well nigh passed away.

It was while they lay becalmed in the vicinity of the Bahama Islands, that Solomon and some of his companions were providentially saved from great temptation and crime; a cause of thankfulness to the Almighty as long as he lived. Solomon thus referred to it in after years:—"I thank God, who has since permitted me to escape from the thraldom of slavery, that, through His merciful interposition, I was prevented from imbruing my hands in the blood of my fellow creatures. Let not those who have never been placed in like circumstances judge me harshly. Until they have been chained and beaten—until they find themselves in the situation in which I was placed, stolen from home and family, and borne away to hopeless bondage—let them refrain from saying what they would not do to regain their liberty. How far I should have been justified in the sight of God and

man had I succeeded, it is now unnecessary to specu-
late upon. It is enough to say that I congratulate
myself upon the harmless termination of an affair
which threatened for a time to be attended with
serious results."

While becalmed off Abaco, Arthur and Solomon
were on the bow of the vessel seated on the windlass.
They were conversing together concerning the probable fate which awaited them, and mourning over the
misfortunes which had come upon them through the
villainy of their fellow-men. Arthur said, and
Solomon agreed with him, that death was far less
terrible than the prospect of misery and suffering
which lay before them. For a long time they talked
of their past lives, their homes and wives and children,
and the possibility of making their escape by any
means. Among other schemes, they considered if it
were practicable to take possession of the brig and
make their escape in her to a free land. The possibility of making their way to New York with the
vessel was eagerly discussed. Solomon knew little of
the compass and still less of navigation ; but he was
ready to risk his life in the experiment. If they had
known that the land in sight was free land, and that
they had only, when they had seized the brig, to run
her ashore and make their escape in the boats to land,
where they would have been as much under the
British flag and as securely protected by British
power as if they had been in Canada, no doubt they
would at once have made the attempt, but they were
ignorant of all this.

The chances for and against them in an encounter with the crew were anxiously weighed; who could be relied upon for help and who could not, the time and the manner of making the attempt, were all talked over. From the moment the plot suggested itself to his mind Solomon began to hope that his freedom would be achieved; and as one difficulty after another was suggested by his companion, some expedient was also thought of by which it might be obviated or overcome. While the others were sleeping, the two conspirators were in their own minds revolving and maturing their plans. Whenever they could get together alone, in the bow of the brig, or elsewhere where they were certain of not being overheard, they were conversing on this topic. After awhile Robert was carefully made acquainted with the views and purposes of the others, and he cordially approved them and entered into the conspiracy with a zealous spirit. Nothing could have been more in accordance with his state of mind; outraged as all his feelings were by having been kidnapped from his home and his family, he was willing to take any part in the attempt that might be assigned to him, and anxious to enter upon it at once. There was not another of the slaves they dared to trust. Brought up as they had been in the grossest ignorance and the most debasing fear, it could scarcely be conceived how servilely they would cringe before a white man's look. It was not safe to deposit so important a secret with any of them; and finally Solomon, with Robert and Arthur, resolved to take upon themselves alone the fearful

I

responsibility of the attempt. They knew well that the penalty of failure would be nothing less than death, but that was far preferable to a life of hopeless slavery.

At night all the slaves were driven into the hold and the hatch securely battened down. How to reach the deck was the first difficulty that presented itself. But on the bow of the brig Solomon had observed a small boat lying bottom upwards. It occurred to him that one of them secreting himself underneath the boat, would probably not be missed from the crowd of slaves as they were hurried down into the hold at night. Solomon volunteered to make the experiment, in order that the others might be satisfied of the feasibility of the plan. The one concealed could remove the battens which fastened the hatch, and thus allow the others to come on deck. The next evening, accordingly, Solomon concealed himself under the boat, lying close upon the deck, while himself unobserved, he could see what was going on around him. In the morning when the hatches were opened and the other slaves came on deck, he slipped from his hiding place without being observed. The result was entirely satisfactory, and showed that this part of their scheme could be carried into effect without any difficulty, due caution being observed.

The captain and mate slept in the after cabin. From Robert, who had frequent occasion, in his capacity of waiter, to make observations in that quarter, the conspirators ascertained the exact position of their respective berths. Robert informed them that there were always two pistols and a cutlass lying on the cabin table. The crew's cook slept in the galley on deck—a little house on wheels that could be moved about as convenience required—while the sailors, numbering only six, either slept in the forecastle or in hammocks swung up on the deck below.

The arrangements of the conspirators were all completed, and it only required the night to be fixed for the attempt to be made. Arthur and Solomon were to steal silently to the cabin, seize the pistols and the cutlass, and as quickly as possible despatch the captain and the mate. Robert was to stand, with a heavy club they had got possession of, at the door leading from the deck down into the cabin, and in case of necessity beat back the sailors until Solomon and Robert could hurry to his assistance. They were then to proceed as circumstances might require. Should the attack be so sudden and successful as to prevent an alarm, the hatch was to remain barred down ; otherwise the slaves were to be called up, and with their help all resistance was to be put down and the brig taken possession of by them. Solomon was then to assume the duties of pilot, and steering northward they trusted the vessel would bear them to some land of freedom.

Such a crude and ill-arranged plot was sure to fail ; and it was well for the conspirators that circumstances occurred to prevent the attempt being made. They had left out of consideration altogether that a watch, consisting of half the crew, would be on deck under the command of the captain or mate the whole night, and that they were sure to meet with a determined resistance. Moreover, the course they intended to steer would in all probability have brought them upon some of the banks and shoals of the Bahamas. " The captain," Solomon said, " was a small, genteel kind of man, erect and prompt, with a proud bearing, and he looked the very personification of courage." How very unlikely that such a man would suffer his ship to be taken from him in the manner which these simple-minded, ignorant men had planned! Their plot never had the slightest chance of success.

But it was frustrated by a sad and unforeseen event. When all was prepared, and they were looking for an early opportunity to put their designs in execution, Robert was taken ill. It was soon announced that his disease was small-pox of a very virulent type. He continued to grow worse, and four days before the brig reached New Orleans, the sickness terminated in death. One of the sailors sewed him up in his blanket, with a large stone taken from the ballast at his feet. The body was removed on deck and placed on a hatch reaching the gangway, which being elevated by tackling from above, the body of poor Robert slid off into the sea, there to find a resting place until the morning of the resurrection, when at the sound of the Archangel's trump the sea shall give up its dead.

The slaves were all panic-stricken by this outbreak of the small-pox among them. The captain caused lime to be scattered through the hold, and other precautions to be taken, and the disease spread no fur-

ther.   The death of Robert was a heavy blow to
Solomon; and that, with the presence of such a deadly
malady from which they could none of them flee,
oppressed him sadly, and he gazed over the great
expanse of waters feeling utterly disconsolate.   An
evening or two after Robert's burial, he was leaning
on the bulwarks near the forecastle, full of desponding
thoughts, when a sailor in a kind voice asked him
why he was so downhearted.   The tone and manner
of the man inspired Solomon with a feeling of
confidence, and he replied, " because I am a free man
and have been kidnapped."   He remarked that that
was enough to make anyone feel down-hearted ; and
continued to put questions to Solomon, until he had
learned the particulars of Solomon's whole history.
He was evidently much interested and touched by
Solomon's statement, and in the blunt speech of a
sailor swore, " split my timbers, but I will help you,
my poor fellow, all that is in my power."   Solomon
was overjoyed and said :—

" The best way in which you can aid me is to furnish me with pen, ink and paper, that I may write to
my friends, who will perhaps find means to rescue me."

I'll be glad to help you to them," the sailor replied ;
" but how you can use them without being discovered
is the difficulty."

" Oh, if I can get into the forecastle while you are
off watch and the other sailors asleep, the thing can
be accomplished."   Solomon had in his mind the
expedient of secreting himself under the small boat
for the purpose.

"I think," continued the sailor, "we are not far from the Balize, at the mouth of the Mississippi, and the letter must be written soon or the opportunity will be lost."

Solomon then revealed to his companion the manner in which he intended to accomplish his purpose by concealing himself under the boat, and the arrangement was made for the following night. Accordingly, Solomon secreted himself beneath the boat. The sailor's watch was off at twelve; Solomon saw him pass into the forecastle, and in about an hour followed him. He was nodding half asleep over a table on which a sickly light was flickering, and, to the joy of Solomon's heart, there he saw a pen, an inkstand, and a sheet of paper. As Solomon entered he roused up, beckoned him to a seat beside himself, and pointed to the paper. The letter was written— not a very long one—stating that the writer, Solomon Northup, had been kidnapped and was then on board the brig *Orleans*, bound to the port of New Orleans. It was impossible then for him to conjecture his ultimate destination; but he begged the gentleman to whom he was writing to take such measures as might be in his power to rescue him. The letter was then directed to Henry B. Northup, Esq., of Sandy Hill, New York State; and the sailor, whose name was Manning, having read and sealed it, promised to deposit it in the New Orleans Post Office. Solomon then hastened back to his refuge under the long boat; and in the morning, when the slaves came on deck and were walking round, he crept out unnoticed and mingled with them.

This kind friend was an Englishman, and Solomon regarded him as the most noble-hearted sailor that ever walked a deck. He had lived in Boston, and was under the influence of anti-slavery principles—a tall, well-built man seemingly about twenty-four years of age, with a face expressive of true benevolence.

Nothing further occurred to vary the monotony of the voyage until the vessel arrived at New Orleans. On coming alongside the levee, and before the vessel was well moored, Solomon saw his friend Manning leap ashore and hurry away into the City. As he started he looked back over his shoulder at Solomon in a very significant way, from which Solomon understood that the object of his visit to the City was to dispose of the letter. He was only a few minutes absent, and when he returned, passing by Solomon, he nudged him with his elbow with a wink, which Solomon understood to mean, "it is all right." The letter reached its destination at Sandy Hill, and Mr. Northup visited Albany and laid it before Governor Seward, who felt a lively interest in the case. But inasmuch as the letter gave no information as to the probable destination of the kidnapped man, it was not at that time considered advisable to institute measures for his liberation. Any inquiries that might be made on the subject were more likely to defeat them than to promote such an object, by leading parties concerned in the transaction so to conceal the stolen man as to render it impossible to ascertain his whereabouts. It was concluded to delay further action, trusting that a knowledge of the place to which Solomon was sent would ultimately be obtained. That, however, did not occur until after the lapse of twelve dreary, suffering years.

As soon as the brig was moored alongside the levee a very touching and happy scene occurred. A moment after Manning left the brig to run to the Post Office, two men came up to the side of the vessel and called loudly for Arthur. The poor fellow hearing his name called came to the side of the vessel, and immediately recognizing the two strangers became almost frantic with delight; for in them he beheld friends who were come as his deliverers. He could hardly be restrained from leaping over the brig's side, and when, soon after he met his two friends, he grasped them by the hand and clung to them like one that was insane. They were two gentlemen from Norfolk, who had come to rescue him, having journeyed to New Orleans by land for that purpose. The manner in which he had been beaten and stolen had got to be known. The matter had been taken in hand by kind and zealous friends who had searched into the truth of the whole story. The kidnappers, they informed him, had been arrested and were then confined in the Norfolk prison, awaiting their trial for the outrage they had committed. The gentlemen conversed a few moments with the Captain and showed him some papers of which they were the bearers, and then took their departure with the rejoicing Arthur.

While he sympathized with his friend Arthur in the good fortune which had befallen him, and rejoiced in his escape from a miserable fate, yet this event tended naturally to increase the gloom that filled the mind of Solomon on his own account. As he gazed over the side of the brig, he felt " in all that crowd which covers the levee, there is no one that knows or cares for me. Not one." No familiar voice greeted his ears, nor was there a single face that he had ever seen before. Arthur would soon be restored to his family, and have the satisfaction of seeing his wrongs avenged on the bad men who would have plundered him of all the rights that belonged to him as a man. But as to himself! what prospect was there that he should ever see his wife and children again, or ever regain his liberty or his home? His heart sank with a feeling of utter desolation, and he almost regretted that he had not, like Robert, found a resting place in the deep, deep sea.

Very soon traders and consignees came on board. One, a tall, thin-faced man with light complexion, and a little bent, made his appearance with a paper in his hand. Burch's gang, consisting of Solomon, Eliza and her children, Henry, Lethe, and some others who had joined them at Richmond, was consigned to him. His name was Theophilus Freeman, and he was engaged in the occupation of slave-dealing in partnership with Burch. Reading from the paper in his hand, he called " Platt." No one answered. The name was called again and again, but still there was no reply. Then Lethe was called, then Eliza and her children, then Henry, until the list was finished, each one stepping forward as the name was pronounced.

" Captain, where's Platt ? " demanded Freeman.

" I cannot tell you," the Captain replied. " There's no one on board bearing that name."

" Who shipped *that* nigger ? " he again inquired, pointing to Solomon.

" Burch," replied the Captain.

" Your name is Platt— you answer my description. Why don't you come forward ? " he demanded in a coarse angry tone, and with an oath.

" Because that is not my name," Solomon answered. " I have never been called Platt before. But I have no objection to the name that I know of."

" Well, I will learn you your name," said Freeman, " and so as you won't forget it."

This was accompanied by a round of oaths, which showed that Mr. Theophilus Freeman was not a whit behind his partner, Burch, in brutality and blasphemy. Though very different in physical conformation, they were kindred spirits and worthy associates. In the vessel Solomon had gone by the name of Steward, in virtue of the office which had been assigned to him, and this was the first time he had ever been designated Platt, a name probably of Burch's own choosing which he had forwarded to his consignee at New Orleans. From the vessel Solomon could see the chain-gang at work on the levee ; and shortly after he was, with his companions in misfortune, driven past them on his way to Freeman's slave-pen. This pen was similar to that of Goodin's at Richmond, except that the more spacious yard was enclosed by strong planks standing upright, with the ends sharpened, instead of brick walls.

Including the new arrivals there were at least fifty slaves in this pen. Solomon and his companions were directed to deposit their blankets in one of the small buildings in the yard; and having been called up and fed were allowed to saunter about the yard until night. Then, wrapping their blankets about them, they lay down in the shed or the yard, or ascended to the loft, as taste or fancy dictated.

Solomon closed his eyes for only a brief period that night. Thought was busy in his brain and prevented sleep. Could it be possible that he was thousands of miles from home?—that he had been beaten and chained without mercy—that he had been driven through the streets like a dumb beast—that he was even then herded with a drove of slaves—a slave himself? Were the events of the last few weeks realities indeed? or was he only passing through the dismal phases of a long, protracted dream? Unhappily it was no illusion! His cup of sorrow was full to overflowing! Then he lifted up his hands and his heart to God; and in the still watches of the night, surrounded by the slumbering forms of his companions, begged and prayed that God would have mercy upon the poor, forsaken captive. To the Almighty Father of all—free man or slave—and to Jesus, the loving and compassionate Saviour, he poured forth the supplications of a broken spirit, imploring strength from on high to bear up against the burden of his troubles, until the morning light aroused the sleepers and ushered in another day of bondage.

CHAPTER VI.

New Orleans.

MR. THEOPHILUS FREEMAN, partner and consignee of Mr. James R. Burch, and keeper of the slave-pen at New Orleans, was out amongst his stock early in the morning. With an occasional kick at the older men and women, and many a sharp crack of the whip about the ears or across the persons of the younger slaves, it was not long before he had them all wide awake and astir. He bustled about among them in a very industrious, swaggering manner, getting his property ready for the sales-room, hoping no doubt with his new arrivals that day to do a rousing and profitable business.

In the first place all were required to wash themselves thoroughly, and those who had beards to shave. They were then furnished each with a new suit of clothes, cheap but clean. The men had hat, coat, shirt, pants, and shoes dealt out to them; the females frocks of calico, and handkerchiefs to wrap about their heads. The dresses were not remarkable either for fit or fashion. All were then conducted into a large room in front of the building to which the yard was attached, in order to be properly trained for exhibition before the admission of customers.

The men were arranged on one side of the room, the women on the other. The tallest was placed at the head of the row, and so on according to their respective heights—little Emily, radiant with youthful beauty, terminating the female line. Freeman charged them to be careful to remember their respective places, and admonished them to be smart and lively, holding out both promises and threatenings as inducements, garnished with abundance of oaths and expletives. During the day they were exercised in the art of looking smart and lively, and taught how to move to their appointed places with exact precision.

After being fed, in the afternoon they were all again paraded in the large room, and made to dance— Bob, a coloured boy, who had for some time belonged to Freeman, played the violin after a rude fashion. Standing near him, Solomon inquired if he could play the " Virginia Reel?" He answered " No." " Can you play the violin, and do you know the tune you spoke of ? " Solomon replied in the affirmative, when the boy handed him the instrument, and requested he would play it. This request being complied with, Freeman's attention was directed to the performer, and he stepped up and ordered him to continue playing. He seemed well-pleased to find that Solomon possessed this accomplishment, telling Bob that he far excelled him in his performance. This remark seemed to grieve poor Bob very much, who had a high appreciation of his own skill as a performer on the violin.

Next day many persons wishing to be customers called to examine Freeman's " new lot."   The slave-dealer was very loquacious, dwelling at great length, and with a clumsy attempt at eloquence, upon the good points and qualities of the slaves.   He would make them hold up their heads and walk briskly to-and-fro across the room, while the customers would feel their hands, and arms, and bodies, turn them about, inquire of them what they corld do, and make them open their mouths and show their teeth as a jockey examines the mouth of a horse he is about to purchase.   Sometimes a man or woman was taken back to one of the small houses in the yard to be stripped and inspected more minutely.   Scars upon a slave's back were regarded as evidence of a rebellious and unruly spirit, and irjured the sale ; although in many instances they were more truly the proofs of cruelty and brutality on the part of former owners.

One old gentleman, who said he wanted a coach-man, appeared to take a fancy to Solomon.   From his conversation with Freeman, Solomon learnt that the old gentleman was a resident of the city; and he felt anxious that he should become his purchaser, because he considered that it would be more prac-ticable to make his escape from New Orleans on some Northern vessel, than it would be if he were carried to any of the plantations in the interior.   Freeman asked fifteen hundred dollars for Solomon.   But the old gentleman said, " Times are very hard, and the price is too high."   Freeman declared that the man was sound and healthy, of a good constitution, and more than ordinarily intelligent. He enlarged too a good deal upon Solomon's musical capabilities. But they could not agree upon the bargain, to Solomon's great disappointment. The old gentleman said, " I see nothing extraordinary about the nigger," and left the place, saying he would call again. During the day, however, a number of sales were effected, and Solomon was parted from several of his travelling companions. David and Caroline were purchased together by a planter from Natchez, and they left, both grinning broadly, showing that they were in a happy state of mind because they were not to be separated, but were still to share each other's lot whether for weal or woe. Lethe was sold to a coarse, rough planter from Baton Ronge, as a field hand; her eyes flashing with anger, as she was led away, at the disappointment her vanity had received in being disposed of after a fashion so contrary to her expectations.

The same man purchased Randall. The little fellow was made to jump and run across the floor, and perform many other feats, to display his activity and healthy condition. All the time this bargain was in course of transaction, Eliza was crying aloud and wringing her hands. She besought the man with tears not to buy the child unless he also bought herself and Emily. She promised in that case to be the most faithful slave that ever lived. The man answered that he could not afford to buy them all; and then the distracted, heart-broken mother burst into a paroxysm of grief, weeping and moaning most plaintively. At last Freeman turned to her savagely with his uplifted whip in his hand, and ordered her instantly to " hush her noise," or he would give her a flogging, intermingling oaths with his threats.

" I'll not have such work—such snivelling. If you don't cease your squalling this minute, I'll take you out into the yard and see if a hundred lashes won't quiet you. I'll take the nonsense out of you pretty quick. If I don't, may I——. " We leave out all the blasphemous and brutal words which gave additional energy to his threats.

Eliza shrunk before him and tried to force back and wipe away her tears ; but in vain. She wanted to be with her children, she said, the little time she had to live. All the scowls and threats of the slave-dealer could not wholly silence the afflicted mother. She kept on begging most piteously, and beseeching them not to separate the three. Over and over again she told them how fondly she loved the boy. A great many times she repeated her former promises— how very faithful and obedient and devoted she would be ; how hard she would labour day and night to the last moment of her life, if he would only buy them all together. But it was of no use. The man could not afford it. He would have bought them all if he could. But he had no means to purchase more than he had already agreed for. The bargain was concluded, and little Randall must go alone.

The poor mother ran to him and embraced him passionately. She kissed him again and again in a frantic sort of way, told him not to forget his mother, and rained showers of tears upon his little upturned face.

Freeman cursed her horribly, bestowing upon her many a vulgar and indecent epithet. He ordered her to go to her place and behave herself properly, and swore that he wouldn't stand such stuff very much longer. He would soon " give her something to cry about if she was not mighty careful, and that she might depend upon."

The Baton Rouge planter was ready to depart with his new purchases. Little Randall, as he drew near the door, looked back with streaming eyes and said, " Don't cry, mamma, I will be a good boy. Don't cry." The door closed, and that was the last time the despairing mother's eyes rested on the form of her lovely and much-loved boy. What became of the lad Solomon never learned; whether he sunk under the hardships of slave life into an early grave, or whether he lived to grow up to manhood, he could never ascertain, though he always made inquiries of any whom he thought were likely to have known or heard of the boy.

That night nearly all the slaves who came in the brig *Orleans* were taken very ill. They complained of violent pains in the head and back. Little Emily— a thing very unusual with her—cried constantly all night. In the morning a medical man was called in, but was unable to determine the nature of the complaint. While examining Solomon, whom he found to be more intelligent than the others, and asking him questions touching his symptoms, he was some-

K

what startled when his patient, begging to be excused for what might seem like forwardness, stated his opinion that the disease from which they were all suffering was small-pox.   He asked him why he thought so; when Solomon mentioned the fact of Robert's death on board the brig, and stated that the symptoms he and others were suffering from were similar to those that marked the earlier stages of Robert's illness.   It might be so, indeed, the doctor thought, and he would send for the head physician of the hospital.   Shortly that functionary made his appearance—a small, self-important, light-haired man, whom they called Dr. Carr.   He pronounced the disease at once to be small-pox, to the great terror of all the denizens of the yard, who all seemed to stand much in dread of that terrible complaint.

By order of Dr. Carr, very soon after he left, Solomon, Eliza, and the child, with Harry, were put into a hack and driven to the hospital—a large white building standing on the outskirts of the City. Solomon and Harry were placed in a room in one of the upper stories, and the former soon became very ill—too ill to comprehend much of what was going on around him.   For three days he was entirely blind.   While lying in that state one day, a slave named Bob came into the room, and said to Dr. Carr, who was in attendance, " Mr. Freeman has sent me to inquire how Platt and the others are getting on ? "

" Tell him," said the doctor, " that Platt is very bad; but if he survives until nine o'clock he may recover."

Solomon expected to die, and the thought of dying among strangers as a slave was very bitter. There was not much in the prospect before him to render life very desirable. But he still hoped to gain his liberty by some means, and end his days amongst his family and friends; and with such a hope he desired that he might be permitted to live.

There was a great number of patients in the hospital, of both sexes and of all ages. In the rear of the buildings coffins were manufactured. When a patient died, the bell tolled, a signal to the undertaker to come and bear away the body to the cemetery to which the dead from the hospital were carried. Many times each day and night this bell sent forth its melancholy sound, announcing that another death had taken place. But Solomon's time had not come. The bell was not called into use on his account. The crisis of his disease having passed, he began to recover; and at the end of two weeks and two days he returned with Harry to the slave-pen, bearing upon his face the marks of the fearful malady which had so nearly made him its victim, and which continued all through his after life somewhat to disfigure him. Eliza and Emily were brought back to the pen the next day, neither of them marked by the small-pox, which had been much lighter in their case than Solomon's; and again they were all paraded in the sales-room for the inspection of intending purchasers. Solomon still indulged the hope that the old gentleman in search of a coachman would call again as he had promised, and purchase him. In that event he felt the fullest confidence that he would soon regain his liberty. Customer after customer entered; but the old gentleman never again made his appearance.

At length one day when the slaves were in the yard, Freeman came bustling out, and ordered them all to their places in the great room. A gentleman was waiting there. He was a man above the ordinary height, somewhat bent and stooping. He was a fine-looking, handsome man, and appeared to have reached about fifty years of age. There was nothing repulsive in his appearance and manners; on the contrary, his countenance was pleasant to look upon. It had an expression of benevolence, very different from what they saw in many faces that made their appearance in that room. His voice was soft and agreeable; and as he moved about the room, he asked many questions in the kindest manner of the various slaves as to what they could do—what kind of labour they had been accustomed to—and if they thought they would like to live with him? And whether they would be good boys if he were willing to buy them? His whole manner and appearance seemed to make a favourable impression on all; and all felt that they would be glad if he would become their purchaser.

After some inspection, which was done in the kindest manner, and some conversation with Freeman touching prices and other matters, he finally offered Freeman a thousand dollars for Solomon nine hundred for Harry, and seven hundred for Eliza.

Whether the small-pox had depreciated their value somewhat since he required fifteen hundred dollars for Solomon, and would not take less, or whether his narrow escape from losing the whole by the disease which had attacked them, had impressed him with the fact that after all there is something risky in holding many slaves, cannot be stated. But after a little careful reflection, Freeman concluded to come down from his high figure for Solomon, and to accept the gentleman's offer for the whole party that he had named.

As soon as Eliza heard this she was in an agony again. By this time she had become haggard and hollow-eyed with sickness and sorrow—a very different person in appearance from what she was when, splendidly attired, she was rudely thrust into the slave-pen at Washington. It is difficult to convey an idea of the anguish and despair of the bereaved mother. Solomon said, " I have seen mothers kissing for the last time the faces of their dead offspring. I have seen them looking down into the grave as the earth fell with its dull rumbling sound upon the little coffins which contained the objects of their dearest love, now hidden from their gaze for ever ; but never have I seen such an exhibition of intense, unmeasured, unbounded grief, as when Eliza was parted from her only remaining child. She broke from her place in the line of women, and rushing to where Emily was standing, caught the child in her arms. Emily conscious of some impending evil, though too young to compre-

hend the true character of the scene, instinctively
fastened her arms around her mother's neck, and
nestled her little head in that loving bosom.
Freeman sternly ordered Eliza to be quiet, but she
did not heed him. He caught her by the arm, and
attempted rudely to pull her away, but she only
clung the more desperately to the child. Then,
with a volley of great oaths, he struck her a heavy,
heartless blow, so that she staggered backward, and
would have fallen to the ground, had not some one
caught her. Oh! how piteously did she beseech,
and beg, and pray that they might not be separated!
Why could they not be purchased together? Why
not let her have one of her dear children? Mercy!
mercy, Master!" she cried, falling on her knees.
" Please, Master, buy Emily. I can never work any
if she is taken from me. I will die."

The hardened slave-dealer again interfered ; but
disregarding him in her despair, she still pleaded
earnestly with her new master, telling how Randall
had been taken from her—her precious boy!—how
she would never see him again ; and how it was too
bad, too cruel, to take her away from Emily, her
pride, her only darling, that could not live, she was
so young, without her mother.

After much more of supplication and entreaty on
the part of the frantic mother, the gentleman who
had purchased her, moved by her overwhelming
distress, and evidently deeply affected, stepped
forward, and said that he would buy Emily, and
inquired of the dealer what price he asked for her ?

"What is her *price? Buy her?*" was the responsive interrogatory of Freeman. Then instantly answering his own questions, he exclaimed with an oath, "I won't sell her. She is not for sale!"

The gentleman remarked that he was not in need of one so young—that it would be of no profit to him to purchase her; but since the mother was so fond of her child, and so unwilling to part from her, rather than see them separated he would pay a reasonable price for the girl. But to this humane proposal Freeman was entirely deaf. He would not sell her on any account whatever, observing, in brutal disregard of the sorrow of the suffering mother:—

"There are piles and heaps of money to be made of her, when she is a few years older. There are men enough in New Orleans who would give five thousand dollars for such an extra, handsome, fancy piece as Emily will be, rather than not get her. No! No! I'll not sell her now. She is a beauty—a picture—a doll—one of the regular bloods—none of your thick-lipped, bullet-headed, cotton-picking niggers." And then he let fly a volley of oaths, calling upon heaven to inflict upon him all kinds of terrible evils if it were not so.

When Eliza heard the slave-dealer's determination not to part with Emily, she became absolutely wild with excitement and grief, exclaiming, "I will not go without her. They shall not take her from me." And then she pierced the air with her shrieks and protestations, the loud angry voice of Freeman commanding her to be silent commingling with the frantic and despairing appeals of the wretched woman.

While this scene was in progress, Solomon and Henry had been to the yard for their blankets, and now made their appearance at the front door ready to leave with their new master. He stood near them with an expression of the deepest commiseration upon his benevolent countenance, and evidently disposed to regret having bought Eliza—at whom he gazed pityingly—at the expense of so much sorrow. They waited for some time, when finally, Freeman out of all patience tore Emily from the arms of her mother by main force, the two clinging to each other with all their might.

"Don't leave me, dear mamma—don't leave me," screamed the child as the mother was pushed harshly forward. "Don't leave me—come back, mamma," she still cried, stretching forth her little arms, imploringly. But she cried in vain. Out of the door and into the street, the newly bought slaves were quickly hurried, Eliza being forced onward by some of Freeman's gang, at his command. Far away they could hear the child calling to her mother —"Come back—don't leave me—Oh, do come back, my dear mamma," until the infant voice died away in the distance, and the mother's ears were closed against those sweet tones for ever.

Poor Eliza never saw either of her children again. But day or night these dearly loved ones were never absent from her memory and her thoughts. In the cotton field, in the cabin, always and everywhere she was talking about her children—her "precious Randall—her sweet Emily." And often she talked to them, as if they were actually present, and could hear the endearing words she addressed to them. Only when absorbed in that kind of illusion, or asleep, did she ever have a moment's comfort after her Emily was torn from her arms.

"She was no common slave," said Solomon. "To a large share of natural intelligence which she possessed, was added a large degree of general knowledge and information, which she had acquired by reading and instruction, and by intercourse with the world. She had enjoyed opportunities of improvement such as were seldom afforded to any of her oppressed class. She had been lifted up, as it were, into the atmosphere of a higher life. Freedom —freedom for herself and for her offspring had been before her vision for years. It had been the cloud going before her by day, and her pillar of fire by night. In her pilgrimage through the wilderness of bondage, with eyes fixed upon that inspiring beacon, she had been lifted up to the summit of Pisgah, and cast eager, longing eyes upon the "land of promise." But in an unexpected hour she was utterly overwhelmed with disappointment and sorrow. The glorious, fondly-cherished vision of liberty faded from her sight; and, led away into hopeless, interminable bondage, and robbed for ever of her children, she gave herself up to the anguish of heart-breaking despair.

CHAPTER VII.

The Pine Woods.

ON leaving the slave-pen in New Orleans, Solomon and Harry followed their new master through the streets; while Eliza, crying and turning back frequently, was forced along by Freeman and his people until they reached the levee, and soon found themselves on board the steamboat *Rodolph*, then lying alongside the levee with her steam up, waiting for her passengers. In the course of half-an-hour she was loosed from her moorings and moving briskly up the Mississippi; Solomon and the rest of the party being bound for some point on Red River. There was a large number of slaves on board besides themselves, all just purchased in the New Orleans slave-market. Amongst the rest Solomon noticed a man who was called Mr. Kelsow, who was said to be a well-known extensive planter, who had in charge a gang of women.

Solomon soon learnt that the name of his new master was William Ford. He resided then in the " Great Pine Woods," in the parish of Avoyelles, on the right bank of Red River, in the heart of Louisiana. He became ultimately a Baptist Preacher; and throughout the whole parish of Avoyelles, and especially along both shores of Bayou Bœuf where he was more intimately known, he was accounted by his fellow-citizens an upright man and a worthy Minister of God.

To minds well instructed in the Holy Scriptures and the duty there inculcated upon all with respect to their fellow-men; and especially to those who have been brought up in Great Britain or in the Northern States of America, where human rights are more truly appreciated than in the Slave States, the idea of a Christian man and a Christian Minister holding his brother man in forced servitude, and buying and selling human flesh, will appear to be utterly incompatible with all that is just and right before God. But there is no doubt that many well-meaning persons, educated in association with the slavery institution, and blinded and misled by the sophistries of time-serving and unfaithful religious instructors, were fully persuaded that it was all right, and that the negroes were really better off in their servitude, when not cruelly treated, than they would be if they were free. Thank God! this illusion has been dispelled by the noble action of President Lincoln in emancipating the slaves, and the eyes of the nation are now opened to the mistake and the evil of slavery. Solomon found in William Ford a different kind of man from Burch and Freeman; and thus he apologized for so good a man being mixed up with a system so fraught with wrong and misery.

" I was some time his slave, and had an opportunity of learning well his character and disposition; and it is but simple justice to him when I say, that in my opinion, there never was a more kind, noble, candid Christian man than William Ford. The influences and associations that had always surrounded him blinded him to the inherent wrong involved in the system of slavery. He never doubted the moral right of one man holding property in another. Looking through the same medium as his fathers before him, he saw things in the same light. Brought up under other circumstances and other influences, his views and feelings on the subject would doubtless have been different. Nevertheless, he was a model master, walking uprightly according to the light of his understanding; and fortunate was the slave who came into his possession. If all slave-holders were such as he, slavery would be deprived of half its bitterness."

They were two days and nights on board the steamer *Rodolph*, and nothing occurred to vary the monotony of a voyage up the Mississippi, except the incurable grief of Eliza. She was indeed like Rachel weeping for her children and refusing to be comforted. Solomon was now known by the name of Platt given to him by Burch: and this name clung to him through all his life of slavery. Eliza was sold by the name of " Dradey." This was the designation given her in the conveyance to Ford, and was invented for her either by Burch or Freeman. Thus poor wretches, whose hapless lot it was to fall into the power of slave-dealers, were literally robbed of all human rights even to their names.

On the passage Solomon was constantly reflecting

on his situation, and pondering in his mind the best course to pursue in order to effect his ultimate escape. Sometimes as the amiable character and disposition of Ford became more obvious and he was impressed with the uniform kindness of the man, he was then, and often afterwards, on the point of disclosing fully to him all the facts of his history. He afterwards thought that had he done so his deliverance might have been effected many years earlier than it was, through that man's sense of justice. The prudence of this course was often considered; but through fear of some miscarriage it was never adopted until, eventually, his transfer to other service, and Ford's pecuniary embarrassments, rendered it evidently unsafe. Afterwards, under other masters very unlike William Ford, he knew well enough that the slightest suspicion of his real character would be sufficient to consign him at once to the remoter depths of slavery. He was too costly and useful a chattel to be lost, and was well aware that he would be taken farther on into some unknown region—over the Texan border perhaps—and sold; that he would be disposed of as the thief disposes of a stolen horse if ever his right to freedom should be whispered. So he resolved to lock the secret closely in his own breast—never to utter one word or syllable as to who or what he was— trusting in Providence and his own unslumbering vigilance to obtain deliverance at last.

They left the steam-boat at a place called Alex- andria, several hundred miles from New Orleans. It s a small town, situated on the southern shore near the mouth of the Red River.   Remaining there all night, they entered the morning train of cars, and were conveyed to Bayou Lamourie, a small town or village some eighteen miles from Alexandria.   This was the termination of the railroad; and it was announced to them that they would have to perform the remainder of the journey to Ford's plantation, some twelve miles further on the Texan road, on foot, there being no public conveyances proceeding further in that direction.   Ford's plantation was in the "Great Pine Woods;" and on foot they set forward to reach this termination of their journey.   Ford walked with them.   It was an exceedingly hot day, and they felt the heat very much, being yet scarcely recovered from their illness at New Orleans.   Harry, Solomon, and Eliza all felt feeble, and the soles of their feet were yet very tender from the effects of the small-pox.   They proceeded slowly, Ford telling them to take their time and to sit down and rest whenever they felt tired—a privilege that was taken, advantage of quite frequently.   After leaving Lamourie and crossing two plantations, one belonging to a Mr. Carnell, the other to a Mr. Flint, they reached the Pine Woods—a wilderness that stretches to the Sabine River.

The whole country about the Red River is low and marshy.   The Pine Woods, as they are called, are on gentle rising ground, with frequent small intervals of marsh running through them.   This upland is covered with numerous trees of valuable timber—the white oak, the chincopin resembling the chestnut, but principally the yellow-pine. The latter are of great size running up sixty or seventy feet and perfectly straight. The woods were full of cattle, very shy and wild, dashing away in herds with a loud sniff as the travellers approached. Some of these were marked or branded; the rest appeared to be in a wild and untamed state. Solomon, with a farmer's eye, observed that they were much smaller than northern breeds. But the peculiarity which most arrested his attention was their horns; these stood out from the sides of their heads perfectly straight, like two iron spikes.

About noon they arrived at a cleared piece of ground of about three or four acres. There they rested to obtain refreshment. In the clearing was erected a small, unpainted wooden house. Near by was a corn crib, or barn, and a log kitchen standing about ten feet from the house. This was the summer residence of a Mr. Martin. Rich planters having large establishments on Bayou Bœuf were accustomed to spend the warm season in these woods. Here they found beautifully clear water, and cool, delightful shades. In fact, these retreats were to the planters of that section of the country what Newport and Saratoga were to the wealthier inhabitants of Northern Cities.

The slaves were sent round to the kitchen and supplied with sweet potatoes, corn-bread, and bacon; while Mr. Ford took his dinner with the master of the house. There were several of Mr. Martin's slaves about the premises. Martin came out with

Ford after dinner to take a look at "the stock," asking Ford the price he gave for each, if they were green or experienced hands, and so on; also making many inquiries in relation to the slave-market generally.

After a long rest, by which they were greatly refreshed, the slaves and their owner set forth again, following what was called the Texas road. They travelled very slowly, and for five or six miles passed through woods continuously which afforded them a delightful shade, without observing a single habitation. At length, just before sunset, they entered another opening or clearing which might contain twelve or fifteen acres. In this clearing stood a house much larger than that of Mr. Martin which they had lately left. It was two stories high, with a piazza in front. In the rear of it there was a spacious log kitchen, poultry house, corn cribs, and several negro cabins. Near the house was a pleasant peach-orchard and gardens of orange and pomegranate trees. The space was entirely surrounded by woods, and covered with a rich rank verdure. It was a quiet, lonely, pleasant place—literally a green spot in the wilderness—an oasis in a desert. This was the abode of Solomon's master, William Ford, and the whole party rejoiced that they had reached the end of their journey.

As they approached, a quadroon girl they saw standing on the piazza—whose name they ascertained was Rose—stared at them for a moment; then recognizing her master, she ran to the door to call her mistress. That lady soon came running out, and hastened to meet her husband. She greeted him heartily; then laughingly demanded if he had "bought all those niggers?" Ford replied that he had, and then turning round to them with a pleasant smile, directed them to go round to Sally's cabin and rest themselves. In obedience to this order they went to the back of the house. Turning the corner, they discovered Sally washing—her two children near her rolling on the grass. The little ones jumped up and toddled towards the strangers, looked at them for a moment like a brace of rabbits, then ran back to their mother, as if they were afraid of the new comers.

Sally conducted them into the cabin, telling them to lay down their bundles and be seated, for she was sure they must be tired. Just then, John, the cook, a boy about sixteen years of age, and black as any crow, came dashing into the cabin. He stared in the faces of the strangers for a minute or two, then without saying so much as "how-d'ye-do," he rushed back into the kitchen laughing loudly with all his might, as if their coming was a grand joke indeed.

After supper darkness soon came on, and Solomon and Harry, much wearied with their walk, wrapped their blankets around them and stretched themselves at length on the cabin floor. Solomon's thoughts wandered to his wife and children. The consciousness of his real situation and the hopelessness of any attempt to escape through the wide forests of Avoyelles, and all the fearful entanglements which

L

surrounded him in that slave land pressed heavily
upon his heart, and he called on the Lord to open
his way, that he might once more be restored to his
loved treasures at Saratoga.

Solomon was awakened early in the morning by
the voice of his master, Ford, calling Rose. She
soon made her appearance, and hastened into the
house to dress the children. Sally went into the
field to milk the cows, while John was busy in the
kitchen looking after the breakfast. Meanwhile
Solomon and Harry were strolling about the yard,
looking at their new quarters, and making themselves familiar with the place which was to be their
home. Just after breakfast, a coloured man driving
three yoke of oxen, attached to a waggon-load of
lumber, came into the clearing from one of the roads
through the forest. He was a slave belonging to
Ford, named Walton, and the husband of Rose.
Rose, Solomon discovered when they became better
acquainted, was a native of Washington, and had
been brought from thence five years before. She
had never seen Eliza there, but had heard of Berry,
and she and Eliza knew the same streets, and were
acquainted with the same people, either personally
or by reputation. These two became fast friends
immediately, and talked a good deal of old times and
of friends they had left behind. This served in
some small degree to modify and alleviate the bitter
sorrow of the bereaved Eliza.

Ford was, at the time he purchased Solomon, a
wealthy man. Besides his farm in the pine woods,

he owned a large lumber establishment on Indian Creek, four miles distant; and also in his wife's right, he was the possessor of a large plantation and many slaves on Bayou Bœuf.

Walton had come with his load of timber from the mills on Indian Creek. Ford directed Solomon and Harry to return with him, saying that he would follow them as soon as possible. Before leaving, Mrs. Ford called Solomon into the store room, and handed to him a tin bucket of molasses for Harry and himself. Eliza was still wringing her hands and deploring the loss of her children. Ford tried as much as possible to console her—told her she need not work very hard, and that she might remain with Rose, and assist Madam in the house affairs.

Riding with Walton in his waggon, Solomon and Harry became well acquainted with him before they arrived at Indian Creek. He was born a slave of Ford's, and had never known any other master. He spoke kindly and affectionately of Ford, as a child would speak of his own father. In answer to his inquiries whence he came, Solomon told him that he had been sent on from Washington. Of that city he had heard much from his wife, Rose; and all the way he sorely tried the patience of Solomon by asking him a multitude of absurd and foolish questions.

On reaching the mills at Indian Creek, Solomon became acquainted with two more of Ford's slaves, whom he met there. Their names were Sam and Antony. Sam also was from Washington, having been brought out in the same gang with Rose. He had worked on a farm near Georgetown. Antony was a blacksmith from Kentucky, who had been in Ford's service about ten years. Sam knew Burch; and when informed that he was the trader who had sent Solomon on from Washington, they both agreed fully upon the subject of his superlative rascality. It was Burch who had sent Sam on to the South.

On Ford's arrival at the mill that day, he set Solomon and Harry to the occupation of piling lumber and chopping logs, in which they continued the remainder of the summer.

The slaves usually spent the Sabbath at the clearing, where Ford's dwelling was situated. On these days the master would gather all his slaves about him, and read and expound the Scriptures. He sought to awaken in the minds and hearts of the ignorant creatures that were under his care feelings of kindness and sympathy towards each other, and encourage them to fear and to trust in God. And he often set before them the rewards promised to those who lead an upright and merciful life, putting their trust in the Lord Jesus Christ as the Saviour of sinners. Seated in the doorway of his house, surrounded by his man-servants and maid-servants who looked earnestly into the good man's face, he spoke of the loving-kindness of the Creator, the redemption which is in Christ Jesus, and the terrors or glories of the life to come. Often did prayer ascend from his lips to heaven—the only sound on the Sabbath that broke the silence of the place.

In the course of the summer, Solomon stated, one of his fellow slaves, Sam, who had hitherto been a man of careless life and habits, was brought under powerful religious impressions; and he became an earnest seeker after the pardon of sin and a change of heart. His mistress gave him a Bible, which he carried with him to his work. Whatever leisure time was allowed him he spent in perusing the holy book, though it was only with great difficulty that he could spell out any part of it so as rightly to apprehend its meaning. Solomon often helped him in his efforts to learn, and frequently read to him such portions of the Bible as he desired to hear; and his fervent expressions of gratitude for the assistance thus rendered to him showed how much he was in earnest to be a true Christian. He found peace with God through believing in the Lord Jesus Christ, and became very happy. His efforts to learn to read the Bible for himself were crowned with success, and he became a good man. Sam's piety was frequently observed, approvingly or otherwise, by white men who visited the mill; and the remark made by some was, that " a man who, like Ford, allows his niggers to have Bibles, is not fit to own a nigger."

Mr. Ford lost nothing by his kindness to his slaves. And so it was with others. Those masters who treated their slaves as human beings, and dealt with them considerately and with kindness, were repaid by a greater amount of cheerful, profitable labour. It became a source of pleasure to Solomon to surprise his kind master with a greater day's work than

was required. The desire to please Ford and win
his approval suggested to Solomon an idea that
resulted much to Ford's advantage. Under a
master of different stamp he would have let the
knowledge and experience he had acquired in the
past remain unknown, and have gone on with his
work after the manner of other slaves, doing only
that which was compulsory. Solomon had wrought
as a lumber-man on the canal and Lake Champlain,
and he soon perceived that his experience might be
turned to his master's benefit. The lumber that was
being manufactured at Ford's mills was contracted
for, to be delivered at Lamourie. Hitherto it had
been transported at great expense by land.

Indian Creek, upon which the mills were situated,
was a narrow, deep stream, running into Bayou
Bœuf. In some places it was not more than twelve
feet wide, and the channel had become choked and
much obstructed with trunks of trees and other
things floating down the stream. Bayou Bœuf was
connected with Bayou Lamourie ; and Solomon
ascertained that if the obstructions in the Creek were
removed, there would be a clear course for rafts ;
and the distance by water was only a few miles
greater than by land. Solomon saw at once that if
the Creek could be opened, the expense of trans-
porting the lumber would be greatly diminished.

Solomon suggested his scheme to the foreman and
superintendent of the mills. He was a little white
man, who had served as a soldier in Florida, and
he had strolled into that interior region, and obtained

employment with Ford. Either because he was indisposed to receive suggestions from a slave, or that he was indifferent to the interests of his employer, he scouted the idea altogether. His name was Adam Taylden. But Solomon turned from him, and laid his plans before Mr. Ford, who regarded them more favourably. As soon as he understood the matter clearly, he gave permission for Solomon to try the proposed experiment.

Solomon found less difficulty than he anticipated in clearing away the obstructions in the Creek. This being effected, he made up a narrow raft, consisting of twelve cribs. At this business he was skilful; for he had not forgotten his experience years before on the Champlain Canal. He laboured hard, being exceedingly anxious to succeed, not only from a desire to please his master, but also to show Adam Taylden that his scheme was not such a visionary affair as that worthy had pronounced it to be. One hand could manage three cribs; and Solomon took charge of the first, as well as the general oversight of the whole, and commenced " poling " down the Creek. In due time the raft entered the Bayou, and finally arrived at its destination in a shorter period of time than even Solomon himself had ventured to anticipate.

The arrival of the raft at Lamourie created quite a sensation; while Mr. Ford was profuse in his praises and commendations. On all sides " Ford's Platt " was pronounced to be " the smartest nigger in the pine woods "—in fact, he was regarded as the

Fulton of Indian Creek. Solomon was not insensible
to the praise bestowed upon him; but he especially
enjoyed his triumph over Taylden, whose half-
malicious ridicule had stung him sorely, and greatly
wounded his self-esteem. From that time the entire
control of bringing the lumber to Lamourie was
committed to his hands until the contract was
fulfilled.

Indian Creek flowed through a magnificent forest,
and there were at that time a tribe of Indians
dwelling on its shores, a remnant of the Chickasaws
or Chicopees. With these Solomon soon became
well acquainted. They lived in simple huts ten or
twelve feet square, constructed of pine poles and
covered with bark. The Indians subsisted chiefly
on what they took in hunting—the flesh of the deer,
coon, and opossum, all of which abounded in those
woods. Sometimes they would exchange their
venison with the planters on the Bayou for corn or
whiskey. Their dress was a pair of buckskin
breeches and a calico shirt—the latter of some
fantastic pattern and bright colours, buttoned from
belt to chin. The dress of the squaws was very
similar to that of the men. They wore brass rings
on their wrists, and many of them also in their noses
and their ears. They were fond of dogs and horses,
owning many of the latter, of a small tough breed,
and were the most skilful riders Solomon ever knew.
Their bridles, girths, and saddles, were all made of
the raw skins of animals, and their stirrups of a
certain description of very tough wood. Mounted

astride their ponies, men or women, they would dash out into the woods at the utmost speed of the animals, following narrow, winding paths, and dodging trees in a manner that would eclipse the most astonishing feats of more civilized equestrians. Circling away in various directions, the forest echoing and re-echoing their loud whoops, they would presently return at the same dashing headlong speed with which they started. Their principal village was on Indian Creek, known as Indian Castle, but their range extended to the Sabine river. Occasionally a tribe from Texas would come over on a visit; and then high carnival was held in "the Great Pine Woods." The chief of the tribe was called Cascalla; the second in rank was John Baltese, his son-in-law. With both of these, and others of the tribe, Solomon formed an intimate acquaintance during his frequent voyages down the Creek with rafts; and Sam and he would often visit them when the day's work was done. The people were very obedient to their Chief. The word of Cascalla was their law. They were a rude but harmless people, and enjoyed their own wild mode of life. They had little liking to the open cleared country on the shores of the Bayou, and preferred to hide themselves within the shadows of the forest. They worshipped the Great Spirit, and were much addicted to whiskey, when they could obtain it.

On one occasion Solomon was present at a dance, when a roving band of Indians from Texas had encamped in their villages. The entire carcase of a deer was roasting at a large fire, which cast its ruddy light long distances among the trees under which they were assembled. When the whole party had formed themselves into a circle, men and squaws alternately, a kind of Indian fiddle set off with a tune altogether indescribable. It was a monotonous, melancholy, wavy sound, with the slightest possible variation. At the first note, if, indeed, there was more than one note in the whole tune, they began to move, trotting after each other in a circle, and giving utterance to a gutteral, sing-song noise, quite as indescribable as the music of the fiddle. At the end of the third circuit they would stop suddenly, whoop until the forest rang again, then break from the ring, man and squaw forming couples, each jumping backwards as far as possible from the other, then forwards. After repeating this feat two or three times, they would again all form the circle and go trotting round again as before. The best dancer was considered to be the one who could whoop the loudest, jump the farthest, and give utterance to the most excruciating noise. At intervals one or more would leave the dancing circle, go to the fire and cut a slice of venison from the roasting carcase, with which they regaled themselves.

In a hole, shaped like a mortar, in the trunk of a fallen tree, they pounded corn with a wooden pestle, and made cakes of the meal. Alternately they danced and fed. Thus were the visitors from Texas entertained by the dusky sons and daughters of the Chicopees—such the description of an Indian ball, as Solomon witnessed it in the pine-woods of Avoyelles!

In the autumn Solomon was taken away from the mills, and employed about his master's premises at the opening. There again he had an opportunity of obliging the kind family he served, and showing that he appreciated the kindly consideration with which he was treated. One day Mrs. Ford was representing to her husband the propriety of getting a loom, in order that Sally might commence weaving cloth for the winter clothing of the slaves. This threw Mr. Ford into a difficulty, as he could not imagine where a loom was to be found that he could purchase or hire. Solomon was standing near, and stepping forward he respectfully suggested that perhaps it would be the easiest way to make one. He was, he said, "a sort of Jack of all trades," and he would attempt the making of a loom, if his master would permit him to do so. The permission was readily conceded, and he was allowed to go to a neighbouring farmer's, to inspect a loom in operation there, before commencing the undertaking. The attempt proved to be a success, and in due time the loom was completed, and pronounced by Sally, who was to have the use of it, "the most parfec' loom I ever did see." She could easily weave her task of fourteen yards, milk the cows, and have leisure for her own concerns each day, which she never could do before. It worked so well, that Solomon was kept to the employment of making looms, which were taken to the plantations on the Bayou.

A change now occured which brought the shadow
of a dark cloud over Solomon's life. A man came to
the opening—so Mr. Ford's clearing was called—to
do some work at the dwelling house. He was a carpenter, and his name was Tibeats. Solomon was
told off to be this man's assistant, because he had
proved himself to be apt and clever with almost all
kinds of tools. For two weeks he was employed in
this man's company, planing and matching boards
for ceilings—a plastered room or ceiling being a rare
thing in that part of the country.

John M. Tibeats, as he wrote his name, was in all
respects the reverse of Ford. He was a small,
crabbed, passionate and spiteful man. He had no
fixed residence, but passed from one plantation to
another, stopping wherever he could find employment. He had no creditable standing in the community, was neither respected nor esteemed by the
whites, and was disliked and despised by the slaves.
He was a coarse, ignorant fellow, who had never been
favoured with the advantages of education, and of a
savage and revengeful disposition, as his brutal conduct to Solomon sufficiently proved. Solomon always
thought it a most unlucky day that brought him into
association with Tibeats. During his residence with
Ford he had seen the brightest side of slavery—if
such an evil system can have really any bright side
at all. Ford's was no heavy hand, crushing poor
suffering creatures to the earth, and making life a
curse to them rather than a blessing, as was the case
with many of the planters around him. He con-

cerned himself about both the temporal and spiritual welfare of his dependents. He addressed to them benign and cheering words, never cursing them, or using harsh, contemptuous language. He always remembered that, though enduring a less favourable lot in life than himself, they were his fellow mortals, and accountable like himself to the Maker and Father of all. Solomon always regarded him with warm affection, and might have borne his gentle servitude all his days with patience. But clouds were gathering on the horizon—forerunners of a pitiless storm of adversity that was soon to break over him. He was doomed, notwithstanding his present comparatively easy and favourable condition, to endure such bitterness of trial as the poor slave only knows, and to enjoy no more the happier life he had led in " the Great Pine Woods."

CHAPTER VIII.

Changed for the Worse.

THE pecuniary embarrassments of planters were often a source of much misery and suffering to their slaves, causing families to be separated, and sometimes throwing them under the power of hard and cruel owners. William Ford unhappily got into difficulties, not, as was often the case, through riotous and extravagant living, but through becoming security for another. He had rendered himself liable to heavy obligations on account of his brother, Franklin Ford, residing on Red River, above Alexandria; and he having failed to meet them himself had cast them upon his brother. As the result of legal proceedings, William Ford had a heavy judgment rendered against him, and this was the more embarrassing as he was owing a considerable amount to Tibeats for services rendered in building the mills at Indian Creek, and also a weaving-house, corn-mill, and other erections on the plantation at Bayou Bœuf, which were still incomplete. It became necessary, in order to meet these demands, to dispose of eighteen of his slaves, in which number Solomon was included. Seventeen of the unfortunate ones—for all felt it to be a misfortune to leave Mr. Ford—including Sam and

Harry, were purchased by a Mr. Peter Compton, a planter also residing on Red River.

It was Solomon's unhappy lot to be sold to Tibeats, in consequence of his skill as a carpenter. When this sale took place, the price agreed upon being more than the whole amount due to Tibeats, Mr. Ford took what is called a chattel mortgage on Solomon for four hundred dollars. Thus, in fact, though placed under the control of Tibeats, Solomon belonged to two men in parts. It was well that it was so, for this mortgage became the means of saving his life from being sacrificed to the brutal violence of his new master.

Solomon bade farewell to his friends at Ford's opening with much regret, and departed with Tibeats to the plantation belonging to Ford on Bayou Bœuf, distant about twenty-seven miles from the Pine Woods; there to assist his new master in completing his contract. Solomon described Bayou Bœuf thus:—"It is a sluggish, winding stream—one of those half-stagnant waters to be found in those regions commonly, and setting back from Red River. It stretches from a point near to Alexandria, in a south-easterly direction, and following its tortuous course, is more than fifty miles in length. Large cotton and sugar plantations line each shore, extending back to the almost interminable swamps. It is alive with alligators, rendering it exceedingly unsafe for thoughtless slave children to stroll along its banks. Upon a bend in this Bayou, a short distance from Cheneyville, was situated the plantation of Mrs.

Ford—her brother, Peter Tanner, a great and well-known land-holder and slave-master living on the opposite side.

On arriving at the plantation at Bayou Bœuf, Solomon had the pleasure of meeting with Eliza, whom he had not seen for several months. She had not pleased Mrs. Ford, who found that she was more occupied in brooding over her sorrows than in attending to her business about the house. She had therefore been sent down to work in the fields on the plantation. She had grown very feeble, and was much emaciated, still mourning for her children. She asked Solomon if he had forgotten them? Many times she inquired if he remembered how handsome little Emily was—how much Randall loved his mother, and how he grieved to be parted from her? She wondered if they were living still, and where the darlings could then be. Her mother's heart was still filled with her children. She had sunk beneath the weight of excessive grief; and her hollow cheeks and drooping form too plainly indicated that she had well-nigh reached the end of her life's weary journey.

Ford's overseer on this plantation was a Mr. Chapin, a native of Pennsylvania, and a well-disposed man. He had the exclusive charge of the plantation, which he managed with kindness and prudence. In common with all around, Chapin held Tibeats in very light estimation; which fact, in connection with the four hundred dollar mortgage, proved to be an advantage to Solomon.

He was compelled to labour very hard. From earliest dawn until late at night he was not suffered to be a moment at leisure. But notwithstanding this, Tibeats was never satisfied. He was continually cursing and complaining, and loading Solomon with abuse. Never on any occasion did he speak a kind word to him. He was his faithful slave, earning for his master large wages every day; yet he went to his cabin nightly loaded with unmerited abuse, and assailed with stinging epithets. The corn-mill and the kitchen were completed, and they were at work upon the weaving-house, when Solomon was betrayed into the commission of an offence that might have cost him his life—an offence which the laws of that State made punishable by death.

The weaving-house on which Tibeats and his slave were at work stood in the orchard, a few rods from Chapin's residence, or "the Great House," as it was called. One night, having worked until it had become too dark to proceed further, Tibeats directed Solomon to rise very early in the morning, procure a keg of nails from the overseer, and commence putting on the clap-boards. Solomon retired to the cabin extremely weary. The occupants of the cabin besides himself were Eliza, Lawson and his wife Mary, and a man named Bristol. Having cooked his supper of bacon and corn-cake, and conversed a while with Eliza, he laid him down upon the ground floor in his blanket, little dreaming of the suffering that was awaiting him on the morrow.

Before daylight he was on the piazza of "the

M

Great House," awaiting the appearance of the overseer, Chapin. To have aroused him from his slumbers in order to state his errand, might have been regarded as an act of boldness; so he waited. At length the overseer made his appearance. Solomon respectfully stated that Master Tibeats had directed him to come to him for a keg of nails. Going into the store-room, he rolled it out, saying, " If Tibeats would rather have a different size, I will furnish them; but you had better use those until you have further directions." Then mounting his horse, which stood saddled and bridled at the door, Chapin rode away into the field, whither the slaves had preceded him. Solomon took the keg of nails upon his shoulder, carried it to the weaving-house, and commenced nailing on the clap-boards as he had been directed.

As the day began to open Tibeats came out of the house, and directed his steps to the place where Solomon was hard at work. Never very amiable, he seemed to be that morning more morose and disagreeable than usual. He was Solomon's master, owning his flesh and blood, and entitled by law to exercise such tyranny over his chattel as his mean and ferocious nature prompted. But there was no law that could prevent Solomon looking upon him with profound contempt. Solomon had just approached the keg for a further supply of nails when Tibeats reached the weaving-house.

" I thought," he said, " that I told you to commence putting on weather-boards this morning."

" Yes, Master, and I am now about it," the slave replied.

" Where ? " he demanded.

" On the other side," was the answer.

He walked round to the place and examined Solomon's work, muttering to himself in a grumbling and ill-tempered tone.

" Didn't I tell you last night to get a keg of nails from Chapin ? " he broke out again.

" Yes, Master, and so I did ; and the overseer said he would get another size for you if you wanted them, when he comes back from the field."

Tibeats walked to the keg, looked a moment at the contents, and then kicked it with great violence, probably hurting his foot in doing so. Then, advancing towards Solomon in a great passion, with many fierce imprecations on the eyes and liver, and other parts of his person, he exclaimed, " I thought you knowed something."

Solomon answered, " I tried, Master, to do as you told me. I didn't mean anything wrong. Overseer said——" Here he was interrupted with such a volley of curses that he was unable to finish the sentence.

After a few moments' storming and blaspheming, having wrought himself up into an uncontrollable rage, he ran towards the house, and going to the piazza took down one of the overseer's whips. The whip had a short wooden stock braided over with leather, and was loaded at the butt. The lash was three feet long, or thereabouts, made of raw hide.

At first Solomon was somewhat frightened, and

his impulse was to run. There was no one about but Rachel the cook and Chapin's wife, neither of whom was to be seen. All the rest were in the field. He knew that Tibeats was intending to flog him, which no one had attempted since his arrival at Avoyelles. He felt that he had faithfully obeyed the orders which had been given him, and that he had done no wrong; but deserved commendation rather than punishment. His fear changed to a feeling of anger, and he made up his mind that he would not be whipped let the result be what it might.

Winding the lash around his hand, and taking hold of the small end of the stock, intending to strike his victim with the heavy loaded butt, he walked up to Solomon, and with malignant curses ordered him to strip.

"Master Tibeats," said Solomon, looking him boldly in the face, " I will not."

He was about to say something further in explanation and justification of his conduct, when Tibeats, with concentrated vengeance, sprang upon him, seizing him by the throat with one hand, and raising the whip with the other to strike him. Before the blow descended, Solomon had caught him by the collar of his coat, and drawn him closely to him. Reaching down he seized him by the ancle, and pushing him back with the other hand, Tibeats fell prostrate on the ground. Then putting one arm around his leg, and holding it firmly to his breast, so that Tibeats' head and shoulders only touched the ground, he placed his foot on the neck of his prostrate foe. "My blood was up," said Solomon, as he afterwards related this encounter. "It seemed to course through my veins like fire. I forgot that I was a slave. The spirit of freedom—the freedom in which I was born—nerved my arm. I snatched the whip from his hand. He struggled with all his might, and swore that I should not live to see another day, and that he would tear out my heart. But his struggles and his threats were alike in vain. I cannot tell how many times I struck him. Blow after blow, inflicted with a will, fell fast and heavy upon his wriggling form. At length he screamed—cried murder—and the blasphemous tyrant called upon God for mercy. But he who had never shown mercy did not receive it then. The stiff stock of the whip warped around his cringing body until my arm ached."

Until this time Solomon had been too much occupied to look about him. Desisting from his arduous exercise, he saw Mrs. Chapin looking from the window, and Rachel standing in the kitchen door-way. Their attitudes expressed the utmost excitement and alarm. Tibeats' screams had been heard in the field, and Chapin was hastening to the spot as fast as he could ride. Solomon saw this, and after giving a blow or two more he pushed his antagonist away from him with such a well-directed kick, that he went rolling over on the ground.

Rising to his feet and brushing the dirt from his hair, he stood looking at Solomon almost livid with rage.   They stood glaring at each other without uttering a word until Chapin galloped up.

" What is the matter ? " the overseer cried out.

" Master Tibeats wants to whip me," replied Solomon, "for using the nails you gave me."

" What is the matter with the nails ? " he inquired, turning towards Tibeats.

Tibeats answered to the effect that they were too large, paying little attention, however, to Chapin's questions, but keeping his vicious eyes fastened upon Solomon.

"I am overseer here," Chapin said.   I told Platt to take those nails and use them, and if they were not the proper size I would get others when I returned from the field.   It is not his fault.   Besides, I shall furnish such nails as I please.   I hope you will understand *that*, Mr. Tibeats ? "

Tibeats made no reply ; but grinding his teeth maliciously, and shaking his fist at Solomon, swore that he would have satisfaction, and that it was not " half over yet."   Thereupon he walked away, and entered the house, followed by the overseer, who continued talking to him all the while in a suppressed tone, and with earnest gestures.

Solomon remained where he was ; debating in his own mind whether it would be better for him to fly, or abide the result whatever it might be.   Soon after Tibeats came out of the house, and saddling his horse—the only property he possessed, except his unfortunate slave—he departed on the road to Cheneyville.

When he was gone Chapin came out a good deal excited, telling Solomon not to stir—not to attempt to leave the plantation on any account whatever. He then went to the kitchen, and calling Rachel out, conversed with her some time. Going back to Solomon, he again charged him with great earnestness not to run, saying that his master was "a great rascal." He had left, he said, on no good errand, and there might be trouble before night. At all events Solomon must not leave the place.

Left to himself, reason, which had been overpowered with passion, resumed her sway; and Solomon began to see and feel that he had acted most rashly and unwisely in the affair with Tibeats, and that he had laid himself open to extreme punishment by the ebullition of anger to which he had so foolishly given way. Feelings of unutterable anguish seized upon him, and he yielded to sensations of profound regret. He tried to pray—to beseech his Heavenly Father to pardon his sin, and to sustain and succour him in this sore extremity; but emotion choked his utterance, and he could only bow his head upon his hands and weep bitterly.

For at least an hour he remained in that situation, finding relief only in tears, when looking up, he saw Tibeats, accompanied by two other horsemen, approaching the place. They rode into the yard, jumped from their horses, and approached Solomon, each bearing a large whip. One of them he saw also carried a coil of rope.

"Cross your hands," commanded Tibeats with a blasphemous oath.

"You need not bind me, Mr. Tibeats," Solomon replied. "I am ready to go with you anywhere you please."

One of his companions then stepped forward, swearing that if Solomon made the least resistance he would break his head—tear him limb from limb —cut his —— black throat, and many other things of a similar kind. Perceiving that importunity or resistance would be alike in vain, Solomon did as he was directed, crossing his hands, and submitting himself to be disposed of as they might think proper. Tibeats, finding that he could now approach his slave without danger, stepped up and tied his wrists, drawing the rope around them with his utmost strength. He then bound his ancles in the same manner. Meanwhile, the other two had passed a cord within his elbows, running it across his back, and tying it firmly. Solomon was then in such a condition that he found it impossible to move either hand or foot. With the remainder of the rope Tibeats made a noose, and then placed it around the victim's neck.

"Now then, inquired one of the strangers, "where shall we hang the nigger?"

One of them suggested the limb of a peach tree near at hand. The other objected that it was too weak, it would break with the weight; and pointed to another tree which he thought would answer the purpose better. After a little discussion they fixed upon that.

During the whole conversation between these

worthies, and while they were binding him, Solomon uttered not a word. Overseer Chapin was all the time pacing with hasty strides to and fro in the piazza. Rachel was weeping at the kitchen door, and Mrs. Chapin looking out from the window. Hope seemed to die out in Solomon's heart. Surely his time had now come, and he was to die by the hands of those cruel men. He should never behold the light of another day—never see again the faces of his dear children—the sweet anticipation he had ever cherished with such fondness. He should in that hour struggle through the agonies of death—and such a death! None would mourn for him—none avenge his cruel murder. Soon his form would be mouldering in that distant soil, or perhaps be cast to the slimy, loathsome reptiles that filled the stagnant waters of the Bayou! Tears flowed down his cheeks; but they only called forth the ridicule and laughter of his persecutors.

At length, as they were dragging their helpless victim towards the tree which they had selected, Chapin disappeared for a few moments into the house. He then reappeared with a pistol in each hand, and walked towards the group, with an expression of stern determination on his countenance. Addressing himself to Tibeats and his two companions in a firm, decisive tone, he said:—

"I have a few words to say about this business, and you had better listen to them. Whoever moves that slave another foot from where he stands is a dead man. In the first place he does not deserve this treatment, and it is a shame to murder him in this manner.   I never knew a more faithful boy than Platt.   You, Tibeats, are in the fault yourself.   You are pretty much of a scoundrel, and I know it ; and you richly deserve the flogging you have received. In the next place I have been overseer on this plantation seven years, and in the absence of William Ford I am master here.   My duty is to protect his interests, and that duty I shall perform.   You are not responsible.   You are an utterly worthless fellow. Ford holds a mortgage on Platt for four hundred dollars.   If you were to hang Platt my employer would lose his debt.   Until that debt is cancelled you can have no right to take his life, whatever you may have then.   You have no right to murder him any way.   There is a law for the slave as well as the white man, as you would find to your cost if you were to do what you want to do with him.   You are no better than a murderer.   Ford's interests are in my hands, and therefore I am determined that Platt shall come to no harm."

" As for you," addressing the other two, whose names were Cook and Ramsay, overseers from neighbouring plantations, " As for you, I say, begone from this place.   If you have any regard to your own safety you will make tracks from here a good deal faster than you came."

The men did not wait for further parley.   They did not like the imperious tone in which Chapin addressed them, neither did they much admire the weapons he held towards them, one in each hand.

They thought that the discretion which is the better part of valour demanded obedience to the command which they had received; so without a word they hastily mounted their horses and rode away. Tibeats, overawed and cowed by the decisive language of Chapin, trembled with rage, and sneaking away from the spot like the coward that he was, mounted his horse and rode away after his companions.

Solomon remained standing where they had left him, still bound hand and foot with the rope around his neck. For some reason or other Chapin did not remove the rope or cut his bonds, as Solomon hoped he would do. But as soon as the men were out of sight, and Tibeats had disappeared after them, Chapin called Rachel, ordering her to run to the field, and tell Lawson to hurry to the house without delay, and to bring the brown mule with him; an animal much prized for its unusual fleetness. The boy Lawson soon appeared.

"Lawson," said Chapin, "you must go to the Pine Woods as fast as you can. Tell your master, Ford, that he must come here at once—he must not delay a single moment. Tell him that they are trying to murder Platt. Now hurry boy. Be at the Pine Woods by noon, if you kill the mule in doing it."

Chapin stepped into the house, and wrote a pass for the boy. When he came out, Lawson was at the door mounted on the mule. Receiving the pass, he applied his whip right smartly to the beast, dashed out of the yard, and turning up the Bayou in a hard gallop, was soon out of sight.

CHAPTER IX.

Hired Out.

AS the sun approached the meridian that day it became intensely hot. Its fierce rays scorched the ground, so that it almost blistered the foot that stood upon it. Solomon was without coat or hat, standing bare headed, exposed to its burning blaze. Great drops of perspiration rolled down his face, drenching the scanty apparel wherewith he was clothed. Over the fence, only a little way off, the peach trees cast their cool, delicious shadows on the grass. What would he not have given to be enabled to change the heated oven, in which he was compelled to stand for a seat in that delicious shade. But he was yet bound and helpless, the rope dangling from his neck just where Tibeats and his ruthless companions had left it. He could not move an inch, so firmly had he been tied. To have been enabled to lean against the weaving-house would have been a luxury indeed. But it was far beyond his reach, though distant not more than twenty feet. He wanted to lie down, but knew he could not rise again if he did so, and the ground was so parched and hot that he was aware it would only add to the discomfort of his position. If he could only have changed his position, however slightly, it would have been an unspeakable relief. But the hot rays of the summer sun, beating all day on his bare head, did not cause half the suffering that proceeded from his aching limbs. His wrists and arms began to swell, until the ropes that bound them were buried out of sight by the enlargement they produced, causing excruciating pain.

All day Solomon remained in that condition and in the same place. And all day Chapin walked to and fro in the piazza, but did not approach the sufferer. He seemed to be in a state of great uneasiness, looking first at Solomon, and then turning his gaze anxiously up the road as if he was every moment expecting some arrival. He did not go to the field, as was his custom. It seemed evident from his manner, that he supposed Tibeats would return with more and better-armed assistants to renew the quarrel; and it was equally evident from his manner and his clenched fists, that he had made up his mind to defend Solomon at all hazards.

Why he did not relieve him, Solomon could never clearly understand—why he suffered him to remain in that agony the whole weary day. It was not for want of feeling and sympathy Solomon well knew. Perhaps he wished Ford to see him bound, and with the rope about his neck as they had left him, and thus understand the brutal manner in which he had been treated; or perhaps it was that his interference with another man's property might have been a trespass that would subject him to a legal penalty. Why Tibeats was all day absent was another mystery he could not divine. But Lawson on his return told Solomon that as he passed the plantation of John Cheney, he saw Tibeats and the two overseers, and they turned and looked after him as he flew by upon the mule. Perhaps his supposition was that Lawson had been sent to summon other planters in the neighbourhood to Chapin's assistance, and that therefore it would be discreet on his part to keep away.

Meanwhile Solomon, poor fellow! was growing faint with pain and hunger, and suffering from intolerable thirst. Once only in the hottest part of the day Rachel, half fearful that she was acting contrary to the overseer's wishes, ventured out and held a cup of water to the sufferer's lips saying, "Oh, Platt, how I do pity you!" and then stole back to the kitchen as if she had done some deed to be ashamed of.

Just about sunset the heart of the suffering slave leaped with unbounded joy as he saw Ford riding into the yard with his horse all covered with foam, as if he had been riding hard; which was indeed the fact. Chapin met him at the door, and after a few seconds conversation Ford walked directly to Solomon.

"Poor Platt! you are in a bad state," was the only expression he uttered.

"Thank God! Oh thank God, Master Ford!" said the fainting Solomon, "that you are come at last."

Drawing a knife from his pocket he indignantly cut the cords from the wrists, arms, and ancles of the victim, and slipped the noose from his neck. Solomon attempted to walk, but staggered like a drunken man, and then fell partially to the ground.

Ford returned immediately to the house, leaving Solomon alone again. As he reached the piazza Tibeats and the two overseers rode up. A long discussion followed, in which Solomon could distinguish the mild tones of Ford, and the angry voice of Tibeats, but was unable to distinguish anything that was said. Finally, the three worthies took their departure, apparently not very well pleased with the result of their interview with Ford.

As soon as his blood began to resume its natural course in his veins, Solomon staggered to the weaving-house to resume his work; but the hammer fell from his hand. He was incapable of holding it, and seemed to be feeble as an infant. As it grew dark he crawled into the cabin and lay down. He was in great misery, all sore and swollen—the slightest movement causing him excruciating pain. Then the hands came in from the field. Rachel when she went to fetch Lawson in the morning had partially informed them of what had happened. Eliza and Mary boiled a piece of bacon for the sufferer; but his appetite was gone. Then they scorched some corn meal and made coffee, which was all that he could take. Eliza endeavoured to console him, and all manifested a kindly sympathy. It was not long before the cabin was filled with slaves, and they all gathered about Solomon, asking many questions about the difficulty with Tibeats in the morning, and the particulars of all the occurrences of the day. Then Rachel came in, and she in her simple style repeated it over again, dwelling with a good deal of enjoyable emphasis on the kick that sent Tibeats rolling over on the ground. Upon this there was a general titter throughout the crowd, which seemed to say, "Bravo! Well done!" Then she described how Chapin walked out with his pistols, and how the cowards scampered off, and also how Master Ford, as soon as he came, cut the ropes with his knife "just as if he was mad."

By this time Lawson had returned, and he had to gratify their awakened curiosity with an account of his journey to the Pine Woods. He told them how the brown mule carried him "faster than a streak o' lightning"—how he astonished everybody as he flew along "faster than he eber trabel afore"—how Master Ford started right away—how he said Platt was a good nigger, and they shouldn't kill him, concluding with a pretty broad intimation that there was not another human being in the wide world who could have created such a marvellous sensation on the road, or performed such a marvellous John Gilpin-kind-of-feat as he had done that day with the brown mule.

The kind-hearted slaves loaded Solomon with expressions of their sympathy, saying "that Tibeats is a hard, cruel man," and expressing their hope that "Massa Ford" would soon get Solomon back again. In this manner they passed the time, discussing, chatting, talking over again the exciting affair, until suddenly Chapin presented himself at the cabin door calling for Platt.

"Platt," said he, "you will sleep on the floor in the Great House to-night. Bring your blanket with you, and come along."

Solomon obeyed the mandate as promptly as his swollen, stiffened limbs permitted him, took his blanket in his hand, and followed the overseer. Outside Chapin told him that he would not be surprised if Tibeats was back again before the morning —that he intended to kill him—and he, Chapin, did not mean that he should do it, and do it without witnesses. The laws of the State were such that if Tibeats stabbed him to the heart in the presence of a hundred slaves, not one of them could be allowed to give evidence against him. Solomon laid himself down to rest on the floor of the "Great House," and tried to sleep. Near midnight the dog began to bark. Chapin arose, and looked from the window, but could discover nothing. At length the dog became quiet and the overseer retired to his room. As he was passing in he said, "I believe, Platt, that scoundrel is skulking about the premises, somewhere. If the dog barks again, and I am asleep, be sure to awake me."

Solomon promised that he would do so. After the lapse of an hour or more the dog recommenced his noise, running towards the gate and back again, all the while barking furiously. Chapin was soon out of bed without waiting to be called. On this occasion he stepped into the piazza, and remained stand-

ing there on the look out for a considerable length of
time. Nothing, however, was to be seen, and the
dog returned to his kennel. They were not disturbed again that night. Solomon believed that
Tibeats was about the place on that occasion, but
the caution and vigilance of Chapin prevented him
from effecting his murderous purposes. He had the
spirit of an assassin, cowering before a brave man,
but ready to strike an unsuspecting victim in the
back.

At daylight in the morning Solomon arose sore
and weary, having rested but little. After partaking
of breakfast, which Eliza and Mary kindly prepared
for him in the cabin, he proceeded to the weaving-
house and commenced the labours of another day.
It was Chapin's practice, as with most overseers on
the plantations, immediately on arising to bestride
his horse, always saddled and bridled ready for him
—the duty of one particular slave—and ride into the
field to look over the people at their work. This
morning he came to the weaving-house instead of
proceeding to the field, and inquired of Solomon "if
he had seen anything of Tibeats yet?" Replying in
the negative, the overseer remarked—"There is
something not right about the fellow—there's bad
blood in him," and admonished Solomon to keep a
sharp watch against him, or he would do him some
harm when he was least expecting it.

While Chapin was yet speaking, Tibeats rode in,
hitched his horse, and entered the house. Solomon
had little fear of his oppressor while Chapin and

Ford were at hand; unfortunately they could not be always near. It was now that the iron entered into Solomon's soul as it had never done before, and he felt the terribleness of the yoke of slavery. He sighed for liberty. but the bondman's chain was around him, and could not be shaken off. How wistfully he looked to the North, while he thought of the thousands of miles that stretched between him and the free soil from which he had been torn by ruthless violence, and cruelly plundered of all the rights that belonged to him as a free-born citizen of the United States—as much so as the tyrant who was striving to crush him under his feet, and take away his life.

Tibeats in the course of half an hour walked over to the place where Solomon was at work, looked at him with a scowl, and then returned without opening his mouth even to give utterance to a curse. Most of the forenoon he sat on the piazza reading a newspaper and conversing with Ford. After dinner Mr. Ford left for the Pine Woods, and it was with much regret that Solomon beheld his departure from the plantation. Once more during the day Tibeats approached Solomon, gave him some order about the work, and then turned away.

During that week the weaving-house was completed—Tibeats all the time making no allusion to the quarrel—when Solomon received the agreeable information that Tibeats had hired him to Peter Tanner, to work under another carpenter of the name of Myers. This announcement was very gratifying

N 2

to Solomon ; as any place or arrangement was desirable that would relieve him of the hateful presence of his oppressor.

Peter Tanner was the brother of Mrs. Ford. As already intimated, he lived on the opposite shore of the Bayou. He was one of the most extensive planters in the neighbourhood, and owned a large number of slaves. Thither Solomon proceeded joyfully enough, attended by Chapin's good wishes, who was glad to see Solomon separated from Tibeats. Mr. Tanner had heard of Solomon's late difficulties—in fact the flogging of Tibeats was blazoned about far and wide—and this affair, together with his rafting experiment, had rendered Solomon somewhat notorious.

Peter Tanner endeavoured to impress upon Solomon at their first meeting that he was a very severe master ; but Solomon could perceive that there was more of jocularity than earnestness in his address. He had the reputation of being kind and considerate as a master.

" You're the nigger," he said to Solomon, when they first met—" You're the nigger that flogged your master, eh ? You're the nigger that kicks and holds carpenter Tibeats by the leg, and wallops him, are ye ? I'd like to see you hold me by the leg—I should. You're a 'portant character—you're a great nigger—very remarkable nigger, aint ye ? *I'd* lash you—I'd take the tantrums out of ye. Just take hold of my leg if you please. None of your pranks here, my boy, remember *that*. Now go to work, you *kickin'* rascal." Here Peter Tanner concluded, not able to suppress a comical smile, or rather grin, at his own wit and sarcasm.

After listening to this salutation, Solomon was taken charge of by Myers, and laboured under his direction for a month to their mutual satisfaction.

Like his brother-in-law, William Ford, Tanner was in the habit of reading the Bible to his slaves on the Sabbath, but in a very different way. There was a vein of grotesque humour running through his comments on the Scriptures that often made them very amusing. He thought himself a very impressive commentator on the New Testament. The first Sunday after Solomon went to the plantation, the slaves were all called together, and Peter began to read to them the twelfth chapter in Luke. When he came to the forty-seventh verse he looked very deliberately around him, and continued, " And that servant which knew his Lord's *will* "—here he paused, and looking around again with the utmost deliberation, he went on repeating the words he had just read—" which knew his Lord's *will*, and *prepared* not himself "—here was another pause—" prepared not himself, neither did *according* to his Lord's will, shall be beaten with many *stripes*."

" D'ye hear that ? " demanded Peter, most emphatically. " *Stripes*," he repeated, " D'ye hear that ? —*stripes*." Then slowly and deliberately taking off his spectacles, he prepared himself to give utterance to some very profound remarks.

" That nigger that don't take care—that don't obey his Lord—that's his master—d'ye see ?—that 'ere nigger shall be beaten with many stripes. Now, 'many' signifies a *great* many—forty, a hundred, a hundred and fifty lashes. That's Scripter." In this style he continued to elucidate the subject for a considerable time, much to the amusement if not greatly to the edification of his sable audience, who nevertheless listened with praiseworthy attention.

At the conclusion of the exercises, he called up three of his slaves, Warner, Hill, and Major, and cried out to Solomon—"Now, Platt, you held Tibeats by the legs; see if you can hold these rascals in the same way till I get back from meetin'?"

He then ordered them to the stocks—a common instrument of punishment on plantations in the Red River country. The stocks were formed of two planks; the lower one made fast at the ends of two short posts firmly planted in the ground. At regular distances half-circles are cut in the upper edge. The other plank was fastened to one of the posts by a hinge, so that it could be opened or shut down at pleasure. In the lower edge of this upper plank half-circles were also cut corresponding with the others, so that when the stocks were closed a row of holes was formed large enough to admit a man's leg above the ancle, but not large enough to enable him to draw out his foot. The other end of the upper plank opposite to the hinge was fastened by lock and key to the post. The slave was made to sit upon the ground, when the upper plank was lifted up; his legs just above the ancles were placed in the lower half-circles, then the upper plank was let down and fastened, holding the slave secure and fast. Sometimes the neck is enclosed after a similar fashion; and often the slave is thus secured for whipping.

According to Mr. Tanner's account, the three slaves who had incurred his displeasure, Warner, Hill, and Major, were " melon-stealing, Sabbath-breaking niggers; " and not approving of such wickedness he felt it his duty to put them in the stocks. So they were put in the place of punishment, the key of the stocks handed to Solomon, and then Mr. and Mrs. Tanner, and the children with Myers, entered the carriage and drove away to church at Cheneyville. When they were gone the boys begged hard to be let out of the stocks. Solomon pitied them, exposed as they were to the full heat of the sun ; and remembering his own sufferings when thus exposed a few days before, he let them out on their giving the promise that they would return to the stocks at any moment they were required to do so.

They kept their promise, and shortly before Mr. Tanner's return they were in the stocks again. Driving up to them, he looked upon the prisoners, and said with a chuckle—" Aha ! ye havn't been strolling about much to-day. *I'll* teach you what's what. I'll tire ye of eating water-melons on the Lord's day, ye Sabbath-breaking niggers ! " He then directed their release.

Peter Tanner was a deacon of the church, and prided himself upon the strictness of his religious observances.

CHAPTER X.

The Great Pacoudie Swamp.

AT the end of a month, his services being no longer required by Mr. Tanner, Solomon to his great regret was sent back over the bayou to his master, Tibeats, whom he found engaged in the erection of a cotton-press. This was situated at some distance from the Great House, in a rather retired spot. He commenced working once more with Tibeats, being alone with him most of the time. He always remembered the words of Chapin, and his advice to beware of Tibeats, lest in some unsuspecting moment his enemy might do him some great injury. The overseer's precautions were always in his mind, so that he lived in a most uneasy state of apprehension and fear—one eye was on his work, the other on his master.

Solomon resolved that he would carefully avoid all occasion of offence, work as diligently as possible, and bear in silence and without resentment whatever abuse Tibeats might heap upon him, unless he maliciously attempted to do him some bodily injury; hoping thereby to soften in some degree his feelings towards him, until some favourable arrangement of Providence should deliver him out of such bad hands.

The third morning after his return Chapin left the plantation for Cheneyville, to be absent until night. On that morning Tibeats seemed to be in one of those fits of spleen and ill-humour to which he was frequently subject. But he seemed to be on this particular morning more disagreeable and venomous than usual.

It was about nine o'clock when Solomon was busily employed with the jack-plane on one of the sweeps. Tibeats was standing by the work-bench, fitting a handle into a chisel which he had been previously using.

"You are not planing that down enough," said Tibeats, with an oath.

"It is just even with the line, Master," Solomon replied.

"You're a —— liar," said he with a volley of curses.

"Oh well Master," Solomon said mildly, "I will plane it down more if you say so," at the same time proceeding to do what he supposed his master desired. But he seemed bent upon a quarrel, for before one shaving had been removed he let fly a series of curses and imprecations, saying that he had now planed it too deep—he had spoiled the sweep entirely. Solomon listened in silence to the torrents of abuse that were heaped upon him, and stood holding the plane in his hand, not knowing exactly what to do. The anger of the tyrant seemed to be provoked more and more by the silence with which his reproaches were received. Finally, having wrought himself up into an ungovernable fury until he foamed and raged like a maniac, he gave utterance to a bitter frightful oath, and snatching a hatchet from the work-bench he rushed towards Solomon intending to take him off his guard, and swore he would lay his head open, at the same time aiming a malicious blow at his head with the edge of the weapon.

Life or death depended on a moment. The sharp bright blade of the hatchet glistened in the sun, and in another instant it would have been buried in his brain; for the man was intent on murder. Solomon had but a moment to think; but in that one moment he reasoned, " If I stand still my doom is certain, if I fly, ten to one the hatchet flung from his hand with deadly aim will strike me in the back: there is but one course to take, to stand up for my life." Springing towards him, before the murderer could bring down the blow, with one hand Solomon caught his uplifted arm, and with the other seized him by the throat. As they stood thus looking each other in the eyes Solomon could see murder in his look. He felt as if he had a serpent by the neck, watching the slightest relaxation of his grip to coil itself around him and sting him to death. He thought to scream aloud, trusting that some ear might catch the sound. But Chapin was away, the hands were all in the field, and there was no living soul in sight or hearing.

He felt that the life of his foe was in his power, and that by tightening his grasp upon his throat for a little while the hateful tyrant would fall dead at his feet; but he was graciously restrained. With a vigorous and sudden kick, that brought him with a groan upon one knee, Solomon released his hold upon his neck, wrenched the hatchet from his grasp and cast it away far beyond his reach.

Frantic with rage—maddened beyond control— Tibeats seized a white oak stick about five feet long that happened to be lying near. It was as thick as his hand could well grasp. With this he again rushed upon his slave to strike him to the ground. But again Solomon was more than a match for him. He seized him by the waist and bore him to the ground; and being by far the stronger of the two, while in that position he wrenched the stick from his grasp, and cast it far away as he had done with the hatchet.

As soon as Solomon permitted him to regain his feet, Tibeats ran for the broad axe which lay upon the work-bench. Fortunately there was a heavy plank resting upon its broad blade in such a manner that he could not extricate it before Solomon had sprung upon him, perceiving his object and determined to disappoint it. Pressing Tibeats down closely and with all his weight upon the plank so that the axe was held more firmly in its place, he endeavoured but in vain to loosen his grasp upon the handle. In that position they remained some minutes.

Not able to unloose Tibeats' hold upon the axe Solomon once more seized him by the throat, and this time with a vice-like grasp that soon made him relax his hold, he became pliant and unstrung. His face before white with passion was now black

with suffocation.   Those small serpent-like eyes that
seemed to emit such venom, were now full of horror
—two great white orbs starting from their sockets.
The tempter was at hand, prompting Solomon to kill
the human blood-hound on the spot—to retain his
grip on the blasphemous throat until the breath of
life was gone.   But better feelings prevailed again,
and something like a voice within him seemed to say,
" It will be better to fly than to commit murder."
And to be a wanderer among the swamps, a fugitive
and a vagabond on the face of the earth, was preferable to the life he was compelled to lead with that
man, whose vengeance for the humiliation he had
twice put upon him would be satisfied with nothing
less than taking his life.   .

His resolution was soon formed; swinging the
prostrate tyrant from the work-bench to the ground,
Solomon bounded over a fence near by and hurried
across the plantation, passing the slaves at work in
the cotton-field.   At the end of a quarter of a mile
he reached the wood-postern, and it was a very short
time that he took to do it.   He ran like an antelope,
for he was light on foot as he was strong in his arms
Climbing on to a high fence he could see the cotton
press where his recent quarrel with his master had
taken place, the Great House, and all the space between.   It was a lofty position that he occupied, from-
whence the whole plantation lay spread before his
view.   While he was looking he saw Tibeats cross
the field towards the house and enter it.   Then he
came out carrying his saddle, and presently mounted
his horse and galloped away.

While he sat there he silently lifted his heart to God in thankfulness that his life had been preserved, and that he had been restrained from putting his adversary to death. He prayed, "O God! Thou who gavest me life, and implanted in my bosom the love of life—who filled it with emotions such as other men have—do not forsake me—have pity on the poor slave, and let me not perish. Save me for Christ's sake. If thou dost not protect me I am lost."

He had been there nearly an hour when several of the slaves shouted to him and made signs for him to run. Looking up the bayou, he saw Tibeats and two others on horseback riding swiftly, and followed by a troop of dogs. There were as many as eight or ten dogs; and distant as he was Solomon knew them very well, for they belonged to an adjoining plantation. The dogs used on Bayou Bœuf for hunting slaves were a kind of blood-hound, of a far more savage breed than were found in the Northern States. They would attack a negro at their master's bidding, and cling to him with as much tenacity as the bull-dog would cling to the lips and nose of a bull. Frequently their loud bay was heard in the swamps; and then there would be speculation and betting as to the point at which the runaway would be overhauled. It was seldom or ever known that a fugitive slave escaped with his life from Bayou Bœuf, when the dogs were put upon his track. One reason for this was that the slaves were never allowed to learn the art of swimming in that region, so that they were incapable of crossing a very inconsiderable stream

when they ventured upon running away. In their
flight they could go but a little distance in any
direction without coming to a bayou; when the
alternative was presented of drowning or being torn
to pieces by the dogs. But Solomon in his youth
had practised swimming in the clear streams that
flowed through his native district. He was expert
in the exercise, and felt at home in the watery
element.

He stood upon the fence until the dogs had reached
the cotton-press where he had been at work with
Tibeats; and they were there put upon the scent.
In an instant their loud savage yells announced that
they were on his track—leaping down from his
position he ran towards the swamp. Fear gave him
strength, and he exerted it to the utmost. Every few
moments he could hear the yelping of the dogs. They
were gaining upon him, every howl being nearer and
nearer. Each moment he expected to feel their long
teeth sinking into his flesh. There were so many of
them he knew they would tear him in pieces—they
would soon worry him to death. He gasped for
breath—gasped forth a half-uttered choking prayer
to the Almighty to help him—to give him strength
to reach some wide, deep bayou, where he could
throw the ferocious creatures off his track, or sink in
its friendly waters. Presently he reached a thick
palmetto bottom. As he pushed his way through
them they made a loud rustling noise; not loud
enough, hewever, to drown the voices of the dogs
which were evidently coming nearer.

Continuing his course due south, as near as he could judge, the panting fugitive came at length to water just over his shoes. The hounds at that moment he thought could not have been five rods behind him. He could hear them crashing and plunging through the palmettoes, their loud eager yelp making the whole swamp seem clamorous with the sound. Hope revived a little as he reached the water. If it were only a little deeper they might loose the scent, and thus disconcerted afford him the opportunity of evading them. It grew deeper the further he proceeded—now over his ancles—now half way to his knees—now sinking for a moment to his waist, and then coming presently again to more shallow places. The dogs had not gained upon him since he struck the water. Evidently they were confused. Now their savage intonations grew more and more faint and distant, assuring him that they were leaving him. He stopped to listen; but the long howl came booming on the air again, telling him that he was not yet safe. From bog to bog where he had stepped they might still keep upon his track, though impeded for awhile by the water. At length to his great joy, Solomon came to a wide bayou, and plunging in he soon stemmed its sluggish current and reached the other side. There, certainly, the dogs, if they followed him so far, would be con- founded—the current carrying down the stream all traces of that slight, mysterious scent, which enables the quick-smelling hound to follow so truly in the track of the fugitive.

After crossing the bayou the water in the swamp was so deep he could not run. He was now, as he afterwards ascertained, in the "Great Pacoudie Swamp." It was filled with immense trees—the sycamore, the gum, the cotton-wood and cypress, extending some thirty or forty miles to the shore of the Calcasien River. For thirty miles or more it is without inhabitants save wild beasts,—bears, wild-cats, and tigers, with great slimy reptiles crawling through it everywhere. Long before he reached the bayou, in fact from the time he first struck the water until he emerged from the swamp on his return, noxious and dangerous reptiles surrounded him. He saw hundreds of moccasin snakes. Every log and bog—every trunk of a fallen tree, over which in his rapid flight he was compelled to climb, was almost alive with them. They crawled away at his approach ; but sometimes in his haste he almost placed his hand or foot upon one of these poisonous serpents. Their bite is more deadly than that of the rattlesnake. He had lost one shoe, the sole having come, off leaving the upper leather dangling to his ancle.

He saw also many alligators, great and small, lying in the water or on pieces of floating wood. The noise he made usually startled them, when they moved off and plunged into deeper places. Some-times he would come upon a monster before observing it. In such cases, he would start back, run a short way round, and in that manner shun them. Straight-forward, they will run a short distance rapidly, but they do not possess the power of turning quickly.

In a crooked race there is no difficulty in evading them.

About two o'clock in the day, as far as he could judge by the sun, he heard the last of the hounds. Probably they did not cross the bayou, even if they followed him to its brink. Wet and weary, but relieved from the sense of imminent peril, he continued his journey, more cautious and more afraid of the snakes and alligators than he had been at the commencement of his flight. Now, before stepping into a muddy pool, he would strike the water with a stick. If the waters moved he would go round them, if not he would venture through.

At length the sun went down and gradually night's dark mantle shrouded the great swamp, and made it inexpressibly gloomy. Still he staggered on, fearing every instant that he should feel the dreadful sting of the moccasin, or be crushed within the jaws of some disturbed alligator. The dread of these creatures almost equalled the fear of the hounds that were pursuing him a short time before. After a while the moon arose and sent its mild light creeping through the overspreading branches, which were loaded with long pendant moss and many curious creepers. He kept travelling forwards until after midnight, hoping every moment that he would emerge into some less desolate and dangerous region. But the water grew deeper and the walking more difficult than ever, and he felt that it would be impossible to proceed much further; moreover, he knew not into what hands he might fall should he succeed in reaching any human

o

habitation. Unprovided with a pass any white man would be at liberty to arrest him and place him in prison, until such time as his master should " prove property," pay charges, and take him away. He was " an estray," and if so unfortunate as to meet a law-abiding citizen of Louisiana, the stranger would probably deem it his duty to his neighbour to put him in the pound. Really it was difficult for poor Solomon to determine which he had at that time the most reason to fear—dogs, alligators, or men!

After midnight he came to a halt. The place was indescribably dreary. The swamp was resonant with the quacking of innumerable wild ducks; and Solomon's intrusion on their domain seemed to have awakened the feathered tribes by hundreds of thousands, and they poured forth such multitudinous sounds that he was affrighted and appalled. Since the Creation, probably, no human footstep had ever so far penetrated the recesses of that far-stretching swamp.

The moon was now well up, when Solomon after some deliberation with himself resolved to change his course. Hitherto he had endeavoured to travel as nearly south as possible. Now he resolved to proceed in a north-west direction. That he believed would enable him to strike the Pine Woods somewhere in the vicinity of Master Ford's. With him he felt he would be comparatively safe.

His clothes were in tatters, his hands, face and body covered with scratches, received from the sharp knots of fallen trees, and in forcing his way through the brushwood. His bare foot was full of thorns, and he was besmeared with mud and the green slime that had collected on the surface of the dead stagnant waters, in which he had many times been immersed to the neck during that day and night of painful trial. As he pursued his way in the direction he had chosen, the water gradually became less deep and the ground more firm under his feet. At last he reached the Pacoudie—the same wide bayou he had swum across—but at another point. He swam it again, and shortly after thought he heard a cock crowing; but he might be deceived, the sound was so faint. The water receded from his advancing foot-steps entirely;—he had left the bogs behind him. He was once more on dry land that gradually ascended to the plain, and he knew that he was somewhere in " the Great Pine Woods."

Just at daybreak he came to an opening, or clearing —a sort of small plantation, but one he had never seen before. In the edge of the wood he came upon two men—a slave and his young master engaged in catching wild hogs. The white man Solomon knew would demand his pass; and not being able to give one he expected that he would take him into custody. He was too weary to run, and too desperate to be taken; so he adopted a ruse that proved successful. Assuming a fierce expression he walked directly towards the young man, looking him steadily in the face. As Solomon approached he moved backwards with an air of alarm. It was plain that he was frightened, as if he regarded the stranger as some goblin coming out of the swamp, and truly his appearance was startling.

"Where does William Ford live?" demanded Solomon, in no gentle tone.

"He lives seven miles from here," was the reply.

Which is the way to his place?" he again demanded, trying to look very fierce.

"Do you see those pine trees yonder?" he asked, pointing to two about a mile distant that rose far above their fellows, like a couple of tall sentinels overlooking the broad expanse of the forest.

"Yes, I see them," was the answer.

"At the foot of those pine trees," he continued, must be the Texas road. Turn to the left and it will lead you to William Ford's.

Without any further parley, Solomon hastened on his way in the direction that had been indicated, happy, as no doubt the other was, to part company and place a distance between them. Striking the Texas road, he turned to the left hand as he had been directed, and soon passed a great fire where a pile of logs was burning. He would have stopped to dry his clothes, but was fearful that some white man might observe him, so continuing his travels, about eight o'clock he reached the house of his old master, Ford.

The slaves were all absent from their quarters at their work. Stepping on to the piazza, he knocked at the door, which was opened by Mrs. Ford. Solomon's appearance was so changed—he was in such a forlorn, dirty, woe-begone condition, that the good lady failed to recognize him. Inquiring if Master Ford was at home, that good man made his appearance before the question could be answered. Solomon told him of his flight and all the particulars connected with it. He listened attentively, spoke to the fugitive kindly and sympathizingly, and taking him to the kitchen called John to prepare breakfast for Solomon, who had tasted nothing since daylight the preceding day.

When John had set a substantial meal on the table, Mrs. Ford came out with a bowl of milk, and several little dainties such as rarely regale the palate of a slave. He was hungry and weary, but neither food nor rest afforded him half the pleasure with which the suffering man listened to the voices of those truly Christian friends. It was the oil and wine which the Good Samaritan of the Pine Woods poured into the wounded spirit of the poor slave, who came to him stripped and wounded and half dead.

They then left him in the cabin that he might enjoy the rest he so greatly needed. He felt secure there under the protection of William Ford, and was soon oblivious to all the evils and perils that surrounded him in a profound slumber.

CHAPTER XI.

The Big Cane Brake.

SOMETIME in the afternoon, after a long sleep, Solomon awoke very sore and stiff. Sally came in and talked with him, while John cooked him some dinner. Sally was in great trouble, one of her children being so ill that she feared it would not recover. After dinner he walked about the quarters for awhile, visited Sally's sick child and did all he could to comfort the sorrowing mother. Then he strolled into Madame Ford's garden.

Solomon indulged the most grateful feelings towards both the master and the mistress of the house; and wishing in some manner to show his sense of the kindness with which they treated him, he commenced to work in the garden—trimming the vines, and weeding out the grass from amongst the orange and pomegranate trees. Oranges, peaches, plums, and most other fruits flourished abundantly in the rich soil and warm climate of Avoyelles. The apple is rarely to be seen there, flourishing better in a cooler region.

After awhile Mrs. Ford came out and said that it was very praiseworthy in Solomon thus to make

THE BIG CANE BRAKE.

himself useful ; but she thought he was not in a condition to labour, and had better rest himself in the quarters until Master Ford should go down to Bayou Bœuf. That, however, would not be that day, and it might not be the next. Solomon replied that he felt bad to be sure and was stiff and his foot pained him, the stubs and thorns having so torn it ; but he thought that gentle exercise would not hurt him, and he felt it a great pleasure to work for so good a mistress. She returned to the house, and for three days the grateful fugitive laboured in the garden, cleaning the walks, weeding the flower-beds, and clearing away the rank grass from the jessamine vines which the gentle hand of his protectress had trained to clamber along the walls.

It was on the fourth morning when, having been recruited and refreshed by his sojourn with Master Ford, Solomon was directed to make ready to accompany him to the plantation at the Bayou. There was only one saddle-horse at the opening, all the others with the mules having been sent on to the plantation. Solomon said he could walk, and bidding Mrs. Ford and the other inmates of the house " good bye," he quitted the opening, trotting along by the horse's side. He left the opening in " the Great Pine Woods " with much regret and sorrow—not, however, so overwhelming as it would have been had he then known that he was to return to it no more.

Master Ford urged Solomon to take his place on the horse occasionally to rest him. But Solomon declined very respectfully, saying that he was not tired, and it was better that he should walk than the master, as he was more able to do it. He rode slowly in order that Solomon might keep up with him, and spoke many kind and cheering things to him on the way, pointing out to him his obligations to God, and admonishing him to look up and cast his care upon the Lord. The goodness of God was manifest, he declared, in Solomon's wonderful deliverance from the swamp, which he likened to Daniel's deliverance from the den of lions. For a long time did the benignant man seek to encourage the heart of the oppressed slave, and endeavour to animate his confidence in God as the friend of the suffering and the oppressed.

They had approached to within five miles of the plantation, when they discovered a horseman at a distance riding towards them pretty briskly. As he came near, Solomon's heart began to beat somewhat quicker, when he saw that it was Tibeats. He looked at Solomon for a moment, but did not address him, and turning his horse's head rode along side by side with Ford. Solomon trotted silently along at their horses' heels and paid great attention to their conversation. Ford informed Tibeats of Solomon's arrival at the Pine Woods three days before, of the sad plight he was in and the difficulties and dangers he had encountered.

" Well," exclaimed Tibeats, omitting his usual oaths in the presence of Ford, " I never saw such running in my life, I'll bet him against a hundred dollars he'll beat any nigger in Louisiana. I offered John David Cheney twenty-five dollars to catch him dead or alive; but he outran his dogs in a fair race. Them Cheney dogs ain't much after all. Dan Woodie's hounds would have had him down before he touched the palmettoes. Somehow the dogs got off the track, and we had to give up the hunt. We rode the horses as far as we could, and then kept on foot till the water was three feet deep. The boys said he was drowned, sure. I allow I wanted to get a shot at him mightily. Ever since I have been riding up and down the Bayou, but hadn't much hope of catching him—thought he was dead—*sartin.* Oh, he's a cuss to run, that nigger is."

In this way Tibeats ran on describing his search in the swamp, and the wonderful speed with which the slave fled before the hounds. When he had finished, Master Ford responded, saying " Platt has always been a willing and faithful boy, and according to what he has told me he has been most inhumanly treated; and you, Tibeats, are in fault. To use hatchets and broad axes against a slave is shameful, and must not be allowed. This is no way of dealing with them. It will have a most pernicious influence and set the people all running away; and we shall have the swamps filled with runaway slaves to the great injury and danger of the community. A little kindness would be far more effectual in re-straining them and keeping them in order, as I have proved, than the use of such deadly weapons. Every planter on the Bayou should frown upon such inhumanity. It will be the interest of all to do so. It is quite evident, Mr. Tibeats, that you and Platt cannot live together. You dislike him and would not hesitate to kill him; and knowing that he will run from you again through fear of his life, Mr. Tibeats you must sell him, or hire him out at least. Unless you do so, I shall at once take measures to get him out of your possession."

On reaching the plantation the two entered the Great House and Solomon repaired to Eliza's cabin. The slaves on returning from the field were greatly astonished to find him there; for they had all concluded that he had been drowned in the swamp. That night again they gathered about the cabin to listen to Solomon's adventures. They all took it for granted that he would be terribly whipped; the well-known punishment for running away being five hundred lashes.

"Poor fellow!" said Eliza, taking him by the hand, "it would have been better for you if you had been drowned in the bayou. You have a cruel master, and I am afraid he will kill you yet."

Lawson suggested that it might be that Overseer Chapin would be the person appointed to give "the whipping," in which case it would be severe; but Mary, Rachel, and several others hoped it might be Master Ford, and then it would scarcely be any punishment at all. They all pitied and tried to console Solomon in view of the suffering that awaited him, except John the cook. There were no bounds to his laughter; and the cause of his noisy mirth was the idea of Solomon outstripping the hounds. The thing presented itself to John's view in a comical light. "I know'd dey wouldn't catch him, when he run cross de plantation. O dear, didn't Platt pick his feet right up tho', hey. When dem dogs got whar he was, he wasn't dar—law, law, law." And then John gave way without restraint to one of his boisterous fits.

Early the next morning Tibeats left the plantation. In the course of the forenoon while Solomon was sauntering about the yard, a tall, good-looking man approached him and enquired if he was Tibeats' boy? He took off his hat and answered that he was.

"How would you like to work for me?" enquired the stranger.

"Oh, I would like to very much," said Solomon, inspired with the hope of getting away from Tibeats.

"You worked under Myers at Peter Tanner's didn't you?"

"Yes Massa, and Myers was pleased with me and my work."

"Well boy," said the stranger, "I have hired you of your master to work for me in the Big Cane Brake. It is thirty-eight miles from here down on Red River."

This man was a Mr. Eldret, who lived below Ford's on the same side of the bayou. Solomon at once accompanied him to his plantation, and the next morning started with Sam and a waggon-load of provisions drawn by four mules for the Big Cane Brake; Eldret and Myers having preceded them on

horseback. Sam was a native of Charleston, where
he had left a mother and brothers and sisters. He
" allowed " that Tibeats was a mean, bad fellow,
and hoped, as also Solomon did, most earnestly
that Eldret would buy him from Tibeats.

They proceeded down the south shore of the
bayou, and just at sunset, turning from the highway,
they struck into the Big Cane Brake. They followed
an unbeaten track, just wide enough to admit the
waggon, through a vast extent of wild canes which
were as thick as they could stand. The tracks of
wild beasts ran through them in various directions—
the bear and the American tiger abounding in the
brakes ; and wherever there was a pond of stagnant
water it was full of alligators.

They kept on their lonely course for several miles,
when they entered a clearing known as " Sutton's
Field." Sam related to Solomon the legend connected with this lonely spot. Many years before, a
man of the name of Sutton, a fugitive from justice,
penetrated the wilderness of cane, and settled down
at this spot. Here he lived alone—recluse and
hermit of the swamp—with his own hand planting
and harvesting what he required to supply his wants.
But one day a band of strolling Indians tracked him
to his solitude and massacred him, destroying his
hut by fire. For miles around, in the slaves' quarters
and on the piazzas of great houses where white
children listened to nursery tales, the story was often
told of the tragedy at the Big Cane Brake, and hints
were circulated about its being a haunted place.

For nearly half a century human voices had seldom or ever broken the silence of the clearing. Solomon saw that rank and noxious weeds had overspread the once cultivated field, and serpents sunned themselves where the cabin had stood. It was a dreary picture of desolation.

Two miles further on they reached the termination of their journey. They had arrived at the wild lands of Mr. Eldret, where he contemplated the clearing of an extensive plantation. The two slaves went to work the next morning, and cleared a sufficient space for the erection of two cabins—one for themselves, and one for Eldret and Myers; the one for themselves being made pretty large for the reception of other slaves who were to come after.

They were now in the midst of trees of enormous growth, whose wide-spreading branches almost shut out the light of day, while the space between the trunks was an impervious mass of cane. They cut down oaks, split them into rails, and with these erected their temporary cabins. The roofs were covered with the broad palmetto leaf, an excellent substitute for shingles, although they do not last so long. But they were greatly tormented by gnats and mosquitoes, which swarmed in the brake as Solomon had never seen them before. "A lonelier spot," said Solomon, "or one more disagreeable than the centre of the Big Cane Brake, it would be difficult to conceive; yet to me it was a paradise in comparison with any other place in the company of Master Tibeats. I laboured hard and ofttimes was fatigued and weary, yet I could lie down at night in peace and arise in the morning without fear."

In the course of a week or two four other slaves came down from Eldret's plantation. "They were," Solomon said, "stout able-bodied girls named Charlotte, Fanny, Lucretia, and Nelly. Axes were put into their hands, and they went out with the men to cut trees. They were excellent choppers, the largest oak or sycamore standing but a brief season before their heavy and well-directed blows; and at piling logs they were quite equal to men. Lumber-women were as common as lumber-men in the forests of the South. On the Bayou Bœuf, women perform their share of all the labour of the plantations. Some planters owning large cotton and sugar plantations, would have none other than the labour of slave women.

On their first arrival at the brake, Eldret promised Solomon that if he worked well he might go up to visit his friends at Ford's in four weeks. On Saturday night of the fifth week Solomon reminded him of his promise, when he told him that he had done so well he might go. He was to return so as to commence the labours of the day on Tuesday morning.

While indulging the pleasing anticipation of meeting his old friends again so soon, the hateful form of Tibeats suddenly made its appearance. He inquired how Myers and Platt got along together? and was told "very well," and that Platt was going up to Ford's plantation in the morning on a visit.

"Pooh, pooh," sneered Tibeats, "it isn't worth

while; the nigger will get unsteady. He can't go."
In his malignity he would, if he could, have prevented
Solomon's visit.

But Mr. Eldret insisted that he had worked faithfully—that he, Eldret, had given his promise and
must keep his word, and that under the circumstances
Platt should not be disappointed They entered the
cabin, Tibeats still remonstrating. But Solomon,
thinking it was enough that he had his employer's
leave to go, determined to leave at all hazards. At
daylight he was at his door, with his blanket rolled
up in a bundle and hanging on a stick over his
shoulder, waiting for a pass. Tibeats presently came
out in a very disagreeable mood, and sat down on a
stump near by. After standing there some time,
while Tibeats was busy with his own thoughts,
Solomon started off in the direction in which his
road lay.

" Are you going without a pass ? " Tibeats cried out.

" Yes Master, I thought I would," Solomon answered.

" How do you think you'll get there ? " demanded
the master.

"Don't know," was all the reply that Solomon
gave, " thought I'd try it."

" You'd be taken and sent to gaol, where you ought
to be, before you got half way there," Tibeats remarked
as he passed into the cabin. He came out soon after
with the pass in his hand, and bitterly cursing Solomon as a " worthless nigger that deserved a hundred
lashes " threw it on the ground. Solomon soon picked

it up and hurried away on his journey, glad to leave his tyrant master behind.

A slave caught off his master's plantation without a pass might be seized and whipped by any white man that met him. The paper ran thus:—

"Platt has permission to go to Ford's plantation on Bayou Bœuf, and return by Tuesday morning.

"John M. Tibeats."

On the way he met with several who demanded to see his pass, read it, and then went on. Those who had the air of gentlemen did not notice him beyond a passing look; but shabby-looking fellows and loafers never failed to hail him, scrutinize him carefully, and examine his pass. Catching runaways was a money-making business. A "mean white" therefore—a name applied to a species of loafer—considered it quite a godsend to meet an unknown negro without a pass.

There were no places of refreshment along the road, and Solomon had neither money nor provisions with him. But that did not trouble him; for he only needed to show his pass to the master or overseer of a plantation and state his wants, when he would be sent at once to the kitchen and provided with food and shelter. So with travellers. They had only to stop at any house and call for a meal or lodging, and their wants would be generously supplied. Whatever other faults they had, the inhabitants along the Red River, and around the Bayous in the interior of Louisiana, were not wanting in hospitality.

He arrived at Ford's plantation towards the close

of the afternoon, passing the evening with Lawson, Rachel, and others of his old acquaintances who assembled to welcome him in Eliza's cabin. This was the last time he saw that poor suffering woman. When they left Washington together, Eliza's form was round and plump: she stood erect, and in her silks and jewels presented a beautiful picture of graceful strength and elegance. Now she was but a thin shadow of her former self. Her face had become haggard and ghastly, every trace of its former beauty vanished; and the once straight, graceful, active frame was bowed down as if beneath the weight of a hundred years. Crouching on the cabin floor and clad in the coarse garments of a slave, Elisha Berry, had he seen her, could not have recognized the mother of his children. Solomon did not suppose that that was the last time he would ever look upon her. But so it turned out; and he afterwards took some trouble to acquaint himself with the history of her latter days. Having become useless in the cotton-field through growing weakness, she was bartered for a trifle to some man in the vicinity of Peter Compton's. Grief had gnawed remorselessly at her heart until her strength was utterly wasted; and because of that her last master lashed and abused her unmercifully. But he could not whip back the departed vigour of her youth, nor straighten up that bended body to its full height as when her precious children were around her.

She became at length utterly helpless, for several weeks lying on the earthen floor of a dilapidated

P

cabin, dependent on her fellow-slaves for an occasional drop of water and a morsel of food. Her hard-hearted master did not " knock her on the head," as is sometimes done to put a poor suffering animal out of misery, but left her entirely unprovided for and unprotected, to linger to death in starvation, pain and wretchedness. When the hands returned from the field one night they found her dead. A merciful God had put an end to her sufferings, and poor Eliza was free at last! Her painfully chequered life had reached its termination, and the griefs and sorrows of earth could assail her no more.

The next day Solomon rolled up his blanket, bade his friends farewell, and started on his journey back to the Big Cane Brake. He had travelled about five miles when he encountered again the hateful presence of Tibeats. His heart would have bounded with joy could he have foreseen what was to be the result of their meeting, and that the ties which bound him a slave to that contemptible man were about to be unloosed for ever. Tibeats inquired of Solomon why he was returning so soon, as his pass gave him leave of absence until Tuesday morning. Solomon replied that he was anxious to do as he had been directed, and wished to be ready to go to his work at daylight on the following morning. Tibeats then said he need not go any further than the next plantation, as he had that day sold him to Edwin Epps. They walked down into the yard, where they met Solomon's new purchaser. Solomon was subjected to the usual examination and required to answer many questions, the result of which seemed to be quite satisfactory. Having been duly delivered over to his new master, he was directed by that gentleman to go and make a hoe and axe handles for himself.

He was now no longer the property of Tibeats— his dog—his brute, dreading his wrath and cruelty from day to day. This was balm and consolation to the heart of Solomon. It was blessed news to him when the sale was announced, and with a joyful sense of relief he went to the cabin assigned to him, and sat down in his new abode. Whoever or whatever this new master might prove to be, it was scarcely probable that the change would not be for the better. It was barely possible to sink lower than to be the slave of a wretch like Tibeats.

That worthy soon after disappeared from that section of the country, and only once after selling him to Epps did Solomon catch a glimpse of him. It was many miles away from Bayou Bœuf that he saw Tibeats seated at a low groggery, when he was passing in a drove of slaves through St. Mary's parish.

CHAPTER XII.

The Cotton Plantation.

SOLOMON'S new master, Edwin Epps, was destined in the arrangements of Divine Providence to be his last owner, though his term of service with him was to extend over a series of years. He was a large, portly, heavy-bodied man with light hair, high cheek-bones, and a Roman nose remarkably developed. He had blue eyes, a fair complexion, and stood fully six feet high. He had the sharp, inquisitive expression of a jockey, with manners coarse and repulsive; and he used language which afforded unequivocal evidence that he had never enjoyed the advantages of education. He had the faculty of saying very provoking things—in that respect surpassing old Peter Tanner.

At the time that Solomon came into his possession, Epps was much addicted to excessive drinking—his "sprees" sometimes extending over two whole weeks. But in this respect he became a reformed character, and before Solomon left him, was one of the strictest examples of temperance to be found on Bayou Bœuf. When intoxicated he was a roystering, blustering, noisy fellow; whose chief delight was in dancing with his "niggers," or lashing them about the yard with his long whip, just for the pleasure of hearing them screech and scream as the great welts were planted on their backs. When sober, he was silent, reserved, and cunning; not beating his slaves indiscriminately, as in his drunken freaks, but sending the end of his raw hide to some tender spot of a lagging slave with a sly dexterity peculiar to himself.

He had been a driver and overseer in his younger days; but at this time was in possession of a plantation on Bayou Huff Power, twelve miles from Cheneyville. The property belonged to Joseph B. Roberts and was leased to Epps, Roberts being uncle to Epps' wife. The principal business of Epps was raising cotton.

The ground being previously prepared, the cotton was planted in the months of March and April, the corn having been planted in February. In the course of ten or twelve days the first hoeing was commenced, and in July it was hoed for the fourth and last time. During all these labours the overseer or driver followed the slaves, on horseback, with a whip in his hand, and the lash was flying from morning until night.

About the latter part of August the cotton-picking began. At this time each slave was presented with a sack with a strap fastened to it to pass over the neck, holding the sack breast high, while the bottom reached nearly to the ground. Each slave was also furnished with a large basket that would hold about two barrels. These were to put the cotton in when the sacks were filled. The baskets were placed at the head of the rows.

When a new hand who had been unaccustomed to the business was sent for the first time into the field, he was whipped up smartly, and made for that day to pick as fast as he could. At night it was weighed, so that his capability in cotton-picking was ascertained. He was then required to bring in the same weight each night following. If it fell short, a flogging was the penalty.

An ordinary day's work was two hundred pounds. A slave accustomed to the work was punished if he or she brought in less than that. There was a great difference amongst the slaves as regarded this kind of labour. Some of them seemed to have a knack, or natural quickness, which enabled them with both hands to pick with great celerity; while some, with all the effort of which they were capable, were never able to come up to the usual standard. There was a girl named Patsey in Epps' gang, who was the most remarkable cotton-picker on Bayou Bœuf. She picked with both hands, and with such surprising rapidity that five hundred pounds a day was not unusual with her. Solomon was very clumsy and unskilful as a cotton-picker.

The slaves were required to be in the cotton-field as soon as it was light in the morning; and, with the exception of ten or fifteen minutes given them at noon to swallow their allowance of cold bacon and corn-bread, they were not permitted a moment's relaxation from their toil until it was too dark to see. When the moon was near the full, they were often continued at labour until the middle of the night.

The day's work over in the field, the baskets were "toted." That is, they were carried to the gin-house, where the cotton was weighed. Few of the slaves ever approached the gin-house with their baskets of cotton without fear. They knew that if the cotton fell short in weight, however little, they must suffer. After the weighing followed the whippings. Then the baskets were carried to the cotton-house, and their contents stored away like hay— the slaves having all to assist in tramping it down. If the cotton was wet, it had to be laid upon platforms made for the purpose, and spread out to dry.

After this each slave had to attend to his respective "chores;" one feeding the mules, another the swine, another cutting wood, and so on. Finally, at a late hour they reached the quarters, and there a fire must be kindled in the cabins, the corn ground for supper, and the next day's dinner prepared to carry with them to the field. Then, and not till then, could they lay them down to rest.

All that was allowed the slaves on Epps' plantation was a scanty supply of corn and bacon, which was given out at the corn-crib and smoke-house every Sunday morning. Each one received as his weekly allowance three-and-a-half pounds of bacon, and corn enough to make a peck of meal—no coffee or sugar, and only now and then a slight sprinkling of salt. Solomon thought that after ten years' residence with Master Epps, no slave was ever likely to suffer from gout induced by high living. Master Epps' hogs were fed upon shelled corn; it was thrown out to his slaves in the ear.

The corn-mill stood in the yard beneath a shelter, the hopper holding about six quarts. There was one privilege Epps granted to his slaves. They might grind their corn nightly in such small quantities as their daily wants required ; or they might grind their whole weekly allowance at one time.

The cabins were constructed of logs, without floor or window ; the latter being scarcely necessary, the crevices between the logs admitting both light and air. In stormy weather the rain would drive through these interstices, rendering the cabin damp and disagreeable. At one end was constructed an awkward fire-place. There were no soft couches to be found in these coarse abodes. The bed on which Solomon reclined during the whole ten years he spent in Epps' service was a plank twelve inches wide and ten feet long. His pillow was a log of wood, and his blanket his only covering.

On Solomon's arrival at Epps' plantation, he proceeded at once to obey the order which that gentleman had given him to make an axe-helve and a handle for his hoe. The axe-handles he found in use in that part of the country were simply plain round straight sticks. He made a crooked one, shaped like those he had been accustomed to use at the North. When he finished it and presented it to Epps, that worthy looked at it with astonishment, unable to determine at first what it was. He had never before seen such a handle, and when Solomon explained its conveniences, and the greater power it gave to the instrument to which it belonged, he was forcibly struck with the novelty of the idea. He kept it in his house a long time, and exhibited it to his friends as a great curiosity.

It was now the season of hoeing. Solomon was first sent into the corn-field, and afterwards set to scraping cotton. In this employment he remained until hoeing was nearly done. Then he began to experience symptoms of approaching illness. He was attacked first with chills, and then with burning fever; and these continued until he became weak and emaciated, and frequently so dizzy, that he would reel and stagger like a drunken man. He was, nevertheless, compelled to keep up his row with the other slaves. When in health he found little difficulty in keeping pace with his fellow-labourers; but now it seemed to be an impossibility. Often he fell behind, when the driver's lash was sure to fall upon his back. He continued to decline until the whip became utterly ineffectual, and the sharpest sting of the raw hide could not arouse him. Finally, in September, when the busy season of cotton-picking was at hand, he became unable to leave his cabin. Up to this time he had received no medicine, nor any attention whatever from his master or mistress. The old cook visited him occasionally, preparing for him corn-coffee, and sometimes boiling a bit of bacon when he had become too feeble to do it for himself. When it began to be said the sufferer was likely to die, **Mr.** Epps, unwilling to bear the loss of an animal that was worth at least a thousand dollars, concluded to incur the expense of sending for a medical attendant.

So Dr. Wines was summoned from Holmesville to
see the patient. He announced to Epps that it was
the effect of the climate, and it was very probable
that he would lose his slave. He directed Solomon
to eat no meat, and partake of no more food than was
absolutely necessary to sustain life.

Whether it was the scanty diet or the effect of
some medicine the doctor gave him, after the lapse of
several weeks he began to recover. One morning,
long before he was in a fit state to work, Epps
appeared at his cabin door, and presenting Solomon
with a sack, ordered him to the cotton-field. At this
time he had no experience whatever in cotton-
picking. It was to him an awkward business indeed.
While others used both hands, snatching the cotton
and depositing it in the mouth of the sack with a
precision and dexterity marvellous and incomprehen-
sible to Solomon, he had to seize the boll with one
hand, and deliberately draw out the white gushing
blossom with the other.

Depositing the cotton in the sack, moreover, was a
difficulty that demanded the use both of hands and
eyes. He was compelled to pick it from the ground,
where it would fall very frequently instead of into the
mouth of the sack, almost as often as from the stalk
where it had grown. Then he made havoc with the
branches, loaded with the yet unopened bolls,—the
long cumbersome sack swinging from side to side in
a manner not allowable in the cotton-field. After a
very laborious day he arrived at the gin-house with
the result of his day's toil. When the scale deter-

mined its weight to be only ninety-five pounds—not half the quantity required of the poorest picker—Epps threatened the severest flogging; but in consideration of his being a raw hand, he concluded to pardon him on that occasion.

The following day, and many succeeding days, he returned at night with no better success,—he was evidently not designed for that kind of toil. He had not the gift—the dexterous fingers and quick motion of Patsey, who was unrivalled in that branch of labour. Practice and whipping were alike unavailing, and Epps satisfied of it, at last swore that Solomon was a disgrace,—that he was not fit to associate with a cotton-picking " nigger,"—that he would not pick enough in a day to pay for the trouble of weighing it, —and that he should go into the cotton-field no more. He was therefore employed in cutting and hauling wood, drawing cotton from the field to the gin-house, and whatever service was required. And he was fully employed—never allowed for a moment to be idle.

A day seldom passed without one or more whippings. This occurred at the time the cotton was weighed. The delinquent whose weight had fallen short was taken out, stripped, and made to lie down upon the ground face downwards, when a punishment was administered in proportion to the offence. The crack of the lash and the shrieking of the slave could be heard from dark to bed time on Epps' plantation every day during the cotton-picking time.

The number of lashes was graduated according to

the nature of the case. Twenty-five was a mere brush, when a dry leaf or a piece of the boll was found in the cotton, or a branch was broken in the field; fifty for all offences of the next grade; a hundred for standing idle in the field; from a hundred and fifty to two hundred for quarrelling with cabin-mates; and five hundred laid on with the greatest possible severity for any attempt to run away.

During the two years that Epps remained on the plantation at Bayou Huff Power, he frequently came home intoxicated from Holmesville. The shooting matches held among the planters invariably concluded with a debauch. At such times he was boisterous and half-crazy, and would smash dishes, chairs, or anything else he could lay his hands on. When satisfied with these freaks in the house, he would seize his whip, and walk forth into the yard. Then it behoved the slaves to be on their guard. The first one that came within reach, felt the smart of the lash. He would keep them for hours scampering in all directions and dodging around the corners of the cabins. If occasionally he could come upon one unawares and succeed in inflicting a fair smart blow, it greatly delighted him. It was the aged and the children who suffered the most.

At other times he would come home in a less brutal mood. Then there must be a dance. All must move to the measure of a tune, and he would dash about in the wildest fashion all through the house. Tibeats had informed Epps that Solomon could play on the violin; and through the importunity of his wife the master had been induced to purchase an instrument for him on one of his visits to New Orleans. The lady being fond of music, Solomon was often called into the house to play before the family; and when Epps came home in a frolicsome mood, he would have all the slaves assembled in the large room of the great house to dance. No matter how worn out and tired they were, there must be a general dance. When all were properly stationed on the floor, he would call upon Solomon to strike up a tune, and then shout with his stentorian voice—" Dance, you cursed niggers, dance," often using oaths and expletives not to be repeated. Then there must be no halting or delay; all must be brisk and lively, his own portly form mingling with those of his dusky slaves moving rapidly in the dance.

Not unfrequently his whip was in his hand ready to fall about the ears of any presumptuous slave who dared to rest a moment to recover breath. When he was himself exhausted, there would be a brief cessation. Then, with a crack and flourish of the whip he would shout again — " Dance, niggers, dance," and away they must go again. Frequently he would keep them dancing until near the dawn of the morning, regardless of their wearied condition. But notwithstanding all this, the slaves were required to be in the field as soon as it was light, and to perform the ordinary and accustomed task; and if there were any deficiency no allowance was made,—

the whippings were just as severe as if they had all been invigorated and strengthened by their usual night's repose.   Indeed, after these frantic revels Epps was always more sour and unreasonable and savage than at other times, punishing for slighter causes, and using the whip with more vindictive energy.

The mistress often upbraided him for his folly, declaring that she would return to her father's house at Cheneyville.   Nevertheless, there were times when she could not suppress her laughter on witnessing his wild and uproarious pranks.

Solomon despised Epps only less than he did his former master, Tibeats.   He understood him well, and gave this estimate of his character.   "He was a man in whom the quality of kindness or justice was not found.   A rough, rude energy, united with an uncultured mind, and a mean avaricious spirit, was his prominent characteristic."   He was known as "a nigger-breaker," distinguished for the faculty he possessed of subduing the spirit of the slave; and he prided himself in his reputation in this respect, as a jockey would in his skill in managing a refractory horse.   He looked upon a coloured man not as a human being responsible to his Creator for the talent entrusted to him, but as a chattel—property—no better except in pecuniary value than his mule or his dog.   Solomon said, " When evidence, clear and indisputable, was laid before him, that I was a free man and as much entitled to liberty as he—when, on the day I left, he was informed that I had a wife and children as dear to me as his own were to him, he only raved and swore, denouncing the law that tore me from him, and declaring he would find out the man who had forwarded the letter that disclosed the place of my captivity, if there was any virtue and power in money, and would take his life. He thought of nothing but his loss, and cursed me for having been born free. He could have stood unmoved and seen the tongues of his poor slaves torn out by the roots—he could have seen them burned to ashes over a slow fire, or torn in pieces by dogs, if it only brought him any profit. Such a hard, cruel, selfish, unjust man was my master Edwin Epps."

"On Bayou Bœuf there was only one more savage than he; that was Jim Burns. His plantation was cultivated only by women, and the barbarian kept their backs so sore and raw by continual flogging that they were often unable to perform the daily labour demanded of them. He boasted of his cruelty, and was famous for it all the country round. Like a fool, he whipped and scourged away the very strength on which his gains depended."

Epps remained on Huff Power two years, when, having accumulated a considerable amount of money, he invested it in the purchase of a plantation on the east bank of Bayou Bœuf. He took possession of it in 1845, after the holidays, and carried with him Solomon and seven other slaves, viz. :—Abram, Wiley, Phœbe, Bob, Henry, Edward, and Patsey.

Abram must have been six feet seven or eight inches high, standing a full head above any common man. In his youth he had been renowned for his great strength, but sixty years of toil and suffering had greatly impaired it. He was a kind-hearted being, and " Ole Abram " was regarded as a sort of patriarch among the slaves, loved and respected by them all. He was fond of entertaining and instructing the younger portion of his fellow-bondsmen, and was deeply versed in such philosophy as is taught in the cabin of the slave.

Wiley was forty-eight. He was born on the estate of a man named William Tassle, and for some years had charge of a ferry over the Big Black River in South Carolina. He was a very silent man, and performed his task without murmur or complaint, seldom indulging in the luxury of speech, except to utter a wish that he was away from Epps, and back once more in South Carolina.

Phœbe was a slave of Burford, Tassle's neighbour, and being married to Wiley, Tassle bought her at Wiley's request.

Bob and Henry were Phœbe's children by a former husband, and were both children of tender age when Solomon first knew them.

Patsey was twenty-three years of age, and gloried in the fact that she was the offspring of a " Guinea nigger," brought over to Cuba in a slave ship, and in the course of trade transferred to Burford. She was slim and straight, and stood perfectly erect, and there was a lofty air about her that neither labour nor punishment could destroy. Her intellect and soul were enshrouded in utter darkness, but she was truly "a splendid animal," as someone remarked concerning her. She could leap the highest fence; and it must have been a very fleet hound that could outstrip her in a race. No horse, however wild, could fling her from his back. She was a skilful teamster, turned as true a furrow as the best on the plantation, and at splitting rails none could excel her. When the order to halt was heard at night, she would have her mules at the crib unharnessed, fed, and curried, sometimes before Uncle Abram had found his hat. But she was chiefly famous as a cotton-picker, and in this respect was queen of the field.

Patsey had a genial and pleasant disposition, and was faithful and obedient. She was a joyous creature, a laughing, light-hearted, playful girl. Yet Patsey wept oftener and suffered more than any of her companions. She had been literally excoriated, and her back bore the scars of a thousand stripes; not because she was backward in her work, or that she was of a perverse and rebellious spirit; but because it had fallen to her lot to be the slave of a cruel and unscrupulous master, and a heartless mistress. The mistress hated her with bitter and cruel hatred, and nothing delighted her so much as to see the poor girl suffer under the whip. More than once when Epps refused at his wife's request to sell Patsey, she offered bribes to Solomon to put her to death secretly, and bury the body in some lonely place on the margin of the swamp. She had to be constantly watchful when near the house or about her own cabin, other-

Q

wise a billet of wood or a broken bottle, or some other missile would strike her violently in the face, hurled by the vindictive hand of Mrs. Epps. What with the wickedness and violence of her master, and the malignant hatred of her mistress, the enslaved girl led a most miserable life.

CHAPTER XIII.

Louisiana Sugar Plantations.

THE first year of Epps' residence on the Bayou, 1845, the caterpillers almost totally destroyed the cotton crop throughout that region. There was but little to be done; so that to the great chagrin of the masters the slaves were necessarily unemployed half their time. Intelligence came, however, that wages were high and labourers in great demand on the sugar plantations in St. Mary's parish. This parish was on the Gulf of Mexico, about a hundred and forty miles from Avoyelles.

On the receipt of this intelligence, the planters on the Bayou Bœuf determined to make up a drove of slaves to be sent down to Tuckapaw, in St. Mary's parish, for the purpose of hiring them out to work in the cane-fields. Accordingly, in the month of September there were a hundred and forty-seven slaves collected at Holmesville, Solomon, Abram, and Bob, being of the number. About half were women. Epps and three other planters were the white men selected to accompany and take charge of the drove. They had a two-horse carriage and two saddle horses for their use.   A large waggon drawn by four horses, driven by a slave from a neighbouring plantation, carried the blankets and provisions, the slaves travelling afoot.

The duty assigned to Solomon was to take charge of the blankets and provisions, and see that none were lost by the way.   The carriage went in advance; the waggon followed.   Behind this the slaves were arranged, and two horsemen brought up the rear.   In this order they moved away from Holmesville and proceeded on their journey.

That night they stopped at a plantation belonging to a Mr. Crow, at a distance of about fifteen miles. Large fires were made, and the slaves laying their blankets on the ground lay down upon them to rest,— the white men lodging in the Great House.   An hour before day they were aroused by the crack of the whip.   The blankets were all delivered to Solomon, who deposited them in the waggon, and after a hasty meal the procession again set forth.   The following night it rained violently, and all were drenched— thoroughly saturated with mud and water.   Reaching an open shed, which had formerly been a gin-house, they sought beneath it such shelter as it afforded. There was not room for all to lie down, so they remained huddled together until the morning, when the cracking of the drivers' whips aroused them to resume their march.   During this journey they passed through Lafayette and other towns to Centreville, where Bob and Uncle Abram were hired to a plantation.   The number now decreased every day as they advanced,—nearly every sugar plantation being in want of hands.

On their route they passed the Grand Coteau, or prairie; a vast space of level monotonous country, without a tree, except occasionally one which had been transplanted from a distance and placed near a dilapidated and now deserted dwelling. It was once thickly populated and had been largely brought under cultivation, but for some cause had been abandoned. The business of the few scattered inhabitants that remained was raising cattle. Immense herds were feeding about as the party passed. " In the centre of the Grand Coteau," Solomon said, " one feels as if he were on the ocean, out of sight of land. As far as the eye can reach it is but a ruined and deserted waste."

Solomon was hired out to Judge Turner, a distinguished man in those parts, and an extensive planter whose large estate was situated on Bayou Lalle, within a few miles of the Gulf. For some days he was employed at " Turner's " in repairing his sugar house, after which a cane knife was put into his hands, and with thirty or forty other slaves he was sent into the field. He found no such difficulty in the art of cutting canes as he had in picking cotton. He soon became quite expert, and could keep up with the fastest in the field. Before the season was over he was transferred to the sugar-house to act there in the capacity of driver. From the commencement of the sugar-making, the grinding and boiling does not cease day or night until the season ends. The whip

was given to Solomon with the intimation that he
was to use it upon anyone whom he caught standing
idle ; and if he failed to obey this order to the letter
the whip would be smartly applied to his own back.
In addition to this, his duty was to call on and off the
different gangs at the proper time. He had no
regular periods of rest, and all the season could only
snatch but a few moments' sleep at a time.

It was customary in Louisiana to allow the slaves
to retain whatever compensation they obtained for
services performed on Sundays. In this way only
were they able to provide themselves with any luxury
or convenience whatever.   When a slave, purchased
or kidnapped in the North, was transported to a cabin
on Bayou Bœuf, he was furnished with neither knife,
nor fork, nor dish, nor kettle, nor any other article of
convenience.   All that was given to him was a
blanket to lie down in, if his master did not happen
to require it for any purpose of his own. He was at
liberty to find a gourd if he could to keep his meal
in, or he could eat his corn from the cob just as he
pleased. To ask the master for a knife or skillet, or
any small article for use for himself, would be
answered with a kick, or laughed at as a joke. Whatever necessary article of this nature might be found
in a slave's cabin had been bought with " Sunday
money."

On the sugar plantations in the crop season there
was no distinction as to the days of the week. There
was no Sabbath. It was well understood that all
hands must labour on Sunday as on any other day ;

and it was well understood also, that those who were hired, as Judge Turner had hired Solomon, should receive remuneration for the extra service on Sunday. In cotton-picking it was usual in the most busy time to require the same extra service, and to give the slaves some remuneration for it. From this source they were able, many of them, to supply themselves with a knife, kettle, tobacco, &c. The females, discarding the use of tobacco, were apt to spend their little earnings in gay ribbons, &c., with which to adorn themselves in the merry season of the holidays.

Solomon remained in St. Mary's until the first of January, when his Sunday money amounted to ten dollars. He met with a piece of good fortune, for which he was indebted to his knowledge of music. There was a grand party of whites assembled at a Mr. Garney's at Centreville, a hamlet in the vicinity of Turner's plantation. Solomon was employed to play for them; and they were so well pleased with his services that a contribution was taken for his benefit, which amounted to seventeen dollars—about sixty-eight shillings.

With this sum in possession he was regarded by his fellow slaves as a sort of millionaire. And it afforded him no small pleasure to look at it, and count it over from day to day. Visions of cabin furniture, of water-pails, pocket-knives, new shoes, and coats, and hats, floated before his imagination, and his heart seemed to swell within him as he thought that he was "the richest nigger on Bayou Bœuf."

At this time Solomon made an effort to regain his freedom. Vessels of large size ran up the Rio Teche to Centreville. One day he was bold enough to present himself before the captain of a steamer, and beg permission to hide himself amongst the freight. He was emboldened to risk the hazard of such a step from overhearing a conversation, in the course of which he ascertained that the captain was from the North. He did not relate to him the particulars of his history, but only expressed his desire to escape from slavery to a free state. The captain pitied him, but said it would be impossible to avoid the vigilance of the Custom House officials at New Orleans, and that detection would subject him to a heavy punishment and his vessel to confiscation. Solomon's earnest pleadings awakened his sympathies, and he would doubtless have yielded to them could he have done so with a chance of safety.

Soon after this the drove of slaves was re-assembled at Centreville, and the owners having arrived and collected the moneys due for their services, they were driven back to Bayou Bœuf much in the same order as before. It was on their return that, passing through a small village, Solomon caught a last sight of Tibeats, looking very shabby and out of repair. He was at the door of a low groggery, and was evidently fast sinking into sottishness and ruin.

During their absence, as Solomon learnt from Aunt Phœbe, Patsey had been getting deeper and deeper into trouble. "Old Hogjaw"—the nickname which the slaves had given to Epps—had

The Cane-Field.

beaten her more severely and frequently than ever. As often as he came from Holmesville inflamed with liquor—which was very often in those days—he would whip her merely to gratify the mistress— punishing her to an extent almost beyond endurance, merely to indulge his wife's hatred of the girl.

Epps treated his wife as considerately as so coarse a nature was capable of doing, and to gratify her he would have sold Patsey, but supreme selfishness overmastered conjugal affection. He was ready to comply with any request—to gratify any whim of hers—provided it did not cost too much. Now Patsey was equal to any two of his slaves in the cotton-field. He could not replace her services with the same money she would bring. The idea of disposing of her, therefore, could not be entertained. This was a source of constant disagreement between Epps and his wife. To place Patsey beyond her sight by sale, or death, or in any other way was the demand of the mistress, who would gladly have trampled out the life of the helpless bondwoman. After a storm of angry words between the master and the wife on this subject, there would follow a calm—often at the expense of poor Patsey's suffering. For Epps would quiet the rage of the malicious woman with a promise that the girl should be flogged —a promise he was sure to fulfil. Thus upon the head of Patsey—the simple-minded slave, in whose heart God had implanted the seeds of virtue—the force of all these domestic tempests would break.

During the summer succeeding his return from

St Mary's parish, Solomon thought of a plan of providing himself with some better food than that allowed to him on the plantation, which succeeded beyond his expectations ; and which, being adopted by many others up and down the bayou, he came to be regarded as a sort of public benefactor.

During that summer worms got into the bacon served out to the slaves, and nothing but ravenous hunger could induce them to swallow it. It was customary with the slaves on the bayou, when their weekly allowance was exhausted before Saturday night, or when it was in such a state as to render it nauseous and disgusting, to hunt in the swamps for the coon and the opossum. The flesh of the coon was palatable, " but verily," Solomon said, " there is nothing that I know in all butcherdom so delicious as a roasted 'possum." This kind of supply was very uncertain, especially as the hunting had always to be done at night, after the day's work was accomplished. For this purpose they used dogs and clubs. There were some planters whose slaves never had any kind of meat for many months together, but what they took in this manner.

Solomon's cabin was situated within a few rods of the bayou bank, and he thought that it would be practicable to obtain from its waters the requisite supply of good wholesome food, without the trouble of resorting nightly to the woods and risking an encounter with moccassin snakes and alligators. So he determined to construct a fish-trap, and make the denizens of the bayou contribute to his support and enjoyment. He pondered the subject in his own mind for a little while, and at the first opportunity set about the construction of the trap. He was perfectly successful, and his contrivance answered admirably. The Bayou Bœuf abounded in ·fish, many of them of large size and excellent quality; and the very first time he set the trap he found a large fish in it, sufficient to repay him for all his trouble. After that he was very rarely in want of fish for himself and his fellow-slaves, who all partook of the benefit. Thus a new mine was opened—a new source of comfort, hitherto never thought of by the enslaved children of Africa who were toiling and hungering along the shores of the sluggish but prolific bayou.

About this time an incident occurred in the neighbourhood which made a deep impression upon Solomon, and gave him a new insight into the state of society there, and the manner in which "white gentlemen" avenged the affronts they received. Directly opposite the slaves' quarters on Epps' plantation, on the other side of the bayou, was situated the plantation of a Mr. Marshall, who belonged to one of the most wealthy and aristocratic families in the country. A gentleman from Natchez had been negotiating with him for the purchase of the estate. One day a messenger arrived in great haste at Epps' saying that a terrible battle was going on at Marshall's —that blood had been spilled—and unless the combatants were forthwith separated the result would be fearful and disastrous.

On repairing to Marshall's house a fearful scene presented itself. On the floor of one of the rooms lay the ghastly corpse of the man from Natchez; while Marshall himself, covered with wounds and blood, was stalking to and fro, breathing out threatenings and slaughter. It appeared that a difficulty had arisen in the course of their negotiations, a quarrel ensued; when having recourse to deadly weapons the strife began that ended in such a dreadful tragedy. Marshall was never placed in confinement for the affair. A sort of trial or investigation took place at Markesville which resulted in his acquittal; he giving such an account of the transaction as cast the whole blame on the slaughtered man. He returned to his plantation more respected if anything than he had been before, none thinking any the worse of him because the blood of a fellow-creature was on his soul.

Epps interested himself very much on behalf of Marshall, accompanying him to Markesville and loudly justifying what he had done. But his services in this respect did not deter a kinsman of this same Marshall, and bearing the same name, from seeking his life also. A brawl occurred between them over a gambling table, which terminated in a deadly feud. Riding up on horseback in front of the house one day, armed with pistols and bowie-knife, Marshall challenged Epps to come forth and make a final settlement of the quarrel, or he would brand him as a coward, and shoot him like a dog the first opportunity. Not through cowardice, much less through any conscientious scruples, but through the influence of his wife Epps was restrained from accepting the challenge. A reconciliation however was effected afterwards, and they met and lived on terms of perfect intimacy.

Such occurrences as would bring upon the parties concerned in them condign punishment in the Northern States were common in Louisiana, and were very frequent on Bayou Bœuf, where they passed without notice and without comment. Every man was in the habit of carrying his bowie-knife and revolver; and when a dispute occurred they would set to work hacking, and thrusting and shooting at each other, more like savages than civilized and enlightened human beings. There were on the bayou some of more humane and peaceable disposition, who never degenerated into bullies and cut-throats, and who dealt with their slaves with some consideration for their comfort and well-being. But men resembling William Ford were few and far between.

CHAPTER XIV.

The Letter.

IN consequence of Solomon's want of expertness in picking cotton, his master, Epps, was in the habit of hiring him out to labour on the neighbouring sugar-plantations during the sugar-making season. He received a dollar a day for Solomon's services, out of which he hired another slave to supply his place in cotton-picking. Cutting canes was an employment that was better suited to his former habits of labour. For three years he held what was called the "lead row" on "Hawkins' plantation," leading a gang of from a hundred to a hundred and fifty hands. He was also frequently employed in the boiling-house and other departments of the work, so that he became thoroughly acquainted with the whole process of sugar-growing and its manufacture.

The only respite from constant labour the slaves had through the whole year was during the Christmas holidays. Epps allowed three days. Some of the planters who were of a more generous disposition gave their slaves four, five, and some even six days, according to the mood they might happen to be in and the state of the work on the plantation. It was the only time to which they looked forward with interest and pleasure. They were glad when the night came, not only because it brought them a few hours repose, but because it brought them one day nearer to Christmas. It was to them what the Easter carnival is in Roman Catholic countries, and was hailed with equal delight by old and young. Even Uncle Abram ceased to glorify General Jackson, who with him was the greatest of all military heroes; and Patsey forgot her many sorrows amid the general hilarity of the holidays. It was the time of feasting and frolicking, and fiddling and dancing—the real carnival season of the children of bondage. These were the only days when they were allowed a little *restricted* liberty; and heartily indeed did they enjoy it.

It was the custom for one of the planters to give a Christmas supper to the slaves, inviting the slaves from the neighbouring plantations to join his own on the occasion. One year it was given by Epps, the next by Marshall, the next by Hawkins, and so on. Usually from three to five hundred were assembled, coming together on foot, in carts, on horseback or on mules, riding double and triple; sometimes a boy and girl, sometimes a girl and two boys; and again a boy and girl and an old woman bestriding the same animal. Uncle Abram astride a mule, with Phœbe and Patsey behind him, trotting towards a Christmas supper was a sight to be witnessed and laughed over on Bayou Bœuf.

Then too, of all days in the year, they would array themselves in their best attire. The cotton coat was cleanly washed, the stump of a tallow candle applied to polish the shoes—the luxury of blacking being unknown to them—and if they were so fortunate as to possess a hat, though brimless or crownless, it would be placed jauntily on the head. But they were welcomed with equal cordiality if they went bareheaded or bare-footed to the feast. As a general thing the women wore handkerchiefs tied about their heads. But if chance had thrown in their way a fiery-red ribbon or a cast-off bonnet of the mistress, or even the mistress's grandmother, it was sure to be displayed on these occasions. Red—deep blood red —was the favourite colour among the enslaved damsels of Bayou Bœuf. If a red ribbon did not encircle their necks, their woolly hair was certain to be tied up with red strings of one sort or another.

The table was spread in the open air and loaded with varieties of meat and piles of vegetables. At such times bacon and corn-meal are dispensed with. Sometimes the cooking was done in the kitchen of the plantation, but more generally under the shade of wide-branching trees. In the latter case a trench was dug in the ground, and wood laid in and burned until the trench was filled with glowing coals. Over these chickens, ducks, turkeys, pigs, and not unfrequently the entire body of a wild ox, were roasted. Flour also was furnished in abundance, of which biscuits and cakes were made and also pies and tarts, for which various kinds of preserves were supplied without stint. Only slaves who had lived all the year on the scanty plantation allowance of meal and bacon could fully appreciate those Christmas suppers. The white people in great numbers would assemble on these occasions to witness the gastronomic performances and enjoyments of the slaves.

They seated themselves at the rustic table, the males on one side, the females on the other—any two between whom passages of tenderness had been interchanged, always managing to sit opposite to each other. Unalloyed and exulting happiness would light up the dark faces of all, the ivory teeth contrasting pleasantly with their black complexion as they smiled at each other. All the sorrows of their ordinary life, the driver's whip, the master's cruelty, the mistress's hatred, were forgotten, and they abandoned themselves without reserve to the present enjoyment. Giggling and laughter, and the clattering of crockery and cutlery would be heard. Cuffee's elbow would be driven into his neighbour's side under the impulse of uncontrollable delight; while Nelly would shake her finger at Sambo and laugh—she knew not why; and so the fun and merriment would flow gaily on.

When the viands had disappeared, and the hunger of the party was fully satisfied, then would follow the Christmas dance. Solomon's business on these occasions was always to supply the music for the dancers. And very different was the dancing of these poor slaves from the studied movements of the fashionable dancing party. There was to be seen, if not the *poetry*, yet the *celerity* of motion—genuine

R

enjoyment free and unrestrained in the moon-light or the star-light of the Christmas night, beneath the ample shades of the wide-stretching trees of Louisiana. Violent as it was, this exercise would be continued all night, until broad daylight gave them notice to disperse.

With the exception of the time occupied by the journey to St. Mary's parish, and the seasons during which he was hired out to labour on the sugar plantations, Solomon was constantly employed on the plantation of Master Epps. His master was looked upon as a small planter, not having a sufficient number of slaves to require the services of an overseer. So he acted in that capacity himself; and not being able to increase his force of labourers by purchase, it was his custom to hire slaves during the hurry of the cotton-picking season.

On larger estates, having from fifty to a hundred and fifty hands, the services of an overseer were regarded as indispensable. These gentlemen rode into the field on horseback, armed with pistols, bowie-knives, and whips, and generally accompanied by several ferocious dogs. Equipped in this manner, they followed in rear of the slaves at their work, keeping a sharp look out upon them all. The requisite qualifications of an overseer were utter heartlessness, brutality, and cruelty. It was his business to produce large crops, no matter what amount of suffering that might entail upon the slaves. The presence of the dogs was necessary to overhaul a fugitive who might take to his heels, when faint or sick he was unable to keep up his row, and unable to endure more of the whip. The pistols were reserved for any dangerous emergency that might possibly arise. There were instances when such emergencies did arise, and slaves, goaded to madness by incessant cruelty and oppression, would turn upon their oppressors and handle them roughly.

For some time the gallows stood at Markesville upon which a slave was executed for killing his overseer. The event occurred a short distance from Epps' plantation, on Red River. The overseer was one of those brutal, unreasonable fellows who were capable of any villainy or cruelty towards slaves entrusted to their care. The slave had his task given him at splitting rails. In the course of the day the overseer sent him on an errand, which occupied so much of his time that it was not possible for him to fulfil the day's task. The next day he was called to account for not having completed his work. He reminded the overseer that he had taken him from it to send him on an errand of his own. But the excuse was disregarded, and with oaths and curses he was ordered to kneel down, and to bare his back for the application of the lash. They were alone in the woods, away from the sight or hearing of all on the plantation. The boy submitted, and lash after lash was laid on with all the might of the burly overseer, until, maddened by such cruel injustice, and writhing with pain, the slave turned furiously upon the oppressor, and seizing the axe with which

R 2

he had been at work he struck him to the ground, and literally chopped him in pieces.

He made no attempt at concealment, but hastening to his master related all that had taken place, and declared his readiness to suffer the penalty due for the crime he had committed. He was led to the scaffold; for such a crime, especially against the sacred majesty of a *white* man, was too great to be punished with anything less than the death of the offender. While the rope was round his neck he maintained a fearless bearing, and declared that he had done no wrong in sending such a wicked monster of cruelty as the overseer was to the hell he had so richly deserved. It would save many from the suffering they would have to endure at his hands if he had been suffered to live.

Besides the overseer, there are drivers under him in proportion to the number of hands in the field. It is their duty to keep the hands to their work without a minute's interruption; and whenever they see the slightest sign of relaxation on the part of the slaves, or any of them falling behind in their row, to apply the lash vigorously to their naked bodies, and thus supply a constant stimulant to labour hard. They are also compelled to do the whipping that may fall to the share of their several gangs.

At Huff Power, when Solomon first became the property of Epps, Tom, one of Roberts' negroes, was the driver hired for the purpose. He was a burly, muscular fellow, and severe in the extreme with the people. When Epps took possession of the

plantation upon Bayou Bœuf that honour was conferred upon Solomon; and up to the time of his
departure, he had to wear a whip coiled about his
neck and shoulders as the emblem of the authority
with which he was invested. But he had an uncon-
querable aversion to the cruelty which usually
attended the fulfilment of the office, and resolved
that it should not be so with him.

If Epps were present he dared not show any lenity
or indulgence. But he had an understanding with
his fellow-slaves that they should do all that was
possible to avoid provoking the punishment of the
lash. He could not always avoid using the whip;
but on the whole, much suffering was prevented by
the manner in which he exercised the authority of
his position. It was perfectly understood that Epps,
whether he were actually in the field with his slaves
or not, had his eyes pretty generally upon them.
From the piazza, from behind some adjacent tree, or
other concealed point of observation, he was perpetually on the watch. If any one had been backward
or idle through the day, he was sure to be told of it
on returning to the quarters. "And as it was," he
said, "a matter of principle with him to rebuke every
offence of that kind that came to his knowledge,"
not only was the offender certain to receive a castiga-
tion for his indolence, but the driver was also
punished for permitting it.

If, on the other hand, he had seen the driver use
the lash pretty freely he was satisfied. "Practice
makes perfect," the old proverb says, and Solomon,

during his long experience as a driver, had learned to handle the whip with marvellous dexterity and precision. He could throw the lash within a hair's-breadth of the back, the ear, the nose, without touching either of them. If Epps was observed at a distance, or they had reason to believe that he was sneaking about in the neighbourhood on the watch, the driver would commence plying the lash vigorously, when according to arrangement they would shrink and screech as if in agony, although not one of them had in fact been really grazed. Patsey would take occasion, when he made his appearance, to mumble in his presence complaints that Platt was lashing them the whole time; and Uncle Abram, with an appearance of honesty peculiar to himself, would declare that Platt had been whipping them worse than General Jackson whipped the enemy at New Orleans, when Abram was in attendance upon his master. If Epps was not drunk and in one of his most beastly humours, this generally proved to be satisfactory. If he was in liquor and in a surly mood, some of them must suffer as a matter of course. His violence sometimes assumed a dangerous form, placing the lives of his human stock in jeopardy. On one of these occasions the drunken madman sought to amuse himself by cutting Solomon's throat. He had been absent at Holmsville at a shooting match, and none of the people were aware that he had come back; but while they were at work in the field, hoeing, Patsey, addressing Solomon in a low voice, without looking up, said, " Platt, d'ye see old

Hogjaw there in the edge of the field?" Solomon advised that no notice should be taken of him, neither of them looking off from their work. Suspecting, if he had not overheard what had passed between them, Epps staggered up to Solomon and demanded with a brutal oath, "What was that you said to Pats?" Some evasive answer was returned, which only had the effect of increasing his violence and calling forth a torrent of profanity.

"How long have you owned this plantation, you cursed black nigger?" he inquired with a malicious sneer, at the same time grasping Solomon's collar with one hand, and thrusting the other into his pocket. "Now I'll cut your infernal black throat, and finish with you: that's what I'll do." With one hand he was not able to open the clasp-knife he had drawn from his pocket, until he finally seized it with his teeth, when the slave saw that he was about to get it open and felt the necessity of getting away from him; for in the reckless state in which he then was he was bent on killing the man. Solomon's shirt was open in front, and as he turned round quickly with a wrench and sprang away from him while he still retained his grip, the shirt was torn away and left in his hand. There was then no difficulty in eluding him. Epps would chase his intended victim till he was out of breath, then stop and give utterance to a volley of curses and renew the chase. He would command Solomon to come to him with a voice of drunken authority; then he would have recourse to coaxing. But Solomon always kept at a respectful distance. In that manner they made the circuit of the field several times, the drunken master making desperate plunges, the fugitive always dodging them, more amused than frightened; well knowing that when the drunken wretch recovered his sober senses he would laugh at and be ashamed of his folly.

This scene was at length put an end to by Mistress Epps who appeared at the fence. She beckoned to Solomon, who shooting past the drunken husband ran to the wife, and in answer to her inquiries related all that had taken place. After wandering for an hour about the field, Epps started towards the house walking as demurely as he could with his hands behind his back, and attempting to look as innocent as a child.

As he approached the mistress berated him soundly, heaping upon him many not very respectful epithets, and demanding for what reason he had attempted to cut Solomon's throat? Epps affected to have forgotten it altogether; and began, to the utter surprise of Solomon, to swear by all the saints in the calendar that he had not spoken a word to the nigger that day.

"Platt, you lying nigger, have I spoken a word to you?" was his appeal to the man he addressed.

It was not safe to contradict a master even by the assertion of the truth, so he remained silent; and when Epps entered the house he returned to the field and the danger passed by. But there is no doubt that Epps would, in his drunken fury, have murdered his slave had he not escaped from his hands.

Shortly after this a circumstance occurred that came near bringing out Solomon's real name and history, which he had so long and carefully concealed, and on which concealment he believed that his final escape depended. Soon after he passed into Epps' possession, his master inquired if he could write or read. On being informed that he had received some instruction in those branches, he assured Solomon with emphatic curses that if ever he caught him with a book, or with pen and ink, he would give him a hundred lashes. "I want you to understand that I buy niggers to work, and not to educate." He never inquired a word of his past life or whence he came. The mistress, however, questioned him frequently about Washington, which she supposed to be Solomon's native city; and more than once remarked that he did not talk nor act like the other niggers, and she was sure that he had seen more of the world than he admitted."

Solomon's great object, constantly kept in view, was to devise means of getting a letter into the post-office, directed to some of his friends or family at the North. The difficulty of such an achievement can scarcely be comprehended by persons unacquainted with the severe restrictions imposed upon the slaves. In the first place they were deprived of pen, ink, and paper. In the second place a slave could not leave the plantation without a pass, nor would a post-master mail a letter for a slave without written in-

structions from his owner. He was in slavery nine
years, though always watchful and alert, before he
met with the good fortune of obtaining a sheet of
paper, and then he stole it. While Epps was away
in New Orleans one winter disposing of his cotton,
the mistress sent Solomon to Holmesville for several
articles, and among them a quantity of foolscap
paper. He appropriated a sheet to himself, concealing it in the cabin under the board on which he
slept.

After various experiments he succeeded in making
ink by boiling white maple bark, and from a feather
abstracted from the wing of a duck he manufactured
a pen. When all were asleep in the cabin, by the
light of the coals, lying on his plank couch, he
managed to complete a somewhat lengthy epistle. It
was directed to an old acquaintance at Sandy Hill,
stating his condition, and urging his friend to adopt
measures to restore him to liberty. This letter he
kept by him a long time, pondering day and night
measures by which it could be safely deposited in the
post-office. At length a low fellow by the name of
Armsby, hitherto a stranger, came into the neighbourhood seeking a situation as an overseer. He
applied to Epps, and was about the plantation several
days. He next went over to Shaw's, near by, and
there he remained for several weeks. He became so
much reduced at last that he was compelled to labour
with the slaves. A white man working in the field
with slaves was a rare and unusual spectacle on
Bayou Bœuf. Solomon improved every opportunity

of showing him kindness, and cultivating his acquaintance privately, hoping to gain his confidence so far as to be able to entrust the precious letter to his keeping to be placed in the post-office. He visited Markesville repeatedly, a town some twenty miles distant; and there Solomon proposed to himself that his letter should be mailed, could he venture to entrust it to such a bearer.

After most careful deliberation as to the proper manner of approaching him on the subject, Solomon concluded finally to ask him simply if he would drop a letter for him in the Markesville post-office the next time he visited that place, without reposing in him any further confidence; not telling him that the letter was already written, or any of the particulars it would contain. He had fears that the man was not to be trusted, and that he would be likely to betray him. And he also knew that the man was likely to require an inducement, and that some pecuniary consideration must be offered him before he would be likely to render such a service. As late as one o'clock one night, Solomon stole noiselessly from his cabin, crossed the field to Shaw's, and found the man he sought sleeping on the piazza. His worldly possessions amounted to only a small sum—the proceeds of his fiddling performances; but all he had in the world he promised the fellow if he would do the favour required, and begged him not to expose him if he could not grant his request. He assured Solomon on his *honour* he would deposit it in the Markesville post-office, and that he would keep it an inviolable secret for ever.

The letter was in Solomon's pocket at the time, but he dared not deliver it then for he had serious misgivings about the man. He told the fellow " Good night," said he would have the letter ready for him in a day or two, and returned to his cabin. All night he lay awake revolving the subject in his mind and perplexed in the extreme. He was willing to risk a great deal to accomplish his purpose ; but should the letter by any means fall into the hands of Epps, it would not only bring upon him a terrible punishment, but it would be a death-blow to all his hopes and aspirations, and his chances of freedom would be gone for ever.

His suspicions turned out to be too well founded. The next day but one, while he was scraping cotton in the field, Epps seated himself on the line-fence between Shaw's plantation and his own, in such a position as to overlook the labours of the slaves. Soon after, Armsby made his appearance and took a seat beside him. They entered into conversation, in which they were engaged for two or three hours. All this time poor Solomon was in an agony of apprehension, for he had no doubt that he and his letter were the subjects of their discourse.

That night while Solomon was broiling his bacon, Epps entered the cabin with a raw hide in his hand, and subjected Solomon to a rigid cross-examination about the letter. It was not without much trouble, and no little violation of truth and conscience, that Solomon prevailed on Epps to believe that it was not possible for him to procure writing materials, and that Armsby was trying to prevail on him to believe that the negroes were disposed to run away, in order that Epps might give him employment as an overseer. This he succeeded in doing at last, and Epps left the cabin. All that night Solomon was greatly troubled in his conscience for the falsehoods he had uttered. He burnt the letter as soon as he was alone, and with a desponding and despairing heart, saw the paper which had cost him so much anxiety and thought, and which he had fondly hoped would be his forerunner to the land of freedom and home, writhe and shrivel on its bed of coals, and dissolve into dust and ashes. Armsby, who had so cruelly betrayed him, was shortly after driven from the neighbourhood, and Solomon saw his departure with great joy; for so long as the fellow remained about there, he was under constant apprehension that the conversation about the letter might be renewed, and Epps ultimately induced to believe his statement.

He now knew not where to look for deliverance. Hope had sprung up in his heart only to be blighted. The summer of his life was passing swiftly away. He felt that he was growing prematurely old; that in a few years more, toil and grief and the poisonous miasma of the swamps would accomplish their work upon him, and consign him to an obscure grave, there to moulder and be forgotten. Repelled, betrayed, cut off from the hope of succour, he could only prostrate himself on the earth and groan in unutterable anguish. The hope of rescue was the only light that had cast a ray of comfort on his heart; that was now flickering, faint and low. Another breath of disappointment would surely extinguish it altogether, leaving him to grope in midnight darkness and despair to the end of life.

Solomon prayed to God, especially in times of great and pressing trouble, but he was a stranger to the consolations of experimental religion. His prin-cipal source of comfort and enjoyment during the years of his slave-life was his violin. On Sabbath days when an hour or two of leisure was allowed, he would take his instrument to some quiet spot on the Bayou bank, and there endeavour to draw consola-tion from its sweet tones. Often at midnight, when sleep was not to be had, and his soul was troubled and disquieted by the contemplation of his gloomy fate, he would have recourse to his violin, and make it sing to him a song of peace. "Had it not been for my violin," he said, "I scarcely can conceive how I could have endured the long years of my bondage. It introduced me to the great houses of the plantations; relieved me of many days labour in the field; supplied me with conveniences for my cabin, with pipes and tobacco and extra pairs of shoes; and ofttimes led me away from the presence of a hard master to scenes of jollity and mirth. It was my companion, the friend of my bosom,— triumphing loudly when I was joyful, and uttering its soft melodious consolations when I was sad. My master often received letters, sometimes from a dis-tance of ten miles, requesting him to send me to play at a ball or festival of the whites. He received his compensation, and usually I also returned with many picayunes jingling in my pockets, the extra contributions of those to whose enjoyment I had ministered. In this manner I became more acquainted with the Bayou and its inhabitants up and down, than would otherwise have been the case. My violin heralded my name round the country; made me friends who otherwise would not have noticed me ; gave me an honoured seat at the yearly festivals ; and secured for me the loudest and heartiest welcome at the Christmas dance. The young men and maidens of Holmesville always knew there was to be some pleasure party, whenever ' Epps' Platt ' was seen passing through the town or village with his instrument under his arm. ' Where are you going now, Platt ? ' ' What is coming off to-night ? ' ' What and where is the row ? ' would be the interrogations that would assail me from many a door and window. Many a time when there was no special hurry, yielding to the pressing importunities brought to bear upon me, I would draw out my fiddle and bow, and sitting astride a mule discourse musically to a crowd of children gathered around me in the street.''

CHAPTER XV.

The Bitterness of Bondage.

THE years rolled on and still found and left poor Solomon in his bondage, with little prospect of ever regaining his freedom. The failure of his plans for getting a letter posted had left him more sad and hopeless than before. The year 1850 dawned upon Solomon in slavery, and found the same scenes of cruelty and oppression exhibited daily, as had for many years been witnessed upon the plantations on Bayou Bœuf. On Epps' plantation the lash was wielded as vigorously as it had ever been, and the blood of slaves flowed as freely. Humanity and mercy were strangers to the place.

There was not a day that Solomon did not consult with himself on the possibility of making his escape. He laid many plans which at the time seemed feasible and excellent; but on mature reflection he had to abandon them all. None but those who have been in the situation can comprehend the thousand obstacles thrown in the way of the flying slave. Every white man's hand is against him; the patrollers are watching for him; the hounds are ready to follow on his track; and the nature of the country is such as to render it almost impossible to pass through it with safety. Solomon thought the time might come when he should be flying through the swamps again, and resolved in that case to be prepared for Epps' dogs if they should pursue him. Epps possessed several of these creatures, one of which was a notorious slave-hunter, and the most fierce and savage of his breed. When out with the dogs hunting the coon and the opossum, Solomon took every opportunity of whipping them soundly; and in this manner succeeded in subduing them completely. They learned to fear him and to obey his voice, when others could exercise no control over them; and had they followed and overtaken him they would have shrunk from an attack.

Notwithstanding the certainty of being captured, the woods and swamps were often filled with runaways, driven from the plantations by cruelty and oppression. Sick, weary, and miserable, many would risk the heavy punishment always inflicted on the runaway, for the sake of obtaining a few days or a few weeks' rest in the swamp; and not a few lost their lives in the attempt.

Epps' plantation was bounded on one side by Carey's, a very extensive sugar plantation, with more than one hundred and fifty field hands and a large number of children. With one of the negro drivers of this place, a pleasant, intelligent fellow named Augustus, Solomon had during the holidays, and

occasionally while at work in adjoining fields, cultivated an acquaintance which ripened into a warm
and mutual attachment. Augustus was so unfortunate as to incur the displeasure of the overseer, a
coarse, heartless brute, who whipped him most unmercifully. As he threatened even worse punishment Augustus ran away. Reaching a cane-rick on
Hawkins' plantation, he secreted himself on the top
of it. All Carey's dogs, some fifteen of them, were
put on his track. They soon scented his footsteps to
his hiding place, and surrounded the rick, baying
and scratching, but could not reach the fugitive.
Presently, guided by the clamour of the hounds, his
pursuers came up, when the overseer mounting to
the top of the rick drew the fugitive from his hiding
place and cast him down. As he rolled to the
ground the whole pack fastened upon him, and
before they could be beaten off had torn and muti-
lated him in the most shocking manner ; their teeth
having penetrated to the bone in a hundred places.
He was taken up, tied upon a mule, and carried
home. But this was the last of Augustus. He
lingered in great agony until the next day, when
death came to his relief, and the poor murdered
victim found rest in the grave.

The case of a girl named Celeste, also from Carey's,
was a remarkable instance of successful evasion of
dogs and hunters. She was about nineteen or
twenty years of age, and far whiter than her owner
or any of his children. It required close inspection
to distinguish in her the slightest trace of African

blood. A stranger would never have thought for a moment that she was the descendant of slaves. Solomon was sitting in his cabin late one night, playing a low air on the violin, when the door was cautiously opened, and Celeste stood before him. She was pale and haggard. If an apparition had risen out of the earth Solomon could not have been more startled.

" Who are you ? " he demanded after gazing at her for a moment.

" I'm hungry; give me some bacon," was her only reply.

Solomon's first impression was that she was some white girl with deranged intellect, who having escaped from home, and wandering she knew not whither, had been attracted to his cabin by the sound of his violin. The coarse cotton slave-dress she wore however soon dispelled this supposition.

" What is your name? " he again interrogated.

" My name is Celeste," she answered. " I belong to Carey, and have been two days among the palmettoes. I am sick and can't work, and would rather die in the swamp than be whipped to death by the overseer. Carey's dogs won't follow me; they have tried to set them on. There's a secret between them and Celeste, and they won't mind the devilish orders of the overseer. Give me some food, I'm starving."

Solomon divided his scanty allowance with her; and while eating it she related how she had managed to escape, and described the place of her concealment.

s 2

In the edge of the swamp, not half-a-mile from Epps' house, was a large space, thousands of acres in extent, thickly covered with palmetto. Tall trees, whose long arms intertwined with each other, formed a canopy above so dense as to exclude the beams of the sun. It was perpetual twilight there, even in the middle of the brightest day. In the centre of this great space, which nothing but serpents ventured to explore—a sombre and solitary spot—Celeste had erected a rude hut of the dead branches that had fallen from the trees, and covered it with the leaves of the palmetto. This was the abode she had selected. She had no fear of Carey's dogs, any more than Solomon had of Epps'. It is a fact not easily explained that there are some whose tracks the hounds will absolutely refuse to follow. Celeste was one of these.

For several nights she went to Solomon's cabin for food, which his fish-traps enabled him to furnish in sufficient quantity. On one occasion the dogs barked as she approached, which aroused Epps and induced him to search the premises. He did not discover Celeste ; but after that it was not deemed prudent for her to come to the yard. When all was silent, Solomon carried the provisions to an appointed spot where she would find them.

In this manner the girl passed the summer. She regained her health and became strong and hearty. At all seasons of the year the howlings of wild animals could be heard at night along the borders of the swamps. Several times they made Celeste a midnight call, awakening her from her slumbers by fearful growls. Terrified by these unwelcome visitors, she finally concluded to abandon her lonely dwelling. Returning to her master she was fastened in the stocks and severely scourged, after which she was sent to the field again.

About this time Wiley, the husband of Phœbe, unhappily incurred the vengeance of the cruel tyrant who ruled the plantation. Alway a man of taciturn and retiring habits, he seldom opened his mouth to speak, and revolved in his obscure and unpretending orbit without even grumbling. " Nevertheless," said Solomon, " the warm elements of sociability were strong in that silent nigger."

Disregarding the philosophy of Uncle Abram, and setting at nought the counsels of Phœbe, Wiley, with a kind of foolhardiness none would have expected from him, determined to venture on a nocturnal visit to a neighbouring cabin belonging to another planta-tion, without a pass. He found the society of his friends so attractive that he took little note of the passing hours, and the light began to break in the east before he was aware of it. Speeding homewards as fast as he could run, he hoped to reach the quarters before the horn would sound ; but unhappily he was spied on the way by a company of patrollers.

On Bayou Bœuf there was an organization of " patrollers," as they were styled, whose business it was to seize and whip any slaves they might find wandering from the plantations. They rode on horseback, headed by a captain and accompanied by dogs. They had the right, either by law or by general consent, to inflict discretionary chastisement upon any black man caught beyond the boundaries of his master's plantation without a pass, and even to shoot him if he attempted to escape. Each company had certain distances to ride up and down the Bayou. They were compensated by the planters, who contributed in proportion to the number of slaves they owned. The clatter of their horses' hoofs could be heard as they went dashing by at all hours of the night, and frequently they might be seen driving a slave before them, or leading him by a rope fastened around his neck to his owner's plantation.

Wiley fled before one of these companies thinking he could reach his cabin before they could overtake him. But one of their dogs, a great ravenous hound, seized him by the leg and held him fast. The patrollers whipped him severely and brought him a prisoner to Epps, from whom he received another flagellation even more severe.

The bites of the dogs, which were very painful, and the two heavy floggings he had received, made poor Wiley very sore and stiff and miserable, insomuch that he was scarcely able to move. It was not possible therefore that he should keep up in his row, and consequently there was not an hour of the day but he felt the sting of his master's raw hide upon his already lacerated back, which was bleeding continuously. His sufferings became intolerable. This continual torture was more than he could bear, renewed as it was day after day, and finally he determined to run away. Without disclosing his intention even to his wife, Phœbe, he proceeded to make arrangements for carrying his plan into execution.

Having cooked his whole week's allowance, he cautiously left the cabin on a Sunday night after the other inmates were all asleep. When the horn sounded in the morning Wiley did not appear. Search was made for him in the cabin, the corn-crib, the cotton-house, and every nook and corner of the premises. Each of the slaves was examined touching any knowledge they might have that could throw light upon his sudden disappearance, or his present where-abouts. Epps raved and stormed, and threatened and blasphemed, and then mounting his horse, gallopped to the neighbouring plantations, making inquiries in all directions. The search was fruitless. No tidings could be obtained concerning the missing man. The dogs were led to the swamp, but were unable to strike his trail. They would circle through the forest, their noses to the ground, and invariably return to the place they started from.

Days and weeks passed away and nothing could be heard of Wiley. Epps did nothing but curse and swear. It was the only topic of conversation among the slaves when they were alone. A great deal of speculation was indulged in concerning him. Some supposed that as he was a poor swimmer he had been drowned in some bayou; others conjectured that he had been devoured by the alligators, or stung by the venomous moccasin, whose bite is certain and sudden death. The warm and hearty sympathies of all were with the poor fellow wherever he might be, and many an earnest prayer went up from Uncle Abram imploring safety for the wanderer.

After the lapse of several weeks when all expectation of seeing him again had passed away, to the great surprise of all he one day appeared on the plantation. He told them that when he left it was his purpose to make his way back to South Carolina, to the old quarters of Mr. Burford. During the day he remained secreted, sometimes in the branches of a tree; and at night pressed forward through the swamps. He reached the shore of Red River one morning, but while standing on the bank considering how he should cross it, a white man accosted him and demanded his pass. Being without one and evidently a runaway, he was taken to Alexandria and confined in prison. It happened that several days after, Joseph B. Roberts, uncle to Mr. Epps, visited the jail at Alexandria and recognized him. Wiley had worked on Roberts' plantation. Paying the jail fees and writing him a pass, he also sent a note to Epps requesting that he would not whip the fugitive on his return. So Wiley went back to Bayou Bœuf. It was the hope inspired by the knowledge of this request, and the assurance of Roberts that Epps would not flog him, that sustained him as he approached the plantation. The request, as may be supposed, was disregarded. After being kept in suspense three days, Wiley was stripped and compelled to endure one of those inhuman floggings to which the poor runaway was generally subjected. It was the first and last attempt of Wiley to make his escape. The long scars upon his back, which he would carry to his grave, would perpetually remind him of the danger of such a step.

Severely as Wiley had suffered at the hands of Epps for his unfortunate attempt to escape, he fared but little worse than his unfortunate companions who were under the same control. "Spare the rod," was not an idea suited to the hardened nature of the man. He was always brutal and cruel at his best; and he was constitutionally subject to fits of ill-humour and passion. At such times, however slight the provocation might be, a severe amount of punishment was inflicted without mercy. The circumstances attending the last flogging but one to which Solomon was subjected, will serve to show how trivial a cause was sufficient for resorting to the whip.

A Mr. O'Niel, residing in the vicinity of the Big Pine Woods, called upon Epps one day with the view of negotiating for the purchase of Solomon. He was by occupation a tanner and currier, carrying on an extensive business; and he intended to place Solomon, if he could obtain him, at service in some department of the establishment under his control. Aunt Phœbe, while preparing the dinner-table in the Great House, happened to overhear as much of the conversation between Epps and his visitor as made her acquainted with the facts just stated. On Solomon's return to the yard at night she ran to meet him, designing to overwhelm him with the unexpected intelligence. She enlarged upon the fact that "Massa Epps was gwine to sell him to a tanner ober in de Pine Woods" so long and so loudly, that the attention of the mistress was attracted to their conversation.

"Well, Aunt Phœbe," replied Solomon, "I'm glad of it. I'm tired of scraping cotton and would rather be a tanner. I hope he'll buy me."

The purchase was not effected, as the parties could not agree about the price, and the next morning O'Neil departed. He had gone but a short time when Epps appeared in the field. Nothing was more apt to enrage such a master as Epps than the intimation that one of his slaves would like to leave him—as if any one would not be glad to get beyond the reach of such an unfeeling wretch as he often proved himself to be! The mistress had repeated to him Solomon's expressions which she had overheard on the preceding evening. On entering the field Epps walked directly to Solomon.

"So Platt, you're tired of scraping cotton are you? You would like to change your master, eh? You're fond of moving round—traveller—ain't ye? Ah, yes—like to travel for your health may be? Feel above cotton-scraping, I s'pose? So you're going into the tanning business? Good business—devilish fine business! Enterprising nigger! B'lieve I'll go into that business myself. Down on your knees and slip that rag off your back! I'll try my hand at tanning."

Solomon begged earnestly and endeavoured to

soften him with excuses and explanations, but in vain. There was no alternative, so kneeling down he presented his bare back for the application of the lash.

"How do you like tanning?" Epps exclaimed. "How do you like tanning?" he repeated at every stroke. In this manner he gave him twenty or thirty lashes, incessantly repeating the word "tanning" in one form of expression or another. When sufficiently "tanned," he allowed him to rise, and with a malicious laugh assured Solomon that if he still fancied the business he would give him further instruction in it whenever he desired. "This time," he remarked, "I have given you a short lesson in *tanning*—the next time I'll curry you down well."

The effect of such exhibitions of brutality on the family of the slave-holder was seen in the household of Epps. He had a son, an intelligent child, who was at the time of the "tanning" performance about ten or eleven years of age. It was pitiable to see the lad, in imitation of his father's cruelty, chastise the slaves. Even Uncle Abram, venerable in age as he was, and one of the most harmless and faithful creatures in the world, this boy would call to account; and if in his childish judgment it was deserved, he would sentence him to receive a certain number of lashes, and proceed to inflict them with all deliberation. Mounted on his pony, he would often ride into the field with his whip and play the overseer, greatly to his father's delight. He would apply the raw hide to the naked persons of the slaves, urging them

forward with shouts and profane expressions; at
which the father would laugh loudly, and commend
the precocious blasphemer as "a thorough-going
man."

The lad possessed some noble qualities. But no
process of reasoning could lead him to comprehend
that, in the eye of the Almighty, colour makes no
distinction. He looked upon the black man simply
as an animal, differing in no respect from the other
animals employed on his father's estate, save in the
gift of speech and the possession of other qualities
that made them valuable as beasts to labour. To
work like his father's mules; to be whipped and
kicked and scourged through life; to address the
white man in cringing terms, with eyes bent servilely
to the ground, was, as he was taught, the natural
and proper destiny of the slave. Brought up with
such ideas—in the notion that black people were not
within the pale of humanity—it could scarcely be
otherwise than that the families of Southern planters
should generally be a pitiless and unrelenting race.
The influence of the iniquitous system fostered an
unfeeling and cruel spirit, even in those who among
their equals were regarded as amiable and generous.
Hardened as they must be by witnessing constant
exhibitions of cruelty, it could scarcely be otherwise
than that they would gradually learn to look upon
the sufferings and miseries of the slave with entire
indifference.

Sometimes there were attempts at insurrection
among the slaves. The year before Solomon was

first taken to Bayou Bœuf, there was a movement of this kind among the negroes which terminated very tragically. Lew Cheney, a man with whom Solomon was well acquainted, a shrewd, cunning negro, more intelligent than most of the slaves around him, but unscrupulous and full of treachery, conceived the project of organizing a company sufficiently strong to fight their way against all opposition to the neighbouring territory of Mexico.

A remote spot far within the depths of the swamp was selected as the rallying point. Lew flitted from one plantation to another in the dead of night, creating a *furore* of excitement wherever he appeared. At length a large number of runaways were assembled. Stolen mules, corn gathered from the fields, and bacon filched from smoke-houses, had been conveyed to the spot. The expedition was about ready to proceed, when their hiding-place was discovered. Lew Cheney, becoming convinced of the ultimate failure of the project, in order to curry favour with his master and avoid the consequences which he foresaw would follow, deliberately resolved to sacrifice all his companions. Departing secretly from the encampment, he proclaimed among the planters the number assembled in the swamp; and instead of stating truly the object they had in view, asserted that their intention was to emerge from their seclusion and murder every white person along the Bayou.

Such an announcement, exaggerated as it passed from mouth to mouth, filled the whole country with terror. The fugitives were surrounded and captured, then carried in chains to Alexandria and hung without trial by the populace. Many who were suspected, though entirely innocent, were taken from the field and from the cabin, and without any form of trial put to death. The planters on Bayou Bœuf, alarmed at this wide-spread destruction of their slaves, revolted against such a reckless sacrifice of their property. But it was not until a regiment of soldiers arrived from the Texan frontier, demolished the gallows, and opened the doors of the prison at Alexandria, that the indiscriminate slaughter was stayed. Lew Cheney escaped and was even rewarded for his treachery, but his name was despised and execrated throughout all the region.

Among the slaves on Bayou Bœuf the idea of an insurrection was often cherished and discussed. More than once Solomon has been joined in serious consultation with others when the subject was raised ; and there were times when a word from him would have placed hundreds of his fellow-slaves in an attitude of defiance to their owners. But he saw that without arms or ammunition, or even if they had them, such a step would result in certain defeat, disaster, and death ; and he always lifted up his voice against it. During the Mexican war, extravagant hopes were awakened among the slaves. The news of victory to the American arms filled the Great House with rejoicing, but produced only disappointment and sorrow among the slaves. Solomon's opinion was, that there were not fifty slaves on the Bayou but would have hailed with unmeasured delight the approach of an invading army. That delight they realized not many years after, when the victorious armies of the North carried the coveted blessing of freedom to every slave in the South, and raised four millions of negroes from the debasement of chattels to the dignity of men.

CHAPTER XVI.

Hopes and Fears.

THE time was now drawing near when the long term of oppression and wrong to which Solomon had been subjected was to come to a close, and the chains that bound him to a heartless and cruel oppressor were to be snapped asunder. But Solomon knew not of it. All before him was yet unbroken darkness. In the month of June, 1852, in accordance with a contract entered into by him, a Mr. Avery, a carpenter of Bayou Rouge, commenced the erection of a new house on Epps' plantation. There were no cellars to the houses on Bayou Bœuf, the low and swampy nature of the ground not admitting of such a convenience. The great houses were generally built upon piles driven into the ground. They were constructed entirely of wood, and the planks and boards were sawed by the slaves; there being in that neighbourhood no water-power upon which saw-mills could be erected. When a new house was to be built, therefore, it always brought abundance of extra labour to the already over-wrought slaves. As Solomon had had some experience as a carpenter under his former owner Tibeats, he was taken altogether from field work and put to labour as a carpenter with Avery and his people.

Among the hands of Avery, there was one who was destined to become a deliverer to Solomon, and thus confer upon him a life-long obligation. But for this noble-hearted man—this friend in need—doubtless thrown in his way by Divine Providence, Solomon would in all probability have ended his days amid the oppressions and horrors of slavery, none of his family ever knowing how and where he died.

This man, sent of God to be the saviour of the oppressed, and to open the way for Solomon's restoration to his family and home, was named Bass, and at that time resided at Markesville. Solomon described him as " a man whose big, true heart overflowed with noble and generous emotions, simple mechanic as he was." He was a large man, between forty and fifty years of age, with light complexion and light hair. He was very cool and self-possessed, fond of discussion and argument, and always speaking with extreme deliberation. His peculiarity of temper and manner was such, that what he uttered hardly ever gave offence. He could say with impunity what with many other persons would be regarded as intolerably offensive.

There was not perhaps a man all about the Red River and the Bayou Bœuf that agreed with his peculiar views on political and religious subjects;

T

and perhaps there was not another who discussed these subjects half as much as he did. It seemed to be taken for granted that he would always espouse the unpopular side of any question of local or general interest; and it always created amusement, rather than displeasure, among his auditors to listen to the strange and ingenious manner in which he maintained any controversy. He was without ties of kindred, being unmarried, and having no relatives living of whom he knew anything. Neither had he any settled home; wandering from one State of the Union to another as fancy dictated. He was a native of Canada, born under the British flag; but he had wandered in early life from his birth-place, and after visiting all the principal towns and cities in the Northern and Western States, he had, happily for Solomon, in the course of his peregrinations found his way from Illinois to the unwholesome region of the Red River.

He had been living three or four years in Markesville, where he prosecuted his business as a carpenter. His peculiarities had caused him to be well known, and he was respected through all the parish of Avoyelles. He was of generous and liberal disposition, doing many acts of kindness, and even compelling those to hold him in high esteem whose views and opinions he combatted with all his power. But had they known the part he took in obtaining Solomon's freedom, the planters of the neighbourhood would not have scrupled to put him to death. This he very well knew; and not choosing to entrust himself to the tender mercies of the slave-holders, he prudently disappeared from that part of the world as soon as Solomon's deliverance was effected, and was never seen again within reach of the slave-oppressing tribe on Bayou Bœuf.

One day, while working with Bass on Epps' new house, Solomon heard Bass and Epps engaged in earnest controversy on the subject of slavery, and he listened with absorbing interest to what they said, without appearing to do so.

"I tell you what it is Epps," said Bass, "it's all wrong—all wrong, sir—there's no justice nor righteousness in it. I wouldn't own a slave if I was rich as Crœsus, which I am not, as is perfectly well understood, especially among my creditors. There's another humbug—the credit system—humbug, sir : no credit, no debt. Credit leads a man into temptation. Cash down is the only thing that will deliver him from evil. But this question of *slavery*: what right have you to your niggers, when you come to the point?"

"What right?" said Epps, laughing; "why I bought 'em and paid for 'em."

"Of course you did: the law says you have the right to hold a nigger ; but begging the law's pardon, it *lies*. Yes, Epps, when the law says that, it's a liar, and the truth is not in it. Is everything right because the law allows it? Suppose they'd pass a law taking away your liberty, and making you a slave?"

"Oh, that ain't a supposable case," said Epps, still laughing; "hope you don't compare me to a nigger, Bass."

" Well, no, not exactly," answered Bass very gravely. "But I have seen niggers before now as good as I am, and I have no acquaintance with any white man in these parts that I consider better than myself. Now, in the sight of God, Epps, what is the difference between a white man and a black one ? "

" All the difference in the world," replied Epps. " You might as well ask what is the difference between a white man and a baboon. Now, I've seen one of them critters in Orleans that know'd just as much as any nigger I've got. You'd call them fellow-citizens, I s'pose ? " And Epps indulged in a loud laugh at his own wit.

" Look here, Epps," continued his companion ; " you can't laugh me down in that way. Some men are witty, and some ain't so witty as they think they are. Now, let me ask you a question. Are all men created free and equal, as the Declaration of Independence holds they are ? "

" Yes," responded Epps, " all men, but niggers and monkeys *ain't*." And here he broke forth into a more loud and boisterous laugh than before.

" There are monkeys among white people as well as black, if you come to that ; " coolly remarked Bass. " I know some white men who use arguments no sensible monkey would. But let that pass. These niggers are human beings. If they don't know as much as their masters, whose fault is it ? They are not *allowed* to know anything. You have books and papers and can go where you please, and gather intelligence in a thousand ways ; but your slaves have no privileges. You'd whip one of them if you caught him reading a book. They are held in bondage, generation after generation, deprived of mental improvement ; and who can expect them to possess much knowledge ? If they are not brought down to a level with the brute creation, you slave-holders will never be blamed for it. If they are baboons, or stand no higher in the scale of intelligence than such animals, you and men like you will have to answer for it. There's a sin—a fearful sin—resting on this nation that will not go unpunished for ever. There'll be a reckoning yet. Yes, Epps, there's a day coming that will burn as an oven. It may be sooner or it may be later, but it's coming as sure as the Lord is just."

" If you lived up among the Yankees in New England," said Epps, " I expect you'd be one of those cursed fanatics that know more than the Constitution, and go about peddling clocks and coaxing niggers to run away."

" If I was in New England," returned Bass, " I should be just what I am here. I would say that slavery is an iniquity, and ought to be abolished. I would say there is no reason nor justice in the law, or the Constitution, that allows one man to hold another man in bondage. It would be hard for you to lose your property to be sure, but it wouldn't be half as hard as it would be to lose your liberty. You have no more right to your freedom, in exact justice, than Uncle Abram yonder. Talk about black skin and black blood ! Why, how many slaves are there on this Bayou as white as either of us ?   And what difference is there in the colour of the soul ?   Pshaw ! The whole system is as absurd as it is cruel.   You may own niggers and be hanged ; but I wouldn't own one for the best plantation in Louisiana."

" You like to hear yourself talk, Bass," said Epps, " better than any man I know of.   You would argue that black was white, or white black, if anybody would contradict you.   Nothing suits you in this world ; and I don't believe you'll be satisfied with the next if you should have your choice about it."

Solomon heard several discussions between these two disputants on similar topics.   Epps evidently regarded Bass as a man ready to say anything, merely for the pleasure of hearing his own voice. He looked upon him as vain and self-conceited, contending against his own faith and judgment in order to exhibit his skill and dexterity in argument.   Epps therefore frequently introduced such subjects with the view of drawing Bass out, that he might enjoy a laugh at his expense.

Bass remained at Epps' all through the summer, generally visiting Markesville once a fortnight. These conversations with Epps, which Solomon overheard, awakened the thought in his mind that possibly Bass might prove to be the friend whose help he so greatly needed.   And the more he saw of him, the more he became convinced that he was a man in whom he might safely confide.   But his previous ill-fortune disposed him to be very cautious. It was not his place to speak to a white man, except when he was spoken to ; but he omitted no opportunity of throwing himself in Bass's way, and endeavoured all he could to attract his attention. It so happened that, in the early part of August, Solomon and Bass were at work in the new house by themselves ; all the other carpenters having left, and Epps being absent in the field. Now, if ever, was the time, Solomon thought, to broach the subject that filled his mind above all others ; and he resolved to do it whatever consequences might ensue. They were busily at work in the afternoon, when Solomon stopped and said :—

" Master Bass, I want to ask you what part of the country you came from ? "

" Why Platt, what put that into your head ? " he answered, " you wouldn't know if I should tell you." After a moment or two he added—" I was born in Canada ; now guess where that is."

" Oh," said Solomon, " I know where Canada is : I've been there."

" Yes ? " Laughing incredulously, Bass remarked, " I expect you are well acquainted all through that country."

" As sure as I live, Master Bass," Solomon earnestly replied, " I have been there. I have been in Montreal, and Kingston, and Queenston, and a great many places in Canada. And I have been in York State too—in Buffalo, and Rochester, and Albany, and can tell you the names of the villages on the Erie Canal, and the Champlain Canal."

Bass turned round and gazed at Solomon for some time without uttering a word.

" How came you here ? " he inquired at length.

" Master Bass," Solomon replied, " if Justice had been done I never should have been here."

" Well, how's this ? " said Bass. " Who are you ? You've been in Canada sure enough, I know all the places you mention. How did you happen to get here. Tell me all about it."

" I have no friends here that I can put confidence in," was Solomon's reply. " I am afraid to tell you ; though I don't believe you'd tell Master Epps, if I did."

Bass assured Solomon that he would keep every word a profound secret, and showed that his curiosity was strongly excited. Solomon told him it was a long story, and it would take him some time to relate it. Master Epps would soon be back ; but if he (Bass), would see him that night after all were asleep, he would then repeat it to him. Bass readily consented to the proposed arrangement, and directed Solomon to come to the building where they were at work, and he would be waiting to meet him. About midnight, when all was still and quiet, the anxious slave crept cautiously from his cabin, silently entered the unfinished building, and found his friend already there.

After further earnest assurances on Bass's part that Solomon's confidence should not be betrayed, he entered upon a full history of his life and misfortunes. Bass was deeply interested, and asked numerous questions in reference to localities and circumstances. Having ended his narrative, and seeing that his auditor was profoundly interested, Solomon earnestly besought Bass to write to some of his friends in the North, acquainting them with his situation, and begging them to forward to him free papers, or to take such other steps as they might consider proper and necessary to secure his release. Bass promised to do so, but dwelt upon the danger to which such an act would expose him in case of detection; and in his turn impressed upon the other the necessity of the strictest silence and secresy. Before they parted, their plan of operation was agreed upon.

They arranged to meet each other the following night at a specified place among the high weeds on the banks of the bayou, at some distance from the master's dwelling. There Bass was to write down on paper the names and addresses of several parties, old friends of Solomon in the North; and he was to direct letters to them during his next visit to Markesville. It was not considered prudent to meet in the new house, lest the light it would be necessary to use should arrest attention and lead to discovery. In the course of the day Solomon managed, unperceived, to obtain a few matches and a piece of candle from the kitchen during the temporary absence of Aunt Phœbe. Bass had paper and pencil at hand in his tool-chest.

At the appointed hour they met on the bank of the bayou; and creeping among the tall reeds they lighted the candle, and Bass produced the paper and pencil he had prepared for the occasion. Solomon gave him the names of Cephas Parker, William Perry, and Judge Marvin, all of Saratoga Springs, Saratoga

County, New York State. With the latter he had been employed at the United States Hotel, and with the other two he had often transacted business to a considerable extent. He trusted that at least one of them would still be living at that place and would remember him. Bass carefully wrote down the names, and then thoughtfully remarked :—

" It is so many years since you left Saratoga, all these men may be dead, or may have removed elsewhere. You say you obtained papers at the Custom House in New York. Probably there is a record of them there, and I think it would be well to write and ascertain."

Solomon agreed with him, and again repeated the circumstances connected with his visit to the Custom House with Brown and Hamilton. They lingered an hour or more on the bayou, conversing on the subject now engrossing their thoughts. He could no longer doubt the fidelity of his companion, and spoke to him freely on the many sorrows he had borne so long. He spoke of his wife and children, mentioning their names and ages, and dwelling on the unspeakable happiness it would afford him to clasp these loved ones once more to his heart. Catching Bass by the hand, with tears and passionate entreaties he implored him to befriend him—to restore him to his kindred and to liberty—promising that he would never cease to urge his prayers to Heaven for his benefactor, that he might be blessed and prospered in all his ways.

He assured Solomon most solemnly that he would be his faithful friend, observing that he had never met with one before in whose welfare he took so deep an interest. He spoke of himself in a somewhat mournful tone as a lonely man—a wanderer about the world without ties or kindred. He said that he was now growing old, and must soon reach the end of his earthly journey and lie down in the dust without a human being to mourn for him, or to remember him. His life, he observed, was of little value to himself, and henceforth should be devoted to the accomplishment of Solomon's liberty, and to an unceasing warfare against the accursed evils of slavery.

After this time Solomon and Bass seldom spoke to or appeared to recognize each other. Bass was, moreover, less free in his conversation on the subject of slavery. The slightest suspicion that there was any unusual intimacy—any secret understanding between them—never once entered the mind of Epps, or any other person on the plantation.

Solomon was often asked, with an air of incredulity, how he could succeed through so many years in keeping from his daily and constant companions the knowledge of his true name and history? The terrible lesson which Burch had taught him, at Washington, had made an indelible impression on his mind concerning the danger and uselessness of asserting his claim to freedom. There was no possibility of any slave assisting him, but there was a possibility of his exposing him. For twelve years the whole current of his thoughts constantly turned to the contemplation of escape; and that caused him to be always cautious and on his guard. It would have been an act of folly, he justly thought, to proclaim his right to freedom; for that would only have caused him to be subjected to the severest surveillance; probably have consigned him to some more distant and inaccessible region than Bayou Bœuf. Epps was a person utterly regardless of a black man's rights or wrongs, and utterly destitute of any sense of justice, as Solomon very well knew. It was important, therefore, not only as regarded his hope of deliverance, but also for the sake of the few personal privileges he was permitted to enjoy, that Solomon should keep from him the history of his life.

On the Saturday night following this nocturnal interview on the Bayou bank, Bass went home to Markesville. The next day, being Sunday, he employed himself in his own room writing letters. One he directed to the Collector of Customs at New York, another to Judge Marvin, and another to Messrs. Parker and Perry jointly. The latter was the one which led to the happy result of Solomon's liberation. It was written in Solomon's name, his true name being affixed: but in a postcript it was stated that Solomon was not the writer. The letter shows that Bass considered himself engaged in a dangerous undertaking.

"BAYOU BŒUF, *August 15th*, 1852.

"Mr. WILLIAM PERRY, or Mr. CEPHAS PARKER.

"Gentlemen,—It having been a long time since I have seen or heard from you, and not knowing that you are living, it is with uncertainty that I write to you, but the necessity of the case must be my excuse.

" Having been born free just across the river from you, I am certain you must know me, and I am here now a slave. I wish you to obtain free papers for me, and forward them to me at Markesville, Louisiana, Parish of Avoyelles, and oblige,

"Yours, SOLOMON NORTHUP.

" The way I came to be a slave, I was taken sick in Washington City, and was insensible for some time. When I recovered my reason, I was robbed of my free papers, and in irons on my way to this State, and have never been able to get any one to write for me until now; and he that is writing for me runs the risk of life if detected."

When Bass returned from Markesville, he told Solomon what he had done. They continued their midnight consultations occasionally ; but they never spoke to each other by day, except as it was necessary concerning the work they were engaged upon. As nearly as he was able to ascertain, Bass told him, it would require about two weeks for the letter to reach Saratoga, and the same length of time for the answer to return. Within six weeks, they concluded, the answer would arrive if it came at all. A great many suggestions were now made, and much conversation took place between the two conspirators, as to the most safe and proper course to pursue on the arrival of the free papers. They would stand between Bass and harm, and screen him in case the two were overtaken and arrested when leaving the country together ; which they inclined to as the most feasible plan. It would be no infringement of the law, however much it might provoke individual hostility, to assist a free man to regain the freedom of which he had been unjustly deprived.

At the end of four weeks Bass was again at Markesville, but no answer had come. Solomon was grieviously disappointed, but consoled himself with the thought that a sufficient length of time had not elapsed; that there might be delays; and that he could not reasonably expect a reply so soon. Six, seven, eight, ten weeks passed by, and still nothing came. Solomon was in a fever of suspense and anxiety whenever Bass visited Markesville, and could scarcely close his eyes to sleep until his return. Finally, Epps' new house was finished, and the time came when Bass must leave. The night before his departure Solomon was wholly given up to despair. He had clung to Bass as the drowning man clings to the floating spar, knowing that if it slipped from his grasp, he must sink for ever beneath the waves. The all-sustaining hope to which he had clung so eagerly was crumbling and passing away. He felt as if he were sinking down, down, into slavery's bitter, loathsome waters, from whose unfathomable depths he would never rise again.

The generous heart of his friend was touched with pity at the sight of his distress. He endeavoured to cheer him up, promising that he would return the day before Christmas, and if no intelligence was received in the meantime, some further step should be taken to accomplish their design. He exhorted Solomon to keep up his spirits and be hopeful, and to rely on his continued efforts on his behalf; assuring him in most earnest and impressive terms that his liberation should, from that time, be the chief object of his life.

In Bass's absence the time with poor Solomon passed very slowly indeed. He looked forward to Christmas with intense anxiety and impatience, not dreaming that the time of his redemption was so nigh as it turned out to be. He had almost given up the expectation of receiving any answer at all to his letters. All sorts of thoughts presented themselves to his mind. The letters might have miscarried, or might possibly have been misdirected. Perhaps those at Saratoga to whom they had been addressed were all dead; or perhaps, engaged in their own affairs, they did not consider the fate of an obscure, unhappy black man of sufficient importance to engage their attention. His sole reliance was upon Bass. The confidence with which he had inspired Solomon continually reassured him, and enabled him to stand up against the heavy tide of disappointment which had overwhelmed him.

So fully was he absorbed in reflecting on his situation and prospects, that his fellow-labourers in the field observed and remarked upon it. Patsey would ask him if he was sick; and uncle Abram, and Wiley, and Bob, frequently expressed themselves as curious to know what he could be thinking about so steadily. But he evaded all their inquiries, and kept his secret securely locked in his own breast.

Faithful to his word, the day before Christmas just at night-fall Bass rode into the yard.

"How are you," said Epps, shaking him by the hand, "glad to see you." He would not have been *very* glad had he known the real object of his visit.

"Quite well, quite well," answered the visitor. "Had some business out on the bayou, and concluded to call and see you and stay over the night."

Epps directed one of the slaves to take charge of the horse, and with much talk and laughter they passed into the house together ; not, however, until Bass had looked significantly at Solomon, as much as to say "keep dark, we understand each other." It was ten o'clock at night before the labours of the day were finished and Solomon entered his cabin. Uncle Abram and Bob were joint occupants with him. He lay down upon his board, and feigned to be asleep until his companions were enwrapped in profound slumber. He then moved stealthily out of the door, and watched and listened attentively for some sign or sound from Bass. There he stood until long after midnight, but nothing could be heard or seen. It was as Solomon suspected ; Bass was fearful of leaving the house, lest he should awaken the suspicions of some of the family. He would probably rise earlier than was his custom, and take the opportunity of seeing his slave-friend before Epps was stirring. Accordingly, Solomon aroused uncle Abram an hour sooner than usual and sent him into the house to build a fire, which at that season of the year was a part of the old man's duties.

He also gave Bob a violent shake, and asked him if he intended to sleep till noon, saying, "Master

will be up, if you don't take care, before the mules
are fed. He knew very well the consequences that
would follow such a breach of duty, and jumping to
his feet was at the horse pasture in a very few
minutes.

Presently, when both were gone, Bass slipped into
the cabin.

"No letter yet, Platt," said he. The announcement fell upon poor Solomon's heart like lead.

"Oh, *do* write again, Master Bass," Solomon cried
in anguish. I will give you the names of a great
many I know. Surely they are not all dead. Surely
some one will pity me."

"No use," Bass replied, "no use. I have made
up my mind to that. I fear the Markesville post-
master will mistrust something. I have inquired so
often at his office. It is too uncertain—too dangerous."

"Then it is all over," exclaimed Solomon. "Oh,
my God, how can I end my days here?"

"You're not going to end them here," Bass said,
"unless you die very soon. I've thought this matter
carefully over, and have come to a determination
which I think you will approve. There are more
ways than one to manage this business, and a better
and surer way than writing letters. I have a job or
two on hand, which can be completed by March or
April. By that time I shall have a considerable
sum of money ; and then, Platt, I am going to Saratoga myself."

Solomon could scarcely trust his own senses as

U

the words fell from the lips of this true and faithful friend. But Bass assured him, in a manner that left no doubt of the sincerity of his intentions, that if his life were spared until the spring he should most certainly undertake the journey, for his heart was set on effecting his deliverance.

" I have lived in this region long enough," Bass continued. " I may as well be in one place as another. For a long time I have been thinking of going back once more to the place where I was born. I'm tired of slavery as well as you. If I can succeed in getting you away from here it will be a good act, that I shall like to think of all my life. And I shall succeed, Platt ! I'm bound to do it. Now let me tell you what I want. Epps will be up soon, and it won't do to be caught here. Think of a great many men at Saratoga and Sandy Hill, and in that neigh- bourhood, who once knew you. I shall make an excuse to come here again in the course of the winter, when I will write down their names. I shall then know who to call upon when I go North. Think of all you can. Cheer up ! Don't be discouraged. I'm with you, life or death, Good bye. God bless you." Saying this he left the cabin quickly and entered the Great House.

It was Christmas morning—the happiest day in the whole year for the slave. On that morning he was not compelled to hurry to the field with his gourd and cotton-bag. Happiness sparkled in the eyes and overspread the countenances of all. The time of feasting and dancing had come. The cane and cotton-fields were deserted. That day the clean dress was to be donned, and the red ribbon displayed. There were to be re-unions, and joy and laughter, and pleasant hurrying to and fro. It was to be a day of *liberty* among the children of slavery. Therefore they were very happy.

After Breakfast Epps and Bass sauntered about the yard, conversing on the price of cotton and various interesting topics.

"Where do your niggers hold Christmas?" Bass inquired.

"Platt is going to Tanner's to-day. His fiddle is in great demand. They want him at Marshall's on Monday; and Miss Mary McCoy on the old Norwood Plantation writes me a note that she wants him to play for her niggers Tuesday."

"He is rather a smart boy, ain't he?" said Bass. "Come here, Platt," he added, looking at Solomon as he walked up to them as if he had never before specially noticed him.

"Yes," replied Epps, taking hold of his slave's arm and feeling it, "there isn't a bad joint in him. There ain't a boy on the Bayou worth more than he is: perfectly sound and no bad tricks. Uttering a flippant curse, he added, "he isn't like other niggers; don't look like 'em; don't act like 'em. I was offered seventeen hundred dollars for him last week."

"And didn't take it?" Bass inquired, with an air of surprise.

"Take it! No; I stood——clear of it. Why he's a regular genius; can make a plough beam, waggon

U 2

tongue—anything, as well as you can. Marshall wanted to put up one of his niggers agin' him, and raffle for them. But I told him I would see the —— have him first."

"I don't see anything remarkable about him," said Bass.

"Why just feel of him now," Epps rejoined. "You don't very often see a boy put together any closer than he is. He's a thin-skinned cuss, and won't bear as much whipping as some. But he's got the muscle in him, and no mistake."

Bass felt Solomon and turned him about, and made a show of a thorough examination, Epps all the while dwelling on the good points of his chattel. But his visitor seemed after a little while to drop all interest in the subject, and consequently it was dismissed. Bass soon departed, giving Solomon another significant look as he rode off.

When he was gone, Solomon obtained a pass, and started for Tanner's; not the Peter Tanner formerly mentioned, but a relative of his. He played during the day and most of the night, spending the next day, Sunday, in his cabin. On Monday he crossed the bayou to Douglas Marshall's; all Epps' slaves accompanying him thither. On Tuesday he went to the old Norwood place, where as at the other plantations his violin was in requisition.

This plantation was owned by a Miss Mary McCoy, of whom Solomon gave a very interesting and pleasing account. "Miss McCoy was a lovely girl, some twenty years of age, and the beauty and glory of Bayou Bœuf. She was the owner of about a hundred working hands, besides a great many house servants, yard boys, and young children. Her brother-in-law, residing on the adjoining estate, was her general agent. She was beloved by all her slaves, and good reason they had to be thankful that they had fallen into such gentle hands. Nowhere on the Bayou were there such feasts—such merry-makings—as at young Madame McCoy's. Thither, more than to any other place, did the old and young for miles around love to repair in the time of the Christmas holidays; for nowhere else could they find such delicious repasts, nowhere else could they hear a voice speaking to them so pleasantly. No one was so well beloved; no one filled so large a space in the hearts of thousands of slaves as young Madame McCoy, the orphan mistress of the old Norwood estate.

" On my arrival at her place, I found two or three hundred assembled. The table was prepared in a long building which she had erected expressly for her slaves to dance in. It was covered with every variety of food which the country afforded, and was pronounced by general acclamation to be the rarest of dinners. Roast turkey, pig, chicken, duck, and all kinds of meat, baked, boiled, and broiled, formed a line the whole length of the extended table; while the vacant spaces were filled with tarts. jellies, frosted cakes, and pastry of all kinds. The young mistress walked around the table smiling upon her guests, and saying a kind word to each one, and seemed to enjoy the scene exceedingly.

" When the dinner was over, the tables were removed to make room for the dancers. I tuned my violin and struck up a lively air. While some joined in a nimble reel, others sang their simple but melo-, dious songs, filling the great room with the sound of voices and the clattering of feet.

" In the evening the mistress returned and stood in the doorway a long time looking at us. She was magnificently arrayed. Her dark hair and eyes contrasted strongly with her clear and delicate complexion. Her form was slender but commanding, and her movements were a combination of unaffected dignity and grace. As she stood there clad in her rich apparel, her face animated with pleasure, I thought I had never looked upon a human being half so beautiful. I dwell with delight upon the description of this fair and gentle lady, not only because she inspired me with emotions of gratitude and admiration, but because I would have it understood that all the slave-owners on Bayou Bœuf are not like Epps, or Tibeats, or Jim Burns. Occasionally can be found, rarely it may be indeed, a good man like William Ford, or an angel of kindness like young Mistress McCoy."

Tuesday concluded the three holidays Epps yearly allowed his slaves, and Solomon had to return to the plantation to commence as he supposed another year of misery and unrequited toil. On his way home on Wednesday morning early, he was hailed as he passed the plantation of Mr. William Pierce by the owner of the place, and informed that he, Pierce, had

a note from Epps authorizing him to detain Solomon
for the purpose of playing for his slaves that night.
Solomon accordingly turned into the plantation and
performed his part in the hilarities of the occasion;
into which, however, he had scarcely heart to enter,
oppressed as he was with a painful sense of disappointment that the letters written by Bass had led
to none of the results he had fondly anticipated.
The party continued their jollification until broad
daylight, when Solomon returned to his master's
estate, wearied with the loss of rest, but rejoicing in
the possession of a goodly number of silver bits and
picayunes, which the whites who were pleased with
his musical performances had bestowed upon him.
His rejoicings would have been largely augmented
had he been aware that it was the last time he was
destined to witness a slave dance on the shores of
Bayou Bœuf!

On Saturday that week Solomon was favoured
with the last whipping he was ever to receive at the
hands of his owner. Wearied out with travelling
and gaiety and loss of rest, he for the first time in
many years overslept the usual hour of rising. He
was frightened, on coming out of his cabin, to find
that the slaves were already in the field, and that he
was fifteen minutes behind them. He hurried after
them as fast as he could move. It was not yet sunrise, but Epps was on the piazza as he left the hut,
and cried out—" A pretty time of day this isn't it for
you to be getting up ? " By extra exertion Solomon's
row was up with the others when the master came

out after breakfast. But this was no excuse for the offence of sleeping too late, and he was bidden to strip and lie down. He obeyed and received about fifteen lashes; at the conclusion of which Epps inquired if he thought after that that he could get up sometime in the morning? Solomon replied that he was satisfied he could, and with his back stinging with pain went about his work.

The following day, Sunday, he was much depressed and discouraged. He thought of Bass and the probabilities and hopes which centred in him. If Bass should die how completely would all his hopes of freedom and restoration to his family be cut off! His sore back did not tend to lessen the gloom which rested upon his mind; and after feeling downcast and unhappy all the day, he laid him down upon his hard board at night with a heart oppressed with such a load of grief it seemed as though it must break. But the night is often darkest just before the dawn. How different would have been his feelings could he have known that there was one close at hand coming to release him from his bondage, and that wretched Sabbath day was to be the last day he should spend in slavery!

CHAPTER XVII.

The Rescue.

ONDAY, January 3rd, 1853, was destined to be a red-letter day in Solomon's history. It was to be the day of his deliverance though he knew it not. He, with the other slaves, was in the field betimes, his heart still heavy with grief and disappointment. It was a raw cold morning, such as is very unusual in that Southern region. Solomon was in advance, Uncle Abram next to him, then Bob, Patsey, and Wiley, and all had their cotton bags about their necks. Epps was early in the field; but he happened that morning, a rare thing with him, to come out without his whip. "He swore," as Solomon said, "in a manner that would shame a pirate," that they were doing nothing. Bob ventured to say that his fingers were "so numb with cold he couldn't pick fast." Epps cursed him in reply, and then cursed himself for not having brought his raw hide, and swore that when he came out again he would warm them to some purpose. Yes, he would make them all hotter than —— that fiery realm in which if the Scriptures speak truth all blasphemers like himself will eventually have their portion.

With his mouth full of cursing and imprecations he left the working slaves. As soon as he was out of hearing they commenced talking to each other, saying how hard it was to be compelled to keep up their tasks with fingers benumbed and disabled by cold; how unreasonable the Master was, and speaking of him generally in no very flattering terms. This conversation was suddenly interrupted by a carriage passing them rapidly in the direction of the Great House. A few minutes afterwards they were further surprised by seeing two strangers coming towards them through the cotton-field. The long looked-for hour of deliverance had come to poor Solomon; for these were the men, thus suddenly breaking in upon the astonished slaves, who had come armed with authority to rescue the kidnapped slave from bondage and wrong, and restore him to the embraces of his wife and children.

The letter written by Bass directed to Parker and Perry, and deposited in the Post office in Markesville on the 15th August, 1852, had reached its destination and done its work. It arrived at Saratoga in the early part of September. Some time previous to this Anne, Solomon's wife, had removed to Glen's Falls, Warren County, where she had charge of the kitchen in Carpenter's Hotel. She still, however, kept her own house for herself and the children, from whom she was absent only at such times as her duties at the hotel required.

On receipt of the letter Messrs. Parker and Perry forwarded it immediately to Anne. Great was the excitement it produced in the family; and Anne and the children hastened with the letter to the neighbouring village of Sandy Hill to consult Henry B. Northup, and obtain his advice and assistance in the matter.

That gentleman at once entered into the case with lively interest. Being of the legal profession he began to search his books, and discovered among the Statutes of the State just what was required—an Act providing for the recovery of free citizens from slavery. It was passed May 14th, 1840, and entituled " An Act more effectually to protect the free citizens of this State (New York) from being kidnapped or reduced to slavery." This Act made it the duty of the Governor, upon the receipt of satisfactory information that any free citizen, or inhabitant of the State, was wrongfully held in another State or Territory of the United States, upon the allegation or pretence that such person was a slave, or by colour of any usage or rule of law was deemed or taken to be a slave, to take such measures to procure the restoration of such person to liberty, as he should consider necessary.

To that end the Act authorized the Governor to appoint and employ an agent, and directed him to furnish such agent with all such credentials and instructions as would be likely to accomplish the object of his appointment. It required the agent so appointed to proceed to collect the proofs necessary to establish the right of such person to his freedom, to perform such journeys, take such measures, institute such legal proceedings, &c., as might be necessary to return such enslaved person to the State to which he belonged ; and directed further that all charges and expenses incurred in carrying the act into effect, should be paid out of moneys not otherwise appropriated in the Treasury of the State.

It was necessary to establish two facts to the satisfaction of the governor before his interference could be counted upon. First, that Solomon was a free citizen of New York State ; and secondly, that he was wrongfully held in bondage. As to the first point, there was no difficulty ; all the older inhabitants in the vicinity being ready to testify to it. The second point rested entirely upon the letter to Parker and Perry written in an unknown hand, and upon the letter penned on board the brig *Orleans*, which unfortunately had been mislaid or lost, as many years had passed since it was received.

A memorial directed to Governor Hunt was prepared on behalf of Anne, Solomon's wife, setting forth her marriage ; Solomon's departure to Washington City ; the receipt of the two letters ; that Solomon was a free citizen ; and such other facts as were deemed important. This was signed and attested by Anne ; and accompanying it were several affidavits of prominent citizens of Sandy Hill and Fort Edward corroborating the statements it contained ; and also a request of several well-known gentlemen to the Governor, that Henry B. Northup should be appointed agent in the case under the Act.

On reading over the memorial and affidavits his Excellency the Governor took a lively interest in the matter; and on the 23rd day of November, 1852, under the Seal of the State, he "constituted, appointed, and employed Henry B. Northup, Esq. an agent, with full power to effect the restoration of the said Solomon Northup to his freedom," and to take all such measures as would be most likely to accomplish that object; also instructing him " to proceed to Louisiana with all convenient despatch."

Mr. Northup's professional engagements delayed his departure until December. On the 14th of that month he left Sandy Hill and proceeded to Washington. There he laid the case before the Hon. Pierce Soule, Senator in Congress from Louisiana, Hon. Mr. Conrad, Secretary of War, and Judge Nelson, of the Supreme Court of the United States. Upon hearing a statement of the facts, and examining his commission and certified copies of the memorial and affidavits which had been laid before the Governor of New York State, these gentlemen furnished Mr. Northup with open letters to other gentlemen in Louisiana, strongly urging them to afford their assistance in accomplishing the object of his appointment.

Senator Soule especially interested himself in the matter, insisting that it was the duty and interest of every planter in his State to aid in restoring Solomon to freedom ; and trusted that sentiments of honour and justice in the bosom of every citizen in the Commonwealth would enlist him at once in behalf of the kidnapped man. Having obtained these valuable letters, Mr. Northup proceeded at once to Pittsburgh, to take his journey down the Ohio and Mississippi. It was his first intention to go directly to New Orleans, and consult the authorities of that city. But on arriving at the mouth of the Red River, he changed his mind. And it was providential that he did so ; for had he gone on to New Orleans he would not have met with Bass, who ultimately rendered the most important service in the case ; and the search for Solomon, concealed as he was under a false name, would probably have been fruitless.

Taking passage on the first steamer that arrived, Mr. Northup pursued his journey up the sluggish, winding stream of the Red River, flowing through a vast region of primitive forests and impenetrable swamps almost destitute of human inhabitants. Arriving at Markesville at 9 A.M. January 1st, he left the steamboat at that town and proceeded directly to Marksville Court House, a small village four miles in the interior.

From the fact that the letter addressed to Messrs. Parker and Perry was post-marked at Markesville, it was inferred that Solomon must be in that place, or its immediate vicinity. On reaching that town Mr. Northup at once laid his business before the Hon. John P. Waddill, a legal gentleman who was eminent in the profession, and a man of fine genius and noble impulses. After reading the various documents and inquiring into the circumstances under which Solomon had been betrayed into captivity, as far as Mr. Northup was acquainted with them, Mr. Waddill at once proffered his services, and entered into the business with great zeal and earnestness. He, in common with all men of character and humanity, regarded the kidnapper with abhorrence. He well understood the importance to all interested in slave property of a valid title, and the observance of good faith in all sales and transfers of such property. He was well aware how the sale of a kidnapped man was calculated to weaken confidence in the integrity of all such transactions; moreover, he was a man of honour, in whose heart emotions of indignation were aroused by the cruelty and injustice which such a case as that of Solomon involved.

Solomon Northup was a name Mr. Waddill had never heard of, but he was confident that if there was a slave bearing that appellation in Markesville or its vicinity, his black boy Tom, would know him. Tom was called in, but in all his extensive circle of acquaintance there was no such person. No wonder! for Solomon in all that region had been known only by the name of "Platt," and his own proper name had been carefully concealed.

The letter to Parker and Perry was dated at Bayou Bœuf. At this place, therefore, it was concluded Solomon must be sought. But here a difficulty suggested itself of a very grave character. Bayou Bœuf, at its nearest point, was twenty-three miles distant from Markesville Court House, and was the name applied to a section of country extending between fifty and a hundred miles on both sides of that stream. Thousands and thousands of slaves resided upon its shores, the remarkable richness and fertility of the

soil having attracted thither a great number of planters.   The information conveyed in the letter was so
vague and indefinite, as to render it difficult to con-
clude upon any specific course of procedure.   It was
finally determined, as the only plan that presented
any prospect of success, that Mr. Northup and the
brother of Mr. Waddill, who was a student in his
office, should repair to the Bayou, and travelling up
one side and down the other its whole length, inquire
for Solomon at each plantation.   Mr. Waddill offered
the use of his carriage, and it was definitely arranged
that they should start upon the excursion early on
Monday morning.

Had this course been pursued it is almost certain
that it would have resulted unsuccessfully.   It would
have been impracticable for them to go into the fields
and examine all the gangs at work.   They were not
aware that the person they sought was known only as
" Platt ; " and had they inquired of Epps himself, he
would have stated truly that he knew nothing of
Solomon Northup.

The arrangement being concluded, there was
nothing further to be done until the Sabbath had
passed by.   The conversation between Mr. Northup
and the lawyer Waddill in the course of the afternoon
turned upon New York politics.

" I can scarcely comprehend the nice distinctions
and shades of political parties in your State," observed
Mr. Waddill.   " I read of soft-shells and hard-shells,
hunkers and barn-burners, woolly-heads and silver-
greys, and am unable to understand the precise difference between them.   Pray, what is it ? "

Mr. Northup refilled his pipe, and entered into quite an elaborate narrative of the origin of these various sections of parties; and concluded by saying there was another party in New York known as "free-soilers," or "abolitionists." "You have seen none of those in this part of the country, I presume?" Mr. Northup remarked.

"Never, but one," answered Waddill with a laugh. "We have one here in Markesville, an eccentric creature who preaches abolitionism as vehemently as any fanatic at the North. He is a generous, inoffensive man, but always maintaining the wrong side of an argument. It affords us a great deal of amusement. He is an excellent mechanic, and almost indispensable in this community. He is a carpenter. His name is Bass."

Some further pleasant conversation was carried on concerning Bass's peculiarities; when, all at once Mr. Waddill fell into a very reflective mood, and after awhile requested to see that mysterious letter again.

It was handed to him. "Let me see—let me see!" he repeated thoughtfully to himself, running his eyes over the letter once more, "Bayou Bœuf, August 15th, August 15th—post-marked here. 'He that is writing for me——.' "Where did Bass work last summer?" he inquired, turning round suddenly to his brother. His brother was unable to inform him, but said he could soon find out. Rising from his seat he left the office, and soon returned with the intelligence that "Bass worked last summer somewhere on the Bayou Bœuf."

X

acquaintance with the kidnapped man, and listened with eager curiosity to the account which Mr. Northup gave of Solomon's family, and the history of his early life. Before they separated, Bass drew a map of the Bayou on a strip of paper with a piece of red chalk, showing the locality of Epps' plantation, and the road leading most directly to it.

Mr. Northup and his young companion returned to Markesville, where it was determined to commence legal proceedings to test the question of Solomon's right to freedom. He was made plaintiff, Mr. Northup acting as his guardian, and Edwin Epps, defendant. The process to be issued was in the nature of replevin, directed to the Sheriff of the parish, commanding him to take Solomon into custody and detain him until the decision of the Court was obtained. By the time the papers were duly drawn up it was twelve o'clock, Saturday night—too late to obtain the necessary signature of the Judge, who resided some distance out of town. Further business was, therefore, suspended until Monday morning.

Everything, apparently, was moving along as favourably as could be desired, until Sunday afternoon, when Waddill called at Northup's room to express his apprehension of difficulties they had not expected to encounter. Bass had become alarmed, and had placed his affairs in the hands of a person at the landing, communicating to him his intention of leaving the State. This person had betrayed the confidence reposed in him to a certain extent, and a rumour began to float about the town that the stranger at the hotel, who had been observed in the company of lawyer Waddill, was after one of old Epps' slaves, over on the bayou. Epps was known at Markesville, having frequent occasion to visit that place during the sessions of the Courts ; and the fear entertained by Mr. Northup's adviser was, that intelligence would be conveyed to him in the night, giving him an opportunity of secreting Solomon before the arrival of the Sheriff.

This apprehension had the effect of expediting matters considerably. The Sheriff, who lived at a little distance from the village, was requested to hold himself in readiness to travel immediately after midnight, while the Judge was informed that he would be called upon at the same time. It is just to say that the authorities at Markesville cheerfully rendered all the assistance in their power.

As soon after midnight as bail could be perfected and the Judge's signature obtained, a carriage containing Mr. Northup and the Sheriff, driven by the landlord's son, rolled rapidly out of the village of Markesville in the direction of Bayou Bœuf.

It was supposed that Epps would strongly contest the issue involving Solomon's right to liberty ; and it therefore suggested itself to Mr. Northup that the testimony of the Sheriff, describing his first meeting with Solomon, might perhaps become material on the trial. It was accordingly arranged during the ride that, before Solomon could have an opportunity of speaking to Mr. Northup, the Sheriff should put certain questions to him which were agreed upon, relating to the name of his wife, the number and names of his children, the name of his wife before their marriage, the places he knew at the North, &c., &c. If Solomon's answers corresponded with the statements already given to the Sheriff, the evidence must necessarily be considered conclusive.

Shortly after Epps had left the field where his slaves were at work, with the consoling assurance that " he would return very soon and warm them to some purpose," after his own favourite method of doing such things, Mr. Northup and the Sheriff came in sight of the plantation and discovered the slaves at work. They alighted from the carriage and directed the driver to proceed to the Great House, with instructions not to mention to any one the object of their visit until they should meet him again. The two late occupants of the carriage then turned from the highway, and directed their course across the cotton-field to the spot where the gang of slaves were busy at their work, in momentary expectation of feeling Epps' raw-hide upon their naked backs.

The slaves looked up from their toil in amazement; for it was a singular and unusual thing to see white men approaching them in that manner, and especially at so early an hour in the morning. Uncle Abram and Patsey made some remarks expressive of their astonishment. The Sheriff was several yards in advance of his companion, as had been previously arranged. Walking up to Bob, he inquired:—

" Where is the boy they call Platt?"

" Thar he is, massa," answered Bob, twitching off his hat, and pointing to Solomon.

Solomon wondered in himself what business the gentleman could possibly have with him when he heard himself thus inquired for, and turning round gazed at the stranger until he approached within a step. During his long residence on the bayou, he had become familar with the face of every planter within many miles; but this was a face he had never seen before—the gentleman was a stranger.

" Your name is Platt, is it ? " he inquired.

" Yes, massa," Solomon responded.

Pointing towards Mr. Northup, who was standing a few rods distant, he demanded, " Do you know that man ? "

Solomon looked in the direction indicated, and as his eye rested on the features of the stranger, a world of images rushed upon and thronged his brain; a multitude of well-remembered faces, Anne's, and the dear children's, and his old dead father's. All the scenes and associations of childhood and youth; all the friends of other and happier days appeared and disappeared, flitting like dissolving pictures before his mind, until after a few moments the perfect remembrance of the man before him recurred to him. Then, throwing up his hands towards Heaven, with a feeling of ecstacy, he exclaimed in loud, thrilling tones :—

" *Henry B. Northup!* " Thank God! Thanks to God! " In an instant he comprehended the nature of the business which had brought the gentlemen there, and felt that the hour of his deliverance was at hand. He started towards Mr. Northup, but the Sheriff stepped before him.

"Stop a moment," said he. "Have you any other name than Platt?"

"Solomon Northup is my name, Master," he replied.

"Have you a family?" the Sheriff continued.

"I *had* a wife and three children."

"What were the names of your children?"

"Elizabeth, Margaret, and Alonzo."

"And your wife's name before her marriage?"

"Anne Hampton."

"Who married you?"

"Timothy Eddy, of Fort Edward."

"Where does that gentleman live?" again pointing to Mr. Northup, who remained standing in the same place where Solomon first recognized him.

"He lives at Sandy Hill, Washington County, New York," was the reply.

He was proceeding to ask further questions, but Solomon, unable to restrain himself longer, pushed past him, and seized his old acquaintance by both hands. He could not speak, and big tears of joy and gratitude rolled down his cheeks.

"Sol," Mr. Northup said at length, for he too was deeply affected, "I am glad to see you."

He essayed to make some answer, but his emotions choked his utterance, and he remained silent. The other slaves utterly confounded stood gazing upon the scene, their open mouths and rolling eyes indicating the utmost wonder and astonishment. For more than ten years Solomon had dwelt among them in the field and in the cabin; borne the same hardships; partaken of the same scanty fare; mingled his griefs with theirs; and participated in their seldom-recurring joys. Nevertheless, not until this hour, the last he was to remain among them, had the remotest suspicion of his true name, or the slightest knowledge of his real character and history been entertained by any one of them.

For several minutes not a word was spoken, during which time Solomon clung fast to the hands of Mr. Northup, looking up into his face, fearful that he should awake to find it all a dream.

" Throw down that sack," Mr. Northup at length said, addressing himself to Solomon, " your cotton-picking days are over. Come with us to the man you live with."

He obeyed, and walking between Mr. Northup and the Sheriff, they all moved onwards towards the Great House. It was not until they had gone some distance, that Solomon recovered voice sufficient to ask if his family were all living? Mr. Northup informed him that he had seen Anne, Margaret, and Elizabeth, only a short time before; that Alonzo was still living, and all were well. His mother, however, he could never see again, as during his long absence the old lady had gone to her rest.

When they entered the yard, Epps stood by the gate in conversation with the driver of the carriage. The young man, faithful to the instructions which had been given him, had refused to give him any information concerning the gentlemen and their business, referring him to the gentlemen themselves.

He repeatedly inquired what was going on, but could obtain no satisfactory explanation ; and by the time the party entered the yard, he was almost as much amazed and puzzled as Bob or Uncle Abram had been.

Shaking hands with the Sheriff, whom he knew very well, Epps was introduced to Mr. Northup, whom he invited with the Sheriff to enter the house. At the same time, wondering what could have brought Solomon away from his work, he directed him to go and bring in some wood to build up the fire. It was some time before Solomon could suc-ceed in getting an arm-full, having lost the power of wielding the axe with anything like precision, from the excitement through which he had lately passed.

When he entered with the fuel he saw the table strewed with papers, and Mr. Northup held a paper in his hand from which he was reading. Solomon took more time than was absolutely necessary to place the sticks in order on the fire, and seemed to be unusually particular as to the exact position of every piece ; all the time opening his ears to the utmost to catch what was going on, in which he felt that he was deeply concerned. He heard the words, " the said Solomon Northup," " the deponent further says," and " free citizen of New York State," re-peated frequently ; and from these expressions, he understood that the secret he had so long retained from Master and Mistress Epps was being revealed, to the dismay of his late owner. He lingered in the room as long as prudence permitted, and was in the act of slowly leaving it when Epps stopped him and inquired :—

"Platt, do you know this gentleman ?"

"Yes, Master," he replied, "I have known him as long as I can remember."

"Where does he live ?"

"He lives in New York State."

"Did you ever live there ?"

"Yes, Master, born and bred there."

"You was free then. Now you cursed nigger," he exclaimed, unable to restrain his profane propensities any longer, "why didn't you tell me that when I bought you ?"

"Master Epps," Solomon answered, in a somewhat bolder tone than that in which he had been accustomed to address him, "Master Epps, you did not take the trouble to ask me. Besides, I told one of my owners —the man that kidnapped me—that I was free, and was whipped almost to death for it."

"It seems there has been a letter written for you by somebody. Now, who is it ?" he demanded in an authoritative manner. Solomon made no reply.

"I say, who wrote that letter ?" he demanded again.

"Perhaps I might have written it myself," Solomon remarked.

"You haven't been to Markesville post-office and back before day-light, I know."

He insisted upon Solomon giving the information he desired; and Solomon, no longer afraid of his tyrant master, as firmly insisted upon refusing to give it. Epps gave utterance to many savage threats against the man, whoever he might be, and intimated the dire vengeance he would wreak upon him when he found him out. His whole manner and language exhibited the utmost ferocity towards the unknown person who had 'written on Solomon's behalf, and his deep vexation at the idea of being deprived of such a valuable piece of property— Solomon being by far the best hand in his gang of slaves. His countenance glared with a fiendish expression, and addressing Mr. Northup he swore, " if he had only had an hour's notice of his coming he would have saved him the trouble of carrying Solomon back to New York; for he would have run him into the swamp, or some other place out of the way, where all the Sheriffs on earth couldn't have found him." Thus was made apparent the wisdom of acting so promptly and so cautiously as the Sheriff and Mr. Northup had done in finding and identifying the stolen man.

As Solomon walked out into the yard he encountered Aunt Phœbe. Running up to him, she whispered in his ear with great earnestness in a confidential manner :—

" Lor a'mity, Platt ! what d'ye think ? Dem two men bin come after you. Heard 'em tell Massa you free ; got wife and three children back thar whar you come from. Goin wid dem ? Fool if ye don't —wish I could go," And Aunt Phœbe ran on in this strain at a rapid rate.

Presently Mrs. Epps made her appearance in the

kitchen. She spoke kindly to Solomon, and wondered why he had not told her who he was. She expressed her regret at losing him, saying that she would rather part with any other servant on the plantation. Now Solomon was going, there would be no one left who could mend a chair or a piece of furniture; no one who was of any use about the house; no one who could play for her on the violin; and Mrs. Epps was affected even to tears.

Epps had called to Bob to bring up his saddle-horse. The other slaves, overcoming their fears of the penalty, had left their work and come to the yard. They were standing about behind the cabins, keeping out of sight of Epps. They beckoned Solomon to come to them, and with eager curiosity questioned him as to what was taking place. Their several attitudes and the expression of their countenances, as their slow minds apprehended the truth, would have formed a most interesting picture. In their estimation, Solomon had risen to an immeasureable height above them, and had become a being of immense importance. Platt, a free man! Platt, no longer the slave of Master Epps! It was too wonderful to be true.

The legal papers having been served upon Epps, and arrangements made with him to meet them the next day at Markesville, Mr. Northup and the Sheriff entered the carriage to return to that place. How wonderful was the revolution which the occurrences of an hour or two had made in the condition and prospects of the kidnapped one! All the dark clouds which seemed hopelessly to enshroud his future destiny had been chased away, and that future had been made radiant with hope, and peace, and joy, and the certainty of a speedy restoration to the society of his loved ones, from whom he had been so cruelly separated for many long and suffering years.

Having said " Good-bye " to his fellow-slaves, he was about to mount to the driver's seat, when the Sheriff suggested that he ought to bid " Good-bye " to Master and Mistress Epps. He ran back to the piazza where they were standing, and taking off his hat, said—

" Good-bye, Missis."

" Good-bye, Platt," Mrs. Epps kindly responded.

" Good-bye, Master."

" Ah ! you —— nigger," muttered Epps in a surly, malicious tone of voice, " you needn't feel so cussed tickled. You ain't gone yet. I'll see about this business at Markesville to-morrow."

Solomon felt as if it would have been a relief to his feelings to administer to the surly, ill-conditioned tyrant a parting kick. But feeling that after all he had the best of it, he simply lifted his hat again and bowed, and then returned to the carriage. But on his way, Patsey ran from behind a cabin and threw her arms about his neck.

" Oh ! Platt," she cried, tears streaming down her face, " you're going to be free—you're going way off yonder where we'll nebber see ye any more. You've saved me from a good many whippin's, Platt. I'm glad your going to be free; but, Oh ! de Lord, de good Lord ! What'll become of me ? "

Bidding the poor girl "Good-bye," Solomon mounted the carriage, the driver cracked his whip, and the vehicle rolled away. He turned for a parting look, and saw Patsey with drooping head half reclining on the ground; Mrs. Epps was still on the piazza; Uncle Abram, and Bob, and Wiley, and Aunt Phœbe, stood by the gate gazing after the carriage. He waved his hand, and then the carriage turning round a bend of the bayou these suffering companions of his slave-life vanished from his sight for ever.

The carriage stopped for a short time at Carey's sugar-house, where a great number of slaves were at work, in order that Mr. Northup might look over the sugar-making process, new to him as a Northern man. While they were there Epps dashed by on horseback at full speed, on the way, as Solomon learned the next day, to the Pine Woods to see William Ford, who had brought Solomon to that part of the country.

On the following day, Tuesday, January 4th, Epps and his counsel, the Hon. H. Taylor, Mr. Northup, Waddill, the Judge, and Sheriff of Avoyelles, with Solomon, met at an appointed hour in a room in the village of Markesville. Mr. Northup stated the facts concerning Solomon, and presented his commission with the affidavits accompanying it. The Sheriff then described what had taken place in the field, and Solomon's prompt recognition of Mr. Northup. Next, Solomon was interrogated at great length concerning his former life, and all the circumstances of his kidnapping, until the whole history of his life had been fully drawn out. Epps' lawyer, Mr. Taylor, then turned round to his client, and assured him that he was fully satisfied Solomon's claim to freedom was just, and that all litigation in the case would not only be expensive, but utterly useless.

In accordance with Mr. Taylor's advice, a paper was then drawn up and signed by the proper parties, wherein Epps acknowledged he was satisfied of Solomon's right to freedom, and formally surrendered him to the authorities of New York. It was also agreed that the document should be entered in the Recorder's office of Avoyelles.

Mr. Northup having thus successfully accomplished his business in a much shorter time than he dared to anticipate, immediately hastened to the landing, with Solomon under his care. Taking passage in the first steamer that arrived, they were soon floating down Red River, up which the now rescued slave, with bitterly desponding thoughts, had been borne more than twelve years before. In strict justice, Solomon was entitled to demand a labourer's full wages at the hands of Epps for the ten years' service he had rendered on his plantation. But he was too glad to get away from the horrors of slave-life, and enter upon the happy future that now opened before him, to be concerned about the past. They soon reached the Mississippi—the father of waters—and had but a short time to wait, before a downward-bound steamer appeared and took them on board.

HOME! SWEET HOME!

CHAPTER XVIII.

Home! Sweet Home!

AS the steamer glided swiftly down the broad Mississippi, Solomon's heart leaped within him for joy, and he found it difficult to restrain himself from dancing round the deck. God had heard and answered his prayers for deliverance ; and now, recognized as a free citizen, he was actually on his way to the home he scarcely dared hope that he should ever see again, and the family for whom he had yearned with intense but hopeless desire. How grateful he felt to Mr. Northup, who had come so many hundreds of miles to seek him out in his miserable condition as a slave, and deliver him from the power of the oppressor ! How eagerly did Solomon hasten to light his pipe, and wait and watch his word, and run at his slightest bidding !

Once more Solomon's feet trod the streets of New Orleans, but no longer the wretched captive that he was when he was first brought to that City, with a band of associates as miserable as himself. Mr. Northup tarried there two days, and Solomon pointed out to him the locality of Freeman's slave-pen where he and the others had been confined, and the room in which Ford had purchased him. They happened

Y

to meet Theophilus Freeman in the street, seedy and shabby ; but Solomon did not feel disposed to renew his acquaintance with him.   He learnt from some who knew Freeman that he had become a low, miserable rowdy—a broken-down, ruined, disreputable man. His trade of villainy and cruelty had not prospered.

They visited the Recorder of the City, a Mr. Genois, to whom Senator Soule's letter of introduction was directed, and found him a liberal-minded gentleman, ready to help them in any way that he could.   He furnished them with a sort of legal pass over his own signature and seal of office, to prevent any possible interruption in the Slave States on their way home. The following is a copy of the document ,—

"STATE OF LOUISIANA—CITY OF NEW ORLEANS.

"Recorder's Office, Second District.

" To all to whom these presents shall come :—

" This is to certify that Henry B. Northup, Esquire, of the County of Washington, New York, has produced before me due evidence of the freedom of Solomon, a mulatto man, aged about forty-two years, five feet, seven inches, and six lines, woolly hair, and chestnut eyes, who is a native-born of the State of New York.   That the said Northup, being about bringing the said Solomon to his native place, through the Southern routes, the civil authorities are requested to let the aforesaid coloured man Solomon pass unmolested, he demeaning well and properly.

" Given under my hand and the seal of the City of New Orleans this 7th day of January, 1853.

[L.S.]   " TH. GENOIS, Recorder."

On the following day they started to go North by railway, and in due time arrived at Charleston, following the usual route. Here, as they were about to resume their journey, Mr. Northup was called upon by a Custom-house official to explain why he had not registered his servant, supposing that Solomon as he was coloured must be a slave as a matter of course. Mr. Northup replied that he had no servant; that as the agent of New York State he was accompanying a free citizen of that State from slavery to freedom; and he did not desire or intend to make any registry whatever. He did not admit the right of the Custom-house officials of Charleston, or any other parties, to interfere with him and his travelling companion. He thought it quite sufficient for all purposes to produce the note furnished to him by the Recorder of New Orleans. They were then permitted to proceed, and passing through Richmond, where Solomon caught a glimpse of Goodin's pen, they arrived at Washington, January 17th, 1853.

They ascertained on inquiry that both Burch and Radburn were still residing in that City. Mr. Northup thought that at least an effort should be made to bring these two ruffians to the punishment which they so richly deserved. A complaint was therefore entered, with a police magistrate of Washington, against James H. Burch for kidnapping and selling Solomon into slavery. He was arrested on a warrant issued by Justice Goddard, and returned before one of the Judges, who held him to bail in the sum of three thousand dollars. When first arrested, Burch was much excited and alarmed, exhibiting in his manner the utmost terror. Before reaching the Justice's office on Louisiana Avenue, and before knowing the precise nature of the complaint alleged against him, he begged the police to allow him to consult Benjamin O. Shekels, a slave-trader of many years standing, who had been at one time his partner in the nefarious business.

A partial Court and perjured witnesses enabled the accused man to escape the punishment the law awarded to the crime of which he had been guilty. Men who traffic in human flesh, and make their wealth by cruelty and wrong, are not likely to be very scrupulous about the truth or the sanctity of an oath. Shekels and two or three others came forward and deposed to things that were absolutely false, so as to make the impression on the Court that Burch came honestly by the possession of Solomon, being imposed upon by others. Solomon was not allowed to give his testimony, which would have shown the falsity of these statements. Burch was consequently discharged.

An attempt was then made by Burch and his friends to get up a charge against Solomon for having conspired with two white men to defraud him. The following extract from a New York daily paper shows the result of this movement :—

" The counsel for the defendant (Burch) had, before the defendant was discharged, drawn up an affidavit, which was signed by Burch, and had a warrant out against the coloured man for a con-

spiracy with the two white men before referred to,
(in the false testimony of the witnesses) to defraud
Burch out of six hundred and twenty-five dollars.
The warrant was served, and the coloured man
arrested and brought before Officer Goddard. Burch
and his witnesses appeared in court, and H. B.
Northup appeared as counsel for the coloured man,
stating that he was ready to proceed as counsel on
behalf of the defendant, and asking no delay whatever. Burch, after consulting privately with Shekels,
then stated to the magistrate that he wished him to
dismiss the complaint, as he would not proceed
further with it. Defendant's counsel stated to the
magistrate that if the complaint was withdrawn, it
must be without the request or the consent of the
defendant. Burch then asked the magistrate to let
him have the complaint and the warrant. Mr.
Northup objected to his receiving them, and insisted
they should remain as part of the records of the
Court, and that the Court should endorse the proceedings which had been had under the process.
Burch delivered them up, and the Court rendered a
judgment of discontinuance by the request of the
prosecutor, and filed it in his office."

Although the man-stealer escaped from the penalty
of the law, yet the publicity given to the proceedings
by the press had the effect of laying open some of
the dark secrets of the prison-house of slavery, and
exposing the villainous character of the trade in
human beings. Solomon's statements of his wrongs
obtained general belief, and few were found to give

credit to the perjuries by which the law had been evaded.

On the 20th January they left Washington, and travelling by way of Philadelphia, New York, and Albany, arrived at Sandy Hill on the night of the 21st. Solomon's heart overflowed with grateful joy as he looked around upon the old familiar scenes. He soon found himself in the midst of friends of other days; but as yet he had not met those who were most fondly beloved. Anne and the children had taken up their residence at Glens Falls, a few miles distant.

On the following morning he started with several friends to that place, and soon found the comfortable cottage that contained his treasures. As yet they had received no notice of his approach. The whole business of Solomon's liberation had been so rapidly carried through, and they had journeyed with so much haste from the South, that no opportunity had been given to apprise Anne and the family of anything that had taken place. They were, therefore, only hoping that the mission of Mr. Northup would be successful, and that the long-lost husband and father would shortly be restored to them.

When Solomon entered the cottage unannounced, his daughter, Margaret, was the first to meet him; but she did not recognize her father in the stranger. When he was taken away into slavery, he left her a little girl seven years of age, prattling over her toys. Now she was grown to womanhood, was married, and a bright-eyed boy was standing by her side, whom she had named in memory of the lost one, Solomon Northup Staunton. When told that the stranger was the father whose disappearance had cost them so many tears, she was overwhelmed with glad emotions, and for some time was unable to speak the words of loving welcome that struggled for utterance as she fondly embraced him. Presently, the other daughter, Elizabeth, entered the room, and folded the returned wanderer to her heart; and soon after Anne, to whom the glad intelligence had been conveyed, came running from the hotel to greet the recovered one. We draw a veil over the scene that ensued, the joy and happiness of which can be more easily imagined than described.

When the violence of their emotions had subsided into calm joy, and gratitude to Him who had so signally favoured them, the happy household gathered round the fire that sent out its grateful warmth to every part of the room, and conversed together on the events which had occurred ; and the hopes and fears, the joys and sorrows, the trials and troubles each had experienced during the long separation. Alonzo was absent in another part of the State. The boy had written to his mother, a short time before, of the prospect of his obtaining sufficient money to purchase his father's freedom. From his earliest years, *that* had been the chief object of his thoughts and his ambition. They knew that the father was somewhere in bondage. The letter which he had written on board the brig that conveyed him to New Orleans, and Jem Ray himself, who had visited them, had put them in possession of this information. But in what part of the wide-spread Southern slave-land he was held in unrighteous thraldom they could only conjecture, until the arrival of Bass's letter indicated the locality. Anne informed her husband that one day Elizabeth and Margaret returned from school weeping bitterly. On inquiring concerning the cause of the children's sorrow, she ascertained that at the school, while studying geography, their attention had been attracted to a picture of a gang of slaves working in a cotton-field, and an overseer following them with his whip. It reminded them of the sufferings their father might be, and, as it happened, actually *was*, enduring in the South. Numerous incidents were related, showing how tenderly and lovingly the memory of the kidnapped one had been cherished by those from whose society he had been ruthlessly torn away.

Leaving him happily restored to his home and family, we now say farewell to Solomon, trusting that the remainder of his life, consecrated to the service of Him whose kind providence was so wonderfully displayed in his restoration to freedom and happiness, may be cheered and brightened by the influences of pure and undefiled religion. Solomon said, and with these words of his we shall close our narrative :—

" I doubt not hundreds have been as unfortunate as myself. Hundreds of free citizens have been kidnapped and sold into slavery, wearing out their unhappy lives on plantations in Texas and Louisiana.

Chastened and subdued in spirit by the sufferings I have borne, and thankful to that good Being through whose mercy I have been restored to happiness and liberty, I hope henceforward to lead an upright and godly, though lowly, life, and rest at last in the churchyard where my father sleeps."

To Abraham Lincoln, the great and good President of the United States of America, belongs the immortal honour of sweeping away the foul system of American slavery, pregnant with so many fearful wrongs, and fraught with such thrilling horrors. This he did, as Captain-General of the American forces, during the slave-holders' Rebellion, which commenced in 1861, and ended in the total overthrow of the oppressors' Confederacy, in 1865 : thus surrounding his name with a halo of glory that will remain as long as the sun and moon endure. The hand of the skulking assassin, which, in the mysterious providence of God was permitted to cut short his life, could cast no shadow upon his fame.

Lightning Source UK Ltd.
Milton Keynes UK
173531UK00006B/63/P